HOW TO DO BUSINESS
WITH THE JAPANESE

HOW TO DO BUSINESS
WITH THE
JAPANESE

MARK ZIMMERMAN

CHARLES E. TUTTLE COMPANY

TOKYO · JAPAN

*Grateful acknowledgment is made to the following for permission to reprint
previously published material:*

D.C. Heath and Company: three tables from *Business Negotiations with the
Japanese*, by Rosalie L. Tung. Lexington, Mass.: Lexington Books, D.C. Heath and
Company, Copyright © 1984, D.C. Heath and Company. Reprinted by permission
of the publisher.

Published by the Charles E. Tuttle Company, Inc. of Tokyo, Japan, with editorial
offices at Suido 1-chome, 2-6, Bunkyo-ku, Tokyo, Japan

English reprint rights arranged with Julian Bach Literary Agency, Inc., N.Y.,
through Japan UNI Agency, Inc.

First Tuttle edition, 1987
Second printing, 1987

ISBN 0-8048-1519-4
Printed in Japan

FOREWORD

Not long after I received the sad news of Mark Zimmerman's death, his wife, Susan, wrote to ask if I would write the foreword to his second book. I immediately agreed, telling her that I considered it an honor to be able to contribute to the memory of a man so dedicated to cross-cultural understanding and communication between the United States and Japan.

On many occasions I have said that the U.S.-Japan relationship is the most important bilateral relationship in the world—bar none. This is obvious when one looks at the breadth of our mutual concerns that encompass the trade, financial, political, security, and cultural realms. The list of shared interests is almost endless. For our two great countries to continue to progress and develop closer relations, communication and mutual understanding are absolutely vital. Although we have had problems in the past due to weaknesses in these areas on both sides of the Pacific, our knowledge and understanding of each other, and our ability to deal in an informed and sensitive manner with each other, are increasing rapidly and dramatically. Today more Americans than ever before are studying about Japan and learning the Japanese language. And the same can be said of Japanese interest in the United States. More and more people are crossing the Pacific, for tourism, business and study. I welcome and fully support these developments. Without such efforts, we are doomed to repeat the mistakes of the past.

Mark Zimmerman was a man who embodied the tremendous potential for continued cooperation and communication between our two societies. Although he arrived in Japan with little prior knowledge of the country, its people, or its language, he departed five years later as an eminently successful Japanese-speaking businessman. He made prodigious efforts to master the Japanese language, recognizing that this ability was vital for living there and achieving his goals. He studied Japanese culture, explored the country, and learned about its long history, thereby gaining a far better understanding of how its society, geography, and past have influenced the Japan of the 1980's and will continue to affect its future development. *How to Do Business with the Japanese* demonstrates clearly that he fully succeeded in reaching his goal.

Based on Mark's own experiences in Japan as the representative of an important American company, this book is a practical guide to doing business in an incredibly dynamic and ever-growing marketplace. But it is much more than just a businessman's guide; it is a road map to understanding, and can be used by anyone who plans to work in Japan or with the Japanese, whether in diplomacy, cultural affairs, academia, the sciences or communications.

During the six decades I have studied this part of the world, I have read innumerable books and articles about how to communicate effectively with the Japanese, but Mark Zimmerman's insights into Japan—its culture, history, business practices, language and philosophy—are unique. In this volume he offers the experience of a pragmatic American businessman, but this is tempered by the sensitive perspective of an internationally oriented intellectual. He was constantly looking for opportunities to implement what he had learned. He sought feedback from those around him—both friends and business associates—for he knew that only by listening to and absorbing what was happening in the local environment could he ever hope to understand Japan and the Japanese.

As president of the American Chamber of Commerce in Japan (ACCJ) in 1981, Mark was the most visible representative of the American business community in Japan. He succeeded admirably in bringing together a widely disparate group of American business leaders and providing them with directions in which to channel their energies. As general manager of Sterling-Winthrop, Inc., his ability to listen to others and learn from them earned him the confidence and respect of his American and Japanese staff. This meant not only achieving greater profits and rapid growth for his company but, perhaps more important, developing close and warm relationships with his Japanese colleagues and counterparts. Mark received great personal satisfaction from his unique ability to bridge what are all too often considered by many people to be unbridgeable gaps between the two cultures.

Perhaps Mark's most significant contribution to breaking down the barriers between our two societies was his attempt to establish productive relationships with Japanese government officials. The fact that these contacts can be a lifeline for foreign businesses is often ignored, but Mark fully recognized their importance. I attribute to Mark's early initiatives and leadership the continuing successful efforts of the ACCJ to build bridges to Kasumigaseki.

In addition to representing his own firm and the entire American business community, Mark had other interests that were broad and varied. Religion played an important role in his life. He was a lay reader of his church and was involved in many religious activities. He was also a patriotic American, serving in the United States Army Reserve. He took his military obligations seriously and considered his military activities an integral part of his career and life. He was also a genuine intellectual who, at the same time, understood the practical world. Thus, he brought an especially broad perspective to his everyday activities.

Mark Zimmerman was a fine individual—gregarious, friendly, sincere, warm, concerned and, quite simply, a pleasure to be with. He was truly interested in people as people, not just as targets of business opportunity. The relationships he developed with those around him demonstrated that this warmth and concern were reciprocated.

It is a tragedy that we lost Mark when he was only forty-five and still in the prime of life. He has, however, left us a legacy in this book that should help other Americans. One of my principal goals as the U.S. ambassador in Japan has been to increase communications between our two countries and peoples. To this effort, Mark Zimmerman made a lasting contribution, and I thank him for it.

—Mike Mansfield
Tokyo, Japan

ACKNOWLEDGMENTS

Although this book is not one that was produced with the direct aid of many different people, I think its author would have wanted to thank not just those who aided in the actual writing of it, but all the many people, Japanese and American, who helped him to learn about Japan. There would have been too many to name, in any case, and now that he is gone it is impossible for us to know whose influence he would have considered paramount. I know he would have wanted to thank those of his colleagues in the American Chamber of Commerce in Japan who over the years have shared their knowledge of Japan with him. Of course, Mark would have wanted to thank his many Japanese friends and colleagues for their generous aid in helping him to understand their country. I think, too, he would have asked their forgiveness if he has seemed critical of Japan or things Japanese. The truth is that Mark was a man who deeply and sincerely admired the Japanese people, and this book was inspired partly by a desire to convey his admiration in terms understandable to the West. If he criticizes certain aspects of modern Japan, it was out of a desire to express an honest dismay at what he perceived as the inevitable negative consequences if Japan and the West continue to pursue outmoded policies in their dealings with each other.

Among those who deserve most thanks for aiding in the production of the book are Fatima Pais, who did much of the typing and collating, cheerfully and all too often under unreasonable expectations of speed in a country where electric typewriters are rare. Promila Barreta stepped in to complete the typing task at a crucial moment.

William Dizer generously contributed his time to critique the early chapters. His suggestions saved Mark from several errors in the difficult opening chapters, although Mr. Dizer shares no responsibility for any errors that may remain. Needless to say, the opinions expressed in this book are the author's alone, based on his experiences and interpretations.

I'm sure that Mark would also have wanted to thank his editors at Random House, as well as Julian Bach, his agent, who gave a great deal of useful advice and unstinting encouragement.

Finally, thanks are due Lynne Hewitt, who worked with Mark on the book from the beginning, researching background material and editing the manuscript, and who was faced with the task of putting the manuscript into its final form after Mark's death.

—Susan P. Zimmerman
May 23, 1984

CONTENTS

Foreword by Ambassador Mike Mansfield   v
Introduction   xiii

PART ONE: UNDERSTANDING THE JAPANESE

Chapter 1   The Basics: Social and Cultural Motivations   3

Chapter 2   Getting the Nuances Right: A Few Matters of
             Etiquette   25

Chapter 3   The Japanese Language: A Key to
             Understanding   41

Chapter 4   They're on a Different Wavelength   55

Chapter 5   Four Essential Concepts: *Nintai, Kao, Giri, On* 64

Chapter 6   The Network That Binds: *Ningen Kankei*   75

PART TWO: NEGOTIATING WITH THE JAPANESE

Chapter 7   The Japanese and Contracts   91

Chapter 8   *"Hai"* Means "I Hear You"   105

Chapter 9   The Decision-Making Process   118

PART THREE: COMPETING WITH THE JAPANESE

Chapter 10   Japanese Business Strategy in Japan   133

Chapter 11   Japanese Business Strategy in Foreign Markets   151

Chapter 12   Japanese Trading Companies and Japanese
             Banks   168

Chapter 13   How to Hold On to Your Market   184

PART FOUR: WORKING WITH THE JAPANESE

Chapter 14   Playing the Harp   205

Chapter 15   Joint Venturing   218

Chapter 16   Exporting to Japan   236

Chapter 17   Working in a Japanese Company   254

Chapter 18   We Need Each Other   269

Glossary   293
Bibliography   299
Notes   303
Index   307

INTRODUCTION

Until recently Westerners in general, and Americans in particular, have been fortunate in their position in the world. When traveling East, we have been able to take along our Western way of doing things, and it has been up to the local inhabitants to adapt to it. From the Englishman of the last century, who dressed for dinner in his tent in the jungle, to the hippies of more recent history, who took along their drugs and ideas on free love on their wanderings throughout Asia, Westerners have seldom found it desirable or necessary to heed the old saw that commends adapting "when in Rome." Indeed, we have been the Romans of our day, exporting our culture to every land on earth, just as the Romans spread their Greco-Roman civilization to every corner of their empire. I doubt they had a proverb along the lines of "When in Carthage, . . ." The world is changing, and we can no longer afford to assume the arrogant self-assurance that the technical and organizational superiority of Western civilization gave us in the eighteenth and nineteenth centuries. Although only one Eastern civilization has so far managed to meet and master the Western economic challenge (several others are fast approaching that level), that one is outstripping Western performance in nearly every market in the world for many categories of consumer goods. It hardly needs to be said that this nation is Japan. Even people in their early twenties can remember when "Made in Japan" was a synonym for merchandise guaranteed to break down or disintegrate shortly after purchase. The Japanese have advanced so quickly that few indeed realize the full implications of their dominance. For decades Americans have been among the most complacent people in the world. It is time to discard this complacency.

Many have begun to wonder how best to meet the unexpected consequences of an event more than a hundred years ago, when the U.S. Navy forced Japan to open its ports to Western trade. The instinctive reaction of many Western nations is to shut off trade with Japan, just as Japan shut off trade with the West when the positions were reversed and Westerners had the upper hand. But erecting tariff barriers, particularly now that the Japanese are lowering theirs, means that the West will be giving up without a fight, tacitly acknowledging its inferiority. After Commodore Perry compelled Japan to open its doors to the West, a revolution in attitudes took place in Japan, and within a few decades the Japanese were furiously studying Western technology and civilization in an attempt to gain a place among the rich and powerful nations of the earth. Despite the disastrous wrong turn taken in World War II, they have managed to achieve that goal. Western ideas breathed new life into their stagnant civilization. Now it's our turn; the process must be reversed.

Unlike some other writers on the subject, it is not my belief that the deterioration of our management techniques is the only cause of the malaise of Western industry. Certainly the old-style adversarial labor-management relations will have to go, along with other outmoded practices, if the West is to emerge from stagnation. But just as important will be a willingness on the part of Westerners to study Japanese civilization with the same intensity the Japanese have devoted to study of the West. And I am not advocating closer study of kabuki drama and ikebana flower-arranging (although these are arts certainly worthy of cultivation). We need to understand how Japanese society works, because it is becoming increasingly clear that its culture can turn out higher-quality goods than our Western cultures are currently producing.

Thus my purpose in writing this book is to help readers understand what competing, negotiating, or working with the Japanese is all about. I do not offer an academic or journalistic perspective. Instead, as a Western businessman who has been intimately involved in doing business with the Japanese for more than six years, I offer a firsthand report from the front lines, coupled with advice on how to succeed in dealings with the Japanese. The time for arrogance is past—gaining an understanding of Japanese culture is a matter of mere survival.

PART

ONE

UNDERSTANDING
THE JAPANESE

CHAPTER
1

THE BASICS:
SOCIAL AND CULTURAL MOTIVATIONS

Almost from the moment I set foot in Japan I realized that I had arrived not at *a* world center of commerce but at *the* world center of commerce. The Japanese believe in big business, and the whole time I was there I felt myself caught in a society that was in an incredible ferment of commercial activity, a society dedicated to the principle of economic growth. In fact, all Japanese are taught even as children at school that Japan's economy must continue growing, and that a favorable balance of trade is the only way for an archipelago poor in natural resources but rich in people to survive. Although growth has slowed in recent years, due to the world recession, rather than retrenching and cutting back, Japanese companies are frantically searching for innovative technology and seeking to penetrate new markets. The Westerner who would fully appreciate this spectacle must come to know the Japanese intimately.

Most Westerners who come to Japan on business or suddenly find themselves dealing with Japanese businessmen may know a little about the country and the people, but seldom does their knowledge come anywhere near approaching adequacy. Far too many of us continue to believe in the geisha–cherry blossom–Mount Fuji stereotype, a line that is still fed to and swallowed by many Western tourists, who are predictably disappointed by the reality. One would expect that executives whose career depends on being well provided with up-to-the-minute information would be considerably more sophisticated, but misinformation continues to be bandied about, largely because, until recently, there has been a persistent lack of serious interest in Japan. There is a new stereotype forming these days, lurking in the back of the minds even of those whose business it is to be well informed about such issues as bilateral trade. That is the notion of the Japanese as "economic animals" or "industrial robots"—a nation of homunculi emerging from "rabbit hutches" each day, marching in lockstep and hell-bent on a mission of world economic domination. Few would seriously maintain the literal accuracy of such a picture, but then again few have entirely forgotten World War II, and such adjectives as "inscrutable," "wily," and "sly" spring very quickly to our minds, even if less often to our lips.

At all economic levels—from the GM or British Leyland auto worker, who faces the prospect of never working again because superior Japanese cars have captured the market for the cars he used to make, to the executive of a consumer appliance or semiconductor company whose market is crumbling away because of Japanese competition—protectionist sentiment is on the rise, and along with it the usual nativist reactions: fear, distrust, hatred. From such emotions arise the "rabbit hutch," "robot," and "animal" stereotypes. But there is another side to our view of the Japanese—grudging admiration, amazement, wonder at their "cleverness." A calculator on a watch, and now a television on a watch! The consumer's vote concerning Japan is certainly "yes"—but there is a tinge of condescension even in our admiration. The Japanese are called not "brilliant" but "clever." Clever is the sort of word one would use to describe a dog that has learned to sit up, roll over, and play dead. Nobody would say "a clever nuclear physicist." In a recently published work on European views of Japan, *Misunderstanding,* by Endymion Wilkinson, the author shows that while the Europeans have always had a quite distorted picture of Japan—at times ludicrously so—the Japanese on the other hand have had a far more accurate picture of Europeans (and Americans, for that matter). This is basically because good information has been more widely disseminated in Japan.

When I first arrived in Japan, like many other businessmen, I thought of culture as a mere cultivation of aesthetic sensibilities, and of sociology and anthropology as abstruse academic specialities of limited practical application. I realized right away that I would have to learn Japanese in order to be effective, but I thought I could learn the ins and outs of Japanese business just by working with Japanese businessmen. But experience changed my original view. I now believe that extensive study of Japanese psychology and the structure of Japanese society is absolutely essential to fruitful dealings with the Japanese. When European and American managers persist in treating Tokyo as if it were Paris or New York, and thinking of Japanese businessmen as almost the same as we are, they very quickly find out that their competitive efforts are outclassed by the Japanese. If, on the other hand, they study the Japanese well enough to be able to anticipate their moves, and learn how to deal with them in the domestic and international marketplace, it may become harder for the Japanese to dominate market after market while we in the West fall like dominoes before the relentless determination and persistence of the Japanese corporation.

In what follows, I attempt to provide an introduction to the factors that have produced the most important—and peculiarly Japanese—economic phenomenon of the latter half of the twentieth century—the Japanese salary man (white-collar worker). It is his dedication—whether he is managing director or assistant to the assistant—that forms the foundation of Japanese success.

In the course of just over a century, Japan has evolved from an agrarian feudal society to a modern industrial one. Certain elements of the old community structure have persisted to the present day, the most important and basic of which is the famous Japanese sense of commitment to the group. Life on the medieval Japanese farm demanded the total involvement of every member of the community. The land-intensive method of producing rice involved backbreaking, never-ending labor and plenty of willing hands. Going it alone was out of the question, so villages were forced to get along with their neighbors. Individual farmers could survive the uncertainties of the weather, meet the heavy burden of the samurai's or daimyo's taxes, and deal with other emergencies only if they submerged themselves into the group and put the welfare of the community before their individual desires. A sense of the village's vulnerability to unpredictable outside forces was prevalent. Moreover, most villages were relatively isolated from their neighbors and were almost self-contained units. Since experimenting with new techniques risked the welfare of everyone, the society tended to be ultraconservative in its decision-making. Group consensus was most easily achieved by pointing out a precedent to the proposed decision. Even today this conservatism is apparent; the countryside is the bastion of the Liberal Democratic Party, the conservatives of Japan (and the leading political party nearly every year since the war).

This image of nervous farmers may contradict the average Westerner's view of the Japanese. Yet I feel that this stereotype is closer to reality than the comic-book image of Japanese as samurai swordsmen. Only a tiny minority of the population ever belonged to the samurai class, when there was such a class—it was eliminated in the nineteenth century during the Meiji Restoration. Up until the twentieth century, the vast majority of Japanese lived and worked on the land.

The two most important events (other than World War II) in the recent history of Japan are the founding of the Tokugawa shogunate and the Meiji Restoration. The Tokugawa shoguns (military dictators) ruled Japan from the seventeenth to the nineteenth centuries. The shogunate consolidated power throughout most of Japan, removing the administrative capital from Kyoto, the traditional seat of the emperor, to Edo (modern-day Tokyo). It banned all contact with foreigners (except for a few Dutch traders authorized to trade in Nagasaki) on penalty of death, and also eventually banned the practice of Christianity as a religion detrimental to the power of the state because it required allegiance to the "King of Rome" (the Pope). (Christianity had been introduced with considerable success by Portuguese missionaries during the preceding century.) The shogun disarmed the populace of the guns imported by the Portuguese merchants who earlier had been allowed to trade in Japan. The Tokugawa society was a combination of a strong central government and a feudal class system of rigid hierarchy.

The Tokugawa shogunate has been called "the closest approximation to a totalitarian system ever to appear in a preindustrial society."[1] Tokugawa Ieyasu, the architect of this social order, was an organizational genius, and is much admired by modern Japanese businessmen. As Albert Keidel has pointed out (in an article on the history of Japan's economic growth in *Business and Society in Japan*), one of the major factors in Japan's successful industrial revolution was that Japan already had a body of highly trained and disciplined managers to draw on:

> Because of the suddenness with which Japan began commerce and
> intercourse with the West it is easy to overlook the long, slow develop-

ment of commercial and managerial skills during the Tokugawa period. ... if there was any single element in Japan's industrialization drive that set her apart from other economies whose growth efforts have failed, it was this network of educated managerial and leadership potential.[2]

This analysis supports the view that a major ingredient in modern Japanese success has been their superior skills in managing people to produce a disciplined and dedicated work force.

The Tokugawa period ended in the 1860's with the restoration of the emperor, supposedly to supreme power, although in fact Japanese emperors have been figureheads for almost their entire history, and those of the nineteenth and twentieth centuries have been no different. But the useful slogan of "Honor the Emperor" gave those responsible for engineering the restoration the excuse they needed to abolish the decadent shogunate. They coupled this with the slogan "Expel the barbarians," meaning the Western traders who began coming to Japan after Commodore Perry and his black ships forced the shogun to open Japan to foreign trade. But rather than try to continue living in isolation, which was no longer a viable option after Perry's arrival, the Japanese decided to embrace all the material and scientific advances of the West, catching up with it economically and militarily while retaining their culture and character. As we all know, they were extremely successful in achieving the material goal. What is important to realize is that they also succeeded in retaining their essential Japaneseness. Despite superficial Westernization, as exemplified by television and innumerable other impressive gadgets, Japanese society has not been Westernized.

One of the best ways to begin seeing this cultural difference is to look at the most popular story of all time in Japan: the "Tale of the Forty-seven *Ronin*" (a *ronin* was a samurai who had lost his master). This is about an incident that occurred in the era of the Tokugawa shogunate and has been told and retold in various versions and media, from traditional kabuki drama to modern movies and TV. The story is probably known to every Japanese in the world who is over the age of seven. It is constantly being cited in Japan, to illustrate a point in a meeting or to enliven a newspaper story.

The forty-seven *ronin* were the retainers of a provincial daimyo (feudal lord), Asano Naganori from Ako. Lord Asano and two other daimyo were appointed by the shogun to receive an envoy from the emperor (residing in Kyoto) at the shogun's court in Edo. The three daimyo were sent to another daimyo, who was an expert on court etiquette, to make sure they learned all the proper forms. The two other daimyo gave the expert, Lord Kira, lavish gifts, but Lord Asano, feeling this to be unnecessary, failed to do so, and as a consequence Lord Kira taunted him with such terrible insults throughout the period of instruction that on April 21, 1701, Lord Asano finally lost his temper and stabbed Lord Kira in the audience hall of the shogun's palace. Lord Kira was only slightly hurt, but the shogun was so angry that he ordered Lord Asano to commit suicide the same day. Lord Asano obeyed the shogun's command.

When Lord Asano's forty-seven retainers heard of their master's death, they called a meeting to decide what to do. Oishi Yoshio, their leader, prevailed upon them to do nothing for the time being so that later they could fall on their enemy Lord Kira when he least expected it. So the forty-seven dispersed for one year. Oishi spent the year drinking and carousing. All the forty-seven were despised as disloyal retainers, even by their own families. Finally, Oishi decided the time was ripe, and on the night of January 30, 1703, the forty-seven took Lord Kira's castle by force and killed their enemy. They placed his head on Lord Asano's grave that night as an offering.

When the shogun learned of this, he decided that although he was sympathetic to their cause, the *ronin* could not be placed above the law. He ordered them to commit *seppuku* (ritual suicide) in March of 1703.

From the first, this incident captured the Japanese imagination. The story of the forty-seven *ronin* is constantly held up to the Japanese as a lesson in behavior and dedication. To Westerners the story may seem brutal and Oishi's waiting tactics cold-blooded. But to the Japanese the forty-seven *ronin* represent an important lesson, because the conflict between loyalty to one's immediate group and loyalty to society in general is solved in this tale. Notice that the Japanese solution to the drama involves dealing with one's immediate obligations first (dispatching the enemy of the daimyo) and worrying about the wider repercussions later. In Western society we tend to idealize those who put the abstract social good—Thou shalt not kill, for example—above all else. We might glorify a revenge killing, but when the avengers are caught and punished, those sympathetic to their cause feel the outcome to be a tragedy. We tend to feel that either they shouldn't have done it, or if they had to do it they should have been able to get away with it. But as many observers have pointed out, it is precisely the *ronins'* willingness to carry out their revenge with no thought of trying to save themselves from the consequences that is most admirable to the Japanese.

It would be a mistake to draw the conclusion from the popularity of this tale that the Japanese people are more fanatically loyal than any other, just as it would be a mistake to conclude from the stories about "Honest Abe" Lincoln that Americans are more likely to be fanatically honest than other nationalities. Loyalty to the group and faithfulness to one's obligations are lauded as abstract principles in the "Tale of the Forty-seven *Ronin,*" but the display of these characteristics in day-to-day life in Japan is based on hardheaded practicalities. To rise in a society composed of groups and factions, you must attach yourself to a group. If you betray one group or faction without first making sure you have another group to fall back on, you will be left out in the cold and despised by all.

Since the source of Japanese ideas about morality does not lie in an absolute code of values, it should come as no surprise that the Japanese have no compunctions about indulging in what we would think of as unethical practices, if such practices will promote the interests of the company/group. The scandal in San Francisco in 1982, when several officials from Hitachi and Mitsubishi Electric were arrested for attempting to bribe employees of IBM firms to steal technical details of the new MVS/XA software (IBM's new operating system software), is one example of the difference in ethical standards. A Japanese firm required new software technology from IBM, and after a first token attempt to license the technology (which IBM obviously refused), it was in their view a logical step to send an industrial espionage team to obtain it. An official of Fujitsu, IBM's number one Japanese rival, was quoted as saying they would gladly have paid for the technology.[3]

Although industrial espionage is by no means unheard of among American firms, it would be very unusual to justify the espionage purely on the grounds of the higher good of loyalty to the company and promotion of its interests above all. Yet that is precisely the Japanese attitude. There is no abstract moral code governing Japanese behavior that exists over and above the individual's commitment to the welfare of the community. Edwin O. Reischauer, the longtime observer of and writer on Japan, has said, "Neither religion, nor ethical principles, nor political and social ideals serve in Japan as the great unifying forces they do in other lands."[4] While this may seem a terrible thing to say about any country, especially to those of us from Judeo-Christian countries, it would be wrong to conclude from this sweeping statement that the Japanese are amoral beings—"economic animals," as they have been called. But they do conceive of right and wrong differently, and it is well to be aware of this.

Another famous case of industrial espionage took place in North Carolina, in 1980, involving Celanese Corporation and another Japanese trading company. The general manager of a Celanese plant in Charlotte was paid $675,000 over a five-year period to methodically "transfer technology" to the Japanese firm. This included showing them around the plant at night and explaining manufacturing processes. It is most unlikely that an American company could find a Japanese willing to betray his company in this fashion. Americans may see themselves as ultimately answerable to a celestial authority for their crimes, but Japanese tend to see themselves as immediately answerable to a very tangible authority—the censure of the members of their group. This does not mean that Japanese never take kickbacks. There is a fine line between graciously receiving gifts and taking bribes. Senior Japanese politicians have become involved in scandals of this kind. One notorious example was former Prime Minister Kakuei Tanaka, who has been accused of using his influence to help Lockheed obtain orders from Japanese airlines. But—and here is the key point—in such examples of corruption the perpetrators are not betraying any specific group loyalties.

I remember one incident, involving one of the large Japanese *zaibatsu* (industrial groups), when I was approached and politely asked to persuade my New York office to stop buying a certain chemical in Europe, and to buy it instead from this particular Japanese group through their chemical subsidiary in Japan. I explained that the decisions for worldwide purchases of chemicals, including purchases in Japan, were made by my New York office, and that the best thing for them to do would be to give me a sample (together with the pricing details) of the chemical. I would see that it was delivered to the right man in our head-office purchasing department. I assured them that in due course the evaluation would be completed and the offer would be considered, providing the quality and price were right. They then explained that they had already been to New York and done all of that, but that my head office would not buy from them because of a long-term commitment to the European supplier of the chemical. I was starting to sympathize with them when they interrupted and said that they wanted the order anyway, and if I didn't arrange it they would see that our business in Japan suffered. They would make a slight technical modification to the chemical to avoid patent-violation prosecution, and sell the chemical at rock-bottom prices to all the Japanese imitator companies, who would then price my company out of the market. I didn't have time to react to this brazen blackmail before they went on to say, "You see, Zimmerman-*san,* it is all for the good of the company, which has a new chemical plant which is operating at only twenty-five percent of capacity. We need the production, so you will please help us." I couldn't believe my ears, and told them in no uncertain terms what to do with their chemical. They left, muttering other threats. Fortunately for us, the Japanese government had passed a new law giving drugs a six-year mandatory side-effect monitoring period, during which time no similar chemical could be introduced. This law effectively stopped the Japanese company. However, it would not surprise me in the least to see them try again, or to actually carry out their threat in 1987, when the six-year period is over.

The reader may be wondering why the Japanese devote themselves so entirely to the interests of their company that they appear to become oblivious to anything beyond these interests. There are several explanations for this behavior. One is that the surface appearance of unity is not the whole story. Factionalism is rife, and the struggle to rise in the company may have nothing to do with the company's welfare. Yet devotion to the group, while perhaps not as perfect as some writers have suggested, is a fact of Japanese society. The most important reason for it is purely pragmatic. If you are lucky enough to be hired by one of the major corporations, which can afford to offer lifetime employment—the smaller companies do not have the resources necessary to commit themselves to this difficult ideal; Jon Woronoff estimates that it is "fully practiced in perhaps a third of the cases"[5]—to risk being fired would be to throw away all the accumulated seniority that is carrying you up the famous Japanese "career escalator," as well as to forfeit the provisions for a huge lump-sum payment on retirement that the company makes for life-time employees. Loss of the material benefits of a secure niche in a major company would be added to the intangible effects of loss of face. And those effects, while "intangible," could be emotionally devastating. It would have to be a very tempting bribe indeed that could lead a Japanese lifetime employee to risk his entire future.

Although I have been emphasizing the practical aspects of Japanese devotion to the group, I do not mean to suggest that there is no true feeling behind the often ostentatious display of love for the company. For example, many Japanese executives tend to wear their company pins even on weekends. (Of course, this is not a universal law; some never wear their company pins at all.) Some writers, such as Woronoff, have suggested that there is a generation gap looming in Japan. The older workers, those responsible for the economic renaissance of Japan in the 1960's, still adhere to the values of self-sacrifice and the company-above-all, while younger employees may feel that life is empty and meaningless when it is all overtime with no chance to be with wife and children. However that may be, the old feelings are still prominently to be seen today in Japan. It is still considered somewhat shameful for a husband to be home before ten o'clock at night on a work day. The neighbors will make his wife miserable by "sympathizing" with her that her husband is not needed at the office. Uniformity and cohesiveness within the firm are actively encouraged by company policy. Company outings are frequent and well attended. Such outings are *not* like the American once-a-year office Christmas party or company picnic, where workers cut loose from their day-to-day routines; they are ritual ceremonies, a sort of group breast beating.

I remember one of our company outings, held at a place near the base of Mount Fuji. It was a dull overcast evening, and the roads were a little slippery, so the bus carrying the employees was delayed and I arrived twenty minutes before they did. As I walked into the reception area of this small country inn I heard shouts of *"Banzai, banzai!"** I looked into the large room that was the source of this uproar, and saw about a hundred young men in black "happi-coats." Their eyes were glowing with pride, and there was a large sign in *kanji* (Chinese ideographs) that said, SALUTING THE GREAT CHIYODA CONSTRUCTION COMPANY. Suddenly the men burst into a military song led by enthusiastic *kachō* (section heads) and *buchō* (department heads). By the time my employees arrived the young men had finished their fourth rendition of the company song and were running to their buses shouting *"Banzai!"* and clapping one another on the back.

---

*Allow me to put at rest for once and all the notion that *banzai* is a war cry. It is not. It merely means "May you live for ten thousand years," and is no more sinister than "Hurray."

How much of this demonstration was feigned by the young office workers, and how much was really heartfelt love of company, is hard to say. Nevertheless, I find it difficult to believe that the display was less than genuine. I think I witnessed a very real demonstration of the employees' devotion to their company. My own staff were informally dressed and far less exuberant than the Chiyoda people, but as the weekend wore on they began to show some of the same signs of dedication and love of company, and it seemed to come naturally to them.

A further extension of the group-loyalty principle is that the Japanese don't like individualists or prima donnas—either inside or outside their firms. The slightest individualistic tendency is frowned on, and two of the top industrialists in Japan were virtually blackballed from the Keidanren (Federation of Economic Organizations), a very powerful industrial association (somewhat similar to the U.S. National Association of Manufacturers, but with much more power and money at its disposal), because of their individualistic tendencies.

When working with the Japanese, one should be wary of the type of man who is most "Westernized" and easy to relate to and understand. He is usually a front man who is used to get rid of or look after foreigners, and to make sure they get trapped at a lower level within the Japanese company. He is regarded as a species of clerk designated to keep foreigners happy. The higher a man's position in the company, the more likely that he will be a humble, self-effacing, "Japanese" executive, who obviously takes pains to hide his ambitions and capabilities and not be seen by others to be a forceful leader. Some such men will seem to be uncomfortable with foreigners—even if they are not—just to show others how "Japanese" they are. This first impression will later change as one gets to know the Japanese executive and discovers that much of the attitude is designed to keep his face with the group.

As mentioned above, Japanese companies tend to be composed of factions. One cause of factionalism stems from the Japanese tradition of *oyabun,* a man who takes on the role of "father" to a coterie of *kobun,* "children," who surround him. The "children" owe obedience and respect to their "godfather," while the father figure is obliged to support and nurture his dependents. The *kobun* will do everything they can to see that their mentor rises, because if he attains a high position, their own future will be secured. These factions are self-limiting in size, because they depend on close personal contact, constantly renewed. So you can imagine the number of such groups there must be in any large Japanese organization. When the company is threatened by competition, a tough marketplace, or recessionary factors, then the factions are less active. When there is an easy market or when leadership of the company is weak, the factions flourish. The Liberal Democratic Party (LDP), the ruling political party of Japan, has four major factions and numerous minor ones. When elections are near, they form temporary alliances and work together for the good of the party, but factionalism is never far beneath the surface. The same holds true to a lesser extent in Japanese companies.

Although factionalism is a reality, don't make the mistake of thinking that the Japanese company is not a closely knit organization. Its components are not individuals, as in the West, but groups of individuals. A Japanese company is an organization that prides itself on group action and presenting a united front. Successful Western business people learn to make use of this fact. The Japanese will view every business venture not only on the basis of its intrinsic merits and profitability but also on its contribution to the group image and prestige. For example, my company had a new drug for treating gonorrhea, but no Japanese company wanted to handle it, because to do so would be to imply that the management of that company thought that Japanese people have gonorrhea. It would damage the image of a reputable company to imply such a slander on the Japanese people. Even doctors will not tell their patients that they have VD. They will inform the patient that he has "a urinary tract infection." This kind of sensitivity, although perhaps once common in the West, seems rather outdated to us nowadays, but it is still an important factor in modern Japanese business.

So far I have been harping on the principle of Japanese loyalty to the group. It has its positive side in the tremendous ability of Japanese people to work together and the high degree of personal fulfillment the average Japanese derives from being dedicated to his job. But groupism also has a negative aspect: xenophobia. Japanese distrust of foreigners is well known. Less well known is Japanese distrust of themselves in a foreign context.

To understand this self-distrust, one must realize that the flip side of devotion to the group is conformity and rigidity of behavioral codes. The result is that Japanese are often tense and wound up.

More muscle-relaxing drugs are sold in Japan than anywhere else in the world. And precisely because of this emphasis on doing what the group expects, Japanese don't feel any shame or embarrassment except within the group—meaning their family or their company. Strangers don't count. So when the Japanese go on a holiday (especially overseas), they seize the opportunity to let loose all that tension. Ask any Manilan or Bangkokite to tell you about the Japanese tourists in their cities! Out of context, the Japanese no longer feel accountable. Japanese who spend too much time outside Japan sometimes find that trust in them as loyal members of the group will be withdrawn, because their fellows feel that they can no longer be relied upon to behave predictably.

However, it would be wrong to imagine that it is only in special circumstances that trust is withdrawn from a member of the group. The very nature of the group means that action is by definition group action. Japanese usually do not trust one another singly; moreover, they don't trust themselves. They prefer always to do business with at least one person there to back them up. The American ideal of the lone operator who doesn't need anybody is simply absent. Even for the most minor details, you will almost never get one man to say yes or no. Leadership in Japan is the art of achieving consensus within one's group, not the ability to take independent decisions and enforce them. Foreign business people are often frustrated by the complications arising from this fact. There's no use in insisting on an answer because it will only confuse and embarrass the fellow who is being pressed for it.

The Japanese need for a backup has a significant emotional component to it. I remember once when a Japanese company with which my company was negotiating an agreement called on me as a backup in an emergency situation when absolutely no one from their group was available. The Japanese were supposed to send a delegation to our New York office for the signing of our first major contract. There were no major decisions to be made—just the clearing up of some minor details, signing the contract with our top brass, and a liaison visit to our Research and Development office. Since none of the major officers were available, they decided to send the *buchō* (department head) of the International Department, together with a researcher. The latter's only function was to accompany the *buchō* on the liaison visit to our R&D center, so essentially the *buchō* was on his own. The *buchō* was, in Japanese terms, relatively young—

under fifty. This situation made them profoundly uneasy.

One morning about a week before the *buchō* was due to leave, the Japanese company's *jōmu* (managing director) called me, and asked me to go with the *buchō*. I was taken aback at this request, but I said I would check with my head office and try to get their approval. In the end, I did go with him, since my New York office wanted to see me anyway. But it was essentially a hand-holding operation; the Japan office needed the emotional security of having sent two men, and the *buchō* needed the emotional security of having a partner. As it turned out, everything went exceptionally well. The *buchō* was extremely well qualified, had been abroad before, and knew how to handle himself. He was an outstanding executive, but the home office still wanted somebody there to serve as a restraint on the individual.

This example taught me the complexities inherent both in Japanese distrust of foreigners and in going abroad. The executives of this Japanese company were driven to the ultimate irony of deputing me, a foreigner, who was working for the company with whom they were negotiating, as a sort of honorary Japanese, not because of their distrust of foreigners but because of their distrust of individual independence. There somehow lurks in the back of many a Japanese executive's mind the fear that a perfectly sober, reliable, committed-to-the-group executive will suddenly lose control or be browbeaten by the other side if he is sent abroad alone. A "team player" must have a team to play on.

In the light of this distrust of those who have gone abroad, it is easier to understand why Japanese dislike dealing with nisei, people born outside of Japan of Japanese-born parents. Some American companies make it a policy to send nisei to manage their businesses in Japan. The nisei has the advantage, in many cases, of the language ability and the ability to mix into street crowds, but he is still regarded with great suspicion and disdain. There are many exceptional nisei and sansei (third generation born abroad) who have done well in Japan, but they have to overcome a lot of suspicion and hostility, more so than a manager of European descent.

The Japanese are an amazingly homogeneous people. They reinforce this characteristic with a social code whose first rule of conduct is "Don't make waves." There are very few times in the life of an average Japanese when he is confronted with people who think differently, have different dietary or other habits, or even who look distinctly different. Although my Japanese friends assure me that they can tell if someone is from Kyushu or Hokkaido (two large islands of the archipelago) by their features or coloring, to my mind the fact that such subtle differences are noted at all makes it the exception that proves the rule.

The homogeneity of its people is a result of Japan's long historical isolation. As the people of an island nation, the Japanese have long cultivated a feeling of uniqueness, vulnerability, and to a certain extent even superiority. This combination of factors has produced xenophobia. The Japanese believe that they are more vulnerable than other nations—certainly more so than any of the other developed nations. Is it any wonder that their market, despite the government's grudging concessions in the face of world pressure, remains extremely difficult to enter?

If the Japanese don't like foreign products invading their market, you're probably wondering what they think of Westerners invading their shores. The answer is that many—in fact, most—Japanese are uncomfortable around foreigners. They call Westerners *gaijin,* "outside people," and find us difficult to deal with and slightly repulsive to look at. This goes double for black people (whom they call *kokujin*). To understand just how far this prejudice goes, consider that in the nightclub *(mizu shōbai)* district of Osaka there is an establishment called the St. Tropez, where all the waiters, including the busboys, are black, and dressed in hokey "negro minstrel" outfits. It is right next to a transvestite bar, and to the Japanese mind has the same sort of outré appeal. Black people are regarded more or less as sideshow freaks by the common people of Japan.

Japanese racism is not reserved for blacks alone; it extends to all foreigners. Leaving Tokyo, one begins experiencing it immediately. Even in Osaka there are few restaurants, clubs, or bars that welcome foreigners by themselves. (Somehow, if one is accompanied by a Japanese, it is all right. I suppose the proprietor views the Japanese accompanying a Westerner as a sort of nursemaid who will guarantee the latter's good behavior.) Foreign women, however, are welcome in a special context—as hostesses in nightclubs, and are well paid for their function of adding an exotic note to the establishment.

Other Asians are not regarded any more warmly than foreigners from more distant lands. Japanese have a deep respect for Chinese culture because much of their own culture has been borrowed from it. But it is at this level that the affinity stops. Despite the "Greater East Asia Co-Prosperity Sphere" during World War II, when the

Japanese promised to deliver Asia from its European colonialist masters, the average Japanese has a low opinion of his fellow Asians. They admire the economic success of the Koreans, but there is no people they hate more. It is a mistake for foreign businessmen to employ Korean interpreters for a party of Japanese visiting their head offices. Although most educated Koreans know how to speak Japanese, many Japanese will resent the presence of Koreans. A clear indication of the scant respect that Japanese have for other Asians is that almost no Vietnamese refugees or boat people were accepted into Japan. Perhaps one reason for this is the popular belief that the Japanese people are a distinct race, racially pure descendants from one original tribal "family."

Anyone who travels to Japan will encounter examples of racism and prejudice. He or she will find that taxi drivers do not like to pick up foreigners. Foreign professional people are not allowed to use their titles in Japan unless they pass all the relevant examinations in the Japanese language—a virtual impossibility.

But my purpose in relating all this is not to imply that every smiling Japanese face conceals implacable hatred. Quite the contrary; Japanese can be very loyal and close friends, and they often go out of their way to help lost and confused *gaijin*. I will treasure the many friendships I have made with Japanese people all my life. Nevertheless, to understand a Japanese competitor or partner, it is necessary to realize that he has to overcome many built-in antiforeign prejudices that are intrinsic to his culture before he can allow himself to become the friend of a Westerner.

The Japanese approach to education has a direct impact on their business success, and on their relations with Western business. Perhaps the best way of summing up this system is to consider that it is not uncommon for seven-year-old children to stay up till midnight studying. Very young children in Japan are allowed a great deal of indulgence, but at the age of five they start going to kindergarten, and immediately the pressure begins. At every stage of their education, Japanese children have to pass rigorous examinations. (This applies even to kindergarten; the latest phenomenon is prep schools for kindergarten to ensure that a child gets into one of the best ones.) If a child fails his entrance exams at any point along the way (but especially at the crucial junctures between junior and senior high, and between senior high and university), he could well be a washout for life, a permanent second-rater. If he fails to get into one of the top government universities, he is very unlikely to be able to land any of the top jobs in government, industry, or academics.

These entrance examinations, and the intense study necessary for preparing for them, are popularly known as "examination hell." Much has been said in praise or blame of the Japanese system (see Woronoff's *Coming Social Crisis* for an extremely negative view, and Vogel's *Japan as Number One* for a positive one). Certainly one very positive thing that can be said for it is that it works; the literacy rate in Japan is the highest in the world, nearly 99 percent. But one major consequence of the system that a business person must be aware of is that the study habits a Japanese salary man began acquiring when he was five make him a compulsive doer of homework. No detail is too small for him to go over; no bit of information is considered irrelevant when studying a problem. He regards absolutely nothing as too much trouble. This capacity for study means that if you are dealing with a Japanese businessman, you can be sure that his preparation for the meetings will always be five steps ahead of yours. They have no concept of the favorite American pastime of "winging it." From preparing for business meetings to preparing to enter a foreign market, the Japanese executive's capacity for sheer doggedness is immense. This is perhaps one of the main reasons why the Japanese know so much more about us and our markets than we do about them.

The impact of Japanese religious beliefs on the way Japanese think and respond to problems of all types tends to be either overestimated or underestimated by foreigners. This is because perhaps the most important aspect of Japanese religion for a foreigner raised in the Judeo-Christian West to understand is that religious life in Japan is not an either/or choice as it is in the West. Put another way, the importance of religion in Japan is its very lack of importance. Reischauer sums it up this way: "The majority of Japanese—some 70 to 80 percent—even though carried on the rolls of one or more religious bodies, do not consider themselves believers in any religion."[6] Woronoff cites the statistics on religion released by the Religious Affairs Section of the Cultural Affairs Agency in Japan in 1975: there were 178,573,950 members of 181,000 registered religious corporations, when the total population of Japan was only about 110 million. The explanation for this is that many people are registered as both Shinto and Buddhist, without having any strong belief in either one. Yet the reader should not take these statistics to mean that Japanese religions have no influence. Perhaps "religion" is the wrong word here; "traditional system of thought" might be a better term.

The ambiguous and laissez-faire attitude toward religion of the Japanese contrasts sharply with the clear-cut labels and yes-or-no choices embodied in our Western religious traditions. It is interesting that Pascale and Athos, in *The Art of Japanese Management*, emphasized the positive virtues that ambiguity and uncertainty have for the Japanese, whereas most Westerners would see these qualities in a negative light. In fact, it is important that one learn to employ the virtues of ambiguity when talking to Japanese people (a point I shall return to in Chapter 5).

Throughout their long history the Japanese have successively absorbed a variety of religious and philosophic thought. Let's look at each of the layers and see how it affects dealings with the Japanese at the everyday business level.

The "bottom layer," the most ancient, is Shintoism. This religion is essentially a form of nature worship, a celebration of being at one with nature. The Japanese love of beauty, *ikebana* and Japanese art in all its forms, as well as the Japanese passion for neatness and order in all things—from the angle of your tie to the pin on your lapel and the papers on your desk—could be traced to the ritualistic perfectionism and precision that stem from the purification rites of Shinto worship. The Creation according to Shinto holds that Japan was created first of all lands, by a goddess who caused it to rise out of the pearly mists of the sea in the dawn of time. All the other islands and continents of the world were scattered around as an afterthought, merely to complement the perfection that is Japan. Despite the apparent gentleness of this nature-loving religion, it played a vital role in uniting the Japanese in World War II. The central premise of the Shinto religion is that Japan is a holy land unlike any other, and "State Shinto" as promoted by the Japanese government formed a very important part of the blind patriotic zeal that led Japan to attack Pearl Harbor and sustains the average Japanese in a deep-seated sense of superiority to all foreigners (a sense that was shaken, but not destroyed, by the events of the Pacific war).

Shintoism forms a more or less constant background to religious life in Japan and manifests itself in the outwardly gentle manner of the Japanese that many Americans interpret as a sign of inferiority.

This outward humility is the *tatemae* (superficial appearance) used to maintain harmony, or *wa,* in human relations, behind which is the steely determination of the Bushido spirit that arose out of the feudal period of constant civil war before the Tokugawa shogunate took control. The shoguns molded the fierceness and loyalty of the samurai into a behavioral code, based largely on Confucian ethics, and kept the warriors in comparative poverty to prevent them from raising the necessary funds to foment a rebellion. Zen Buddhism, with its emphasis on the aesthetic discipline of poverty, appealed to the impoverished samurai. Buddhism can be linked to the traditional Japanese tendency toward austerity, self-discipline, and dislike of ostentation, as well as to the belief in contemplation and silence as essential prerequisites in the development of the human character.

Although Confucianism as a living system of belief was largely supplanted during the nineteenth century by Western rationalism, and is not practiced today in any formal sense, its code of ethics remains an extremely important influence. Reischauer has this to say about Confucianism:

> Confucianism probably has more influence on [the Japanese] than does any other of the traditional religions or philosophies. Any discussion of Japanese religions that overlooks this point would be seriously misleading. Behind the wholehearted Japanese acceptance of modern science, modern concepts of progress and growth, universalistic principles of ethics, and democratic ideals and values, strong Confucian traits still lurk beneath the surface, such as the belief in the moral basis of government, the emphasis on interpersonal relations and loyalties, and the faith in education and hard work. Almost no one considers himself a Confucianist today, but in a sense almost all Japanese are.[7]

The Confucian layer of the Japanese psyche is the basis for the great respect that Japanese have for elders, a respect that may culminate in the virtual worship of the company chairman or president if he is the type who is in the mold of a Confucian elder. I remember the awe and veneration that the employees and executives of the Green Cross Corporation, an Osaka-based Japanese pharmaceutical company, had for their late chairman, Ryoichi Naito, a selfless and dedicated man who epitomized the Confucian tradition. At this point, so soon after his death in 1982, I have yet to hear him being referred to in the reverential tones that, let's say, a Mitsubishi man would use to refer to the founder of the Mitsubishi empire, or a

Mitsui man would to refer to the founders of Mitsui, but it would not surprise me to see Dr. Naito venerated in the future in much the same way. His character is a good example of the three-layered Japanese psychology referred to above. He was intensely nationalistic in the Shinto manner, and served as one of the key officers in the Japanese Army Medical Corps in World War II. He went to the United States and Germany in the thirties to study the pharmaceutical business and bring back as much of the technology as he could in order to help modernize the Japanese pharmaceutical industry in preparation for war. He was also humble, and had a true appreciation of the Japanese ideal, in the Zen tradition, of the self-effacing leader. Underneath, however, was the Bushido spirit of the samurai, and nothing happened in Green Cross without Dr. Naito's knowledge; he understood the virtues of Confucian hierarchy. His exposure to Western thought made him a fanatic for Western as well as locally developed technology. He would take options on every piece of new technology that was remotely connected with the primary business of Green Cross—natural pharmaceuticals and products derived from blood, urine, etc. Dr. Naito was a perfect example of the compleat Japanese man of his generation, in whom all three religious traditions mixed harmoniously.

When the Japanese are seen in the context of these religious and cultural traditions—Shintoism, Confucianism, and Buddhism, overlaid with the rationalism of the West—and the flexible and ambiguous nature of the Japanese attitude toward religion is taken into account, the reasons behind many apparent contradictions in the way they react to messages that a Westerner thinks he has communicated in the most straightforward and logical way become clearer. The key is to remember that a logical Western response is not necessarily the one that the Japanese favor. They have borrowed consciously and successfully from the West and yet have never lost their Japanese character, because the Western layer is the least important in terms of their perception of the world.

Contrary to the stereotype of the inscrutable bland Oriental, the Japanese themselves believe they are a highly emotional people. By this they mean, among other things, that to them personal considerations are important when dealing with people, even on the organizational level. They reject the West in their heart of hearts. A few even crave for a return to the simpler, more traditional ways of the samurai era, but most see no contradictions in the blending of the various influences on Japan. Having never been colonized (unless you count the brief history of the U.S. occupation after World War II), they do not suffer from the inferiority complex that plagues many other Asian peoples. Whatever sense of inferiority may have handicapped them in the past, most Japanese nowadays have become aware of the ills that the West is suffering from, and the best-selling popularity in Japan of such books as Ezra Vogel's *Japan as Number One* is just one sign of renewed Japanese self-confidence. The famous Japanese author Yukio Mishima, who committed *seppuku* (ritual suicide) when his ideas were rejected, wanted to return to the pure, untainted samurai period, but most Japanese do not understand or sympathize with the self-conscious schizophrenia inherent in such a wish.

The contradictions in the Japanese character constantly catch Westerners off-guard. Apparent inconsistencies often make it difficult for the American or European to deal effectively with the Japanese. If one tries to simplify matters by labeling Japanese businessmen as samurai warriors in business suits, or any other of the common stereotypes, one is likely to be caught even more off-base. Modern Japan is a complex reality, and even the omnipresent business culture is not the whole story.

To give an example of how the Japanese operate differently, a typical business decision will evolve on the Japanese side of a Japanese-American joint venture in a manner not at all similar to the way it normally does on the American side. Suppose the American side wants the Japanese company to introduce a new line of products that, while related to the joint-venture business, will involve an unusually large financial commitment of the Japanese parent company's resources. The Japanese will first consider, in a Western rationalistic mode, the market potential for the new product line and organize a task force to conduct exhaustive market research to determine whether the idea makes sound business sense. So far these are the same reactions that an American company would have to a new product or business entry. But after the information-gathering stage, the Japanese practice is markedly different. The next stage will be a kind of consensus building (described in Chapter 8) called *nemawashi,* which leads ultimately to a decision. The influencing elements in the decision will almost certainly include a number of ritualistic, almost religious meetings where the project is not really discussed in the Western sense; rather, the impact of the new venture will be assessed in terms of its "true and pure adherence" to the traditions of the company and its founder. There will then be discussion about the way in which the company's action will be perceived by the business community and by direct and indirect competitors. Will the company lose face by entering this market? How much face will they lose if they fail in the new venture? Intense concentration on these aspects will be likely to have a more important impact than the intrinsic merits (i.e., profitability) of the business itself. Finally comes the execution stage. The Japanese company will make a supreme effort to implement the agreed program because the whole group feels personally committed to making it succeed. Their face is at stake.

To return to the example of Dr. Naito, as president of Green Cross he passed up many opportunities to expand the business of his company, and refused to sever business relationships that would seem nonfunctional to a Western executive. He even kept alive a relationship with a small Indian company that had never done any business with his company simply because the Indian company's founder had once trained for two weeks at Green Cross. Such strict adherence to personal loyalty is at the core of Japanese concern for people rather than for principles or financial profit.

The brief description in this chapter of some of the major factors in Japanese society is, of course, hardly adequate for anyone who plans to spend a lot of time living and working in Japan. In just one short chapter I cannot hope to present a complete account of the "Japanese mind," even if such a goal were possible. Instead of providing a detailed map, I have merely pointed out major landmarks and pitfalls in the maze of modern Japanese society of which a Westerner who wants to do business with it should be aware.

CHAPTER
2

GETTING THE NUANCES RIGHT:
A FEW MATTERS OF ETIQUETTE

When a Westerner meets a Japanese, many factors contribute to a sense of mutual unease. Each has his or her own prejudices to overcome, and there is a cultural gap so wide that many Westerners don't even know it is there. Most people are happiest among their own kind, but the Japanese carry this natural human tendency to an extreme. There are several reasons for this, not least the homogeneity of Japanese society that was referred to earlier. Japanese society demands conformity and predictability in the behavior of its members. Japanese mothers enforce conformity by admonishing their children that people will laugh at them if they behave unacceptably. Unsurprisingly, many Japanese grow up with a horror of committing faux pas. This often makes those Japanese unused to contact with foreigners stiff and awkward when they must meet non-Japanese. Westerners sense their uncertainty, and try to inject warmth into the conversation. Some, anxious to show that they have no prejudice against the Japanese, will adopt a slap-on-the-back joking style that drives the Japanese to distraction. Westerners can avoid such awkward situations by first learning some very basic rules of Japanese etiquette. Westerners who adhere to the forms of Japanese etiquette can relax in the knowledge that they are starting off on the right foot by putting the Japanese they meet at ease.

When meeting someone for the first time, a Japanese wants to find out as soon as possible where that person fits into his or her scheme of things. Socioanthropologist Chie Nakane in her famous study, *Japanese Society*, has claimed that the Japanese are "frame" people, while Westerners are "attribute" people. That is, Japanese tend to want to fit a person into a social context, while Westerners tend to try to find out what a person is like. That is why a Japanese will first ask what company someone works for, while a Westerner will ask what kind of work he does. The easiest way for a Japanese to find out the information he considers to be necessary for smooth social intercourse, with a minimum of embarrassment to both parties, is through the institution of the *meishi* (calling card), which most Japanese adults usually have. The format and mode of presentation of the business meishi is subject to rather fixed rules, and many a Western executive has come to grief for lack of a meishi—like the lack of a horseshoe nail in the old nursery rhyme that resulted in the loss of a kingdom. Western business people should have several hundred meishi printed before boarding the plane to Japan. Preferably the meishi should have English on one side and Japanese on the other. The title printed on it must convey as accurately as possible the level of the person's importance within his or her organization. Small details of rank are meaningful to the Japanese because their society is extremely hierarchical. There will never be two men of exactly the same rank within one department in a Japanese corporation. No matter how close their positions are, there will always be a subtle difference, such as the year of entrance in the company, to distinguish between the two. The Japanese are well aware of these differences; American egalitarianism is quite foreign to them. The ranking system is the major reason why the meishi assumes so much importance.

When meeting a Japanese businessman, meishi are usually exchanged by holding them with the print facing outwards, hands outstretched. Bowing slightly, each accepts the other's meishi in his right hand. Many Westerners feel embarrassed about bowing. Americans suffer most acutely from this problem, for they may not have bowed to anyone since fifth-grade dancing class. Japanese men bow quite stiffly, bending at the hips with the spine held straight, and the hands straight at the sides or holding the meishi outstretched. Women bow similarly, except that they place their palms on their thighs. Learning exactly the right angle (greater or lesser in proportion to the rank of the person being greeted) takes some time, and the nuances can be complex. However, untutored Westerners who make some gesture of respect by lowering their heads will have fulfilled the custom to the satisfaction of their hosts. The Japanese don't expect foreigners to know exactly how to bow, but they do expect a guest to show some inclination to conform to local custom.

When meeting Westerners, the Japanese will consider it their distasteful duty to perform a handshake along with the native bow, but they despise the firm handgrip favored by many Americans. A quick and relaxed handshake is sufficient. Some Westerners are tempted to forgo the handshake, but the Japanese have become so used to dealing with Westerners that they would probably be suspicious of someone who avoids shaking hands with them. I've found that when I get to know a Japanese person quite well I can dispense with the formality of the handshake and then a slight bow is all that is needed. But always remember when meeting Japanese people that a firm grip is physically repulsive to them.

After receiving the meishi, it is important to study its contents, bowing again as one reads it. To ignore a meishi by merely stuffing it in a pocket would be to imply that the person one is meeting is of no importance. The Japanese concept of face applies in this context. Face will be discussed in more detail later, but for present purposes it is enough to say that one must never behave in any way toward a Japanese that might possibly be interpreted as a slight—unless, of course, one means to provoke him deliberately.

Having thoroughly absorbed the contents of the meishi, one utters a usual pleasantry such as "It is so nice to meet you," and repeats the Japanese person's name, followed by *san*, a sign of respect similar to "Mr." in this context (although it is not restricted for use with men). One major difference between *san* and the English "Mr." or "Ms." is that *san* cannot be applied to oneself. It is used only when addressing others. For this reason, Japanese often do not use any title when introducing themselves: "I am Suzuki of Nihon Widgets" (in Japanese they will put the company name first: "Nihon Widgets *no* Suzuki *des*"). The Japanese use first names only with family members and childhood friends, and feel embarrassed when informal Americans slap them on the back and say, "Call me Joe!" Sometimes in the United States one will meet a Westernized Japanese who has adopted the American custom and changed his name to Bill or Ted, but these men are quite rare.

Seniority and ranking once again come into play in the order in which meishi are exchanged. The exchanges proceed from highest to lowest, and it is best to conform to custom because the Japanese will perceive informality as rudeness. The hosts are expected to present their cards first, so the foreign visitor is relieved of the headache of trying to figure out who is senior to whom.

A card file of all meishi received can be a very useful asset for the business person who deals often with the Japanese. They will be insulted if someone who has previously exchanged meishi with them either does not acknowledge the prior meeting or forgets their names. Such a file can also be used to note down impressions of each man met by recording a note on the back of his meishi. By 1982 I had six thousand meishi indexed by company name, with the date of first and subsequent meetings noted on the card. I found this file to be invaluable for keeping track of the people I met.

A typical first meeting with a Japanese company will take place in a large conference room with a gigantic table in the center capable of seating at least two dozen people. The visitor is escorted to this room by a pretty receptionist. When left alone in the room, the chief visitor should proceed to the chair in the center of the table—the seat of honor for the chief guest—which is directly opposite the entrance to the room. As a courtesy, one can remain standing until the Japanese arrive to conduct the guest to his seat. It is a part of Japanese courtesy to deny that one is worthy of receiving the special treatment due the guest of honor, so depending on the circumstances, just sitting down in the seat of honor without waiting to be asked might seem presumptuous. The Japanese will arrive within a few minutes, and they will approach the visitor one by one to perform the meishi-exchanging ceremony.

After everyone sits down, the foreigner must gauge what type of a meeting it is. If it is a formal meeting, as opposed to a working session, the rules are different, and most foreigners find they need all the patience they can muster in order to sit through a formal Japanese meeting without fidgeting. Since the Japanese place so much importance on personal ties and trust, they feel it is necessary to get to know the people with whom they do business. The force of contractual obligations is weak in Japan, and the formal meeting is the place where businessmen begin feeling each other out to determine the trustworthiness of those they are considering doing business with.

Usually in such a meeting fairly high-ranking executives will be present. Executives of the highest rank in Japan are not decision-makers; they are generally elderly by Western standards, and their function is to give direction on major issues, to represent the company among such outside groups as the Chamber of Commerce and Rotary to reinforce the company philosophy, and to appear at ceremonial functions, such as the signing of major deals and first meetings with executives from other companies.

The formal meeting will begin with several minutes of polite inquiries from the Japanese about their guest's trip, health, the health of any of his colleagues they may have met, and other such topics. Sometimes the Japanese will subtly signal their dislike of a particular executive by omitting to ask after him. When they are done, they will pause and expect the visitor to respond in kind. After he has done so, and if this is the first time the Westerner is meeting with this company, the Japanese president (or the most senior man on the Japanese side) will usually recite the entire history of his company's relations with his guest's firm. After patiently listening to this speech, the well-prepared foreigner will respond by conveying greetings from the president of his own company or someone else whose rank is equal to that of the Japanese who has given this speech. Rank is always matched with rank in Japan. If the Westerner has not come equipped with a personal message from the appropriate executive of his company, he must at the very least extend greetings from the home office. And it is essential to express appreciation of the merits of the Japanese company being visited. It is the part of politeness in Japan to praise others and be humble about one's own merits. An extremely polite Japanese host will, for example, disparage his children and complain about their naughtiness, while praising those of his guest, even if the host's children are models of decorum and the guest's are spoiled brats.

Foreign visitors who take the trouble to learn something in advance about the Japanese they are to meet will discover that their efforts will be amply rewarded. The Japanese will be pleased that his foreign guest cared enough to find out, for example, about trips he has made to the United States. Such small gestures signal to the Japanese the Westerner's willingness to establish a genuine relationship.

Sometimes the meeting may end after this formal exchange of greetings, but usually what will happen is that the president and his assistants will leave, indicating that the meeting will now evolve into the second type, the *kaigi* (literally, "discussion meeting"), which is more of a work session. The formal exchange of greetings is often slow going, but so is the *kaigi,* the style of which is low key and nonconfrontational. Many such meetings will be interspersed by silences, during which the Japanese try to sense the mood and true intentions of those with whom they are meeting. Groups of Japanese may come and go, and they may halt the discussion at intervals in order to confer among themselves. These brief asides are for the purpose of maintaining harmony among the Japanese team, to ensure consensus on what is happening in the meeting.

The mistakes most commonly made by Westerners when they first begin dealing with the Japanese all arise from impatience. The Japanese style is almost the opposite of that favored by Western, and particularly American, business. The hard-hitting, confrontational, "no nonsense," impersonal style of Western business people seems rude to the Japanese. Much of the etiquette of Japanese society stems from the strict avoidance of any behavior that might unintentionally be construed as rude, insulting, or emotionally wounding. Moreover, overt displays of anger and impatience are regarded not only as rude behavior but as signs of a weak character.

In light of this the reader can well imagine the distaste Japanese feel for dealing with foreigners unused to their ways. For example, often when Americans become impatient with behavior they regard as foolish or irrelevant, they will tend to display their impatience more or less openly. Indeed, Americans are notoriously unskilled at concealing their true emotions. An all too typical scenario at a first meeting with the Japanese finds a frustrated American trying to hurry the Japanese into some concrete discussion of business, and thereby ruining the chances that such a discussion will ever take place. The Japanese hate to be hurried. In a worst-case example, the frustrated executive will begin speaking too rapidly and using too much jargon even for his interpreter to understand. Often he will begin unconsciously to raise his voice, probably because of a vague feeling that people who don't understand plain English must be deaf. Ultimately, the unhappy fellow will get up and start walking around the room, gesturing with pointed finger in order to emphasize the main points of his monologue. During this display the Japanese will, at some point fairly early on, fall silent, and if the unfortunate American should pause for a minute in his delivery, he will discover that the atmosphere has become positively frosty. The results of such a meeting are invariably negative, and it will take a long time and a great deal of patience on the part of the Westerner who gets off on the wrong foot if he is to build any meaningful relationship with the Japanese at all.

Such a debacle can be avoided by remembering a few common sense rules: Don't shout, don't point, don't get ahead of the interpreter, and don't walk around the room. Punctuality is another must. Japanese keep themselves on a very tight rein, and so must the Westerner who would be successful when working with them. After all, Western individualism has its advantages in that it gives us leeway to adapt ourselves to foreign ways without the terrible wrench to the psyche that Japanese suffer when they are forced to depart from the tried and true.

One mistake should absolutely never be made when dealing with a Japanese company, and that is any attempt to pressure them by remarking that you will also meet with Company X, Y, or Z about the same proposal. The intense competitiveness of Japanese business makes mention of a competitor's name one of the most offensive faux pas possible.

From the very first, the Western business person must be aware of Japanese fanatical devotion to detail. They will have several different people taking notes at any meeting, and unless the Westerner makes a habit of minuting key points in as much detail as possible, he will quickly come to grief. Americans love to go in and wing it, but no matter how skilled one is at this style, Japanese detail work will triumph over it nearly every time. I used to tape-record minutes of a meeting as soon as I left it, and had my secretary transcribe them later. It's even better to have someone with you who will take complete and accurate notes of everything said at the meeting. I used to take my file of meeting minutes with me and surprise and impress the Japanese with my exact recall of previous discussions. Many Americans and some Europeans prefer to treat each meeting as if it were self-contained and have minimal recollection of what has gone before. As mentioned earlier, the Japanese will always be several steps ahead of most Westerners in terms of preparation for meetings. Successful negotiators learn to minimize this difference as much as possible.

Chapter 3 will discuss how to get the most out of an interpreter, but the key is to try to remember not to let one's thoughts run too far ahead, since one should never speak more than two sentences at a time, slowly and clearly, avoiding jargon and technical language as much as possible in order to make the interpretation reasonably accurate. It's easy to take it for granted that the Japanese are following what is being said, but often they aren't. One must be prepared to repeat certain remarks several times over if there's any chance that the Japanese may be missing a key point. The interpreter can tell if the Japanese aren't following, and so can any Japanese-speaking members of the foreign team. Nevertheless, even those who don't know Japanese can learn to gauge the atmosphere. The alert Westerner can pick up on subtle signals when the Japanese are registering confusion, or a desire to linger over a point that may seem trivial to the Western way of looking at things. If such a point is glossed over, it may take several meetings to clear up the problem. One ramification of this need for crystal-clear explanation is that Japanese like to have documents read out loud to them. They also demand endless technical detail, so one is advised to bring along a technical expert if there is to be any discussion of technology, and the senior negotiator and the expert will be expected to go through the data highlights together out loud. (One amusing example of the Japanese love of complete explanations before taking decisions is the way the waiter in a "French style" restaurant is expected to read, translate, and explain each and every item on the menu, including a short dissertation on the natural history of any unusual ingredients.)

To backtrack for a moment, because it is crucially important, it should be reemphasized that *one must speak clear, slower-than-normal, extraprecise English when speaking to a Japanese.* Those who have had the experience of living in a foreign country may easily recognize the polite smiles of noncomprehension, but all too often the native English speaker will fail to notice that his or her host cannot follow what is being said. This is doubly true if one has a strong regional accent or the habit of speaking rapidly. The Japanese will not let on if they aren't following, and it's up to the speaker to make sure that they can understand.

Depending on their purpose, most Japanese business meetings are not really complete without some kind of follow-up social event. When a meeting ends with no invitation to dinner or lunch, then European or American business people have reason to suspect that they have not convinced the Japanese of whatever it is they are proposing. Anyone coming to Japan on a short business trip (which should never be shorter than two weeks if one expects to fly out with a business agreement) must be sure to schedule time for socializing with the businessmen he meets. It would be offensive to Japanese business people if a Westerner refused an invitation from them. This happens sometimes to those on a tight schedule, but Westerners must adjust to a different pace in Japan and not allow themselves to be placed in the position of having to refuse what could be a very valuable invitation. They should have their social commitments structured in a flexible way.

In the context of socializing, it is important not to let our Western love of meat and potatoes interfere with an appreciation for Japanese food. The Japanese are intensely proud of and devoted to their cuisine, which has evolved over centuries. It is rich in the variety of dishes and the many different ways they can be prepared and displayed according to both regional and seasonal preferences. The Western business person who knows something about Japanese food and can appreciate a fine dish not only for its taste but, equally important, for its appearance will gain considerable stature in the eyes of the Japanese. Some of my friends in Tokyo who have frequent visitors from their head offices tell of embarrassing incidents when contracts were either lost or almost lost because of some visiting VP's intense desire to avoid Japanese food.

In reality there are so many kinds of Japanese food that there are bound to be some that even the most Westernized palate will find enjoyable. I am a devotee of raw fish *(sashimi)* and its cousin, raw fish with rice and seaweed *(sushi),* but for the man who prefers a trencherman's lunch or a barbecued steak, there is *teppan yaki* (cubed fillet of steak, grilled, with garlic optional), *shabu shabu* (similar to a good fondue), or *yaki tori* (barbecued pieces of chicken skewered on a stick). *Sukiyaki* is, of course, another Japanese dish palatable to Westerners that is familiar and popular even in the West. If you really don't like octopus, abalone, or raw fish, you can safely pass the word to your hosts, who will take you where dishes that appeal to you can be found, to such restaurants as Zakuro, which is a popular chain, for example. It is as important to learn to appreciate at least some Japanese dishes as it is to play golf in order to get along socially with Japanese businessmen.

In addition to socializing, another unique aspect of Japanese business relations is the custom of giving gifts. Business gift giving in Japan can be an expensive proposition, but the custom is well entrenched, despite recent changes in the tax law that curtail business expenses that may be claimed as deductions. The Japanese can be incredibly generous in their gift giving, and since the practice is nowhere near as widespread in the West, foreign business people, no matter how hard they try, will usually not be able to outdo the Japanese in generosity.

On a first trip to Japan, visitors are not expected to bring gifts because it is the custom for the hosts to give them to their first-time guests. However, after that first visit, when returning to Japan, foreigners should come supplied with gifts for those with whom they expect to establish lasting relations. Also, if the first-time visitor to Japan has already established relations with Japanese through meetings in his home country, it would be appropriate to strengthen the bond by bringing gifts. Gift giving is a way either of greeting a guest or of consolidating good relations. When Japanese visit foreign countries, it is appropriate to give them gifts to show that they are honored guests.

In gift giving, as in everything else, attention to rank is essential. Gifts must be graded according to rank. If the president receives a gift equal to that given to the vice president, the former will feel insulted and the latter embarrassed. In a business situation, Western executives should bring gifts for the top four or five people with whom they will be associated. An appropriate gift for the top executive might be in the $100–$150 range. If one gives the senior man a gift in that range, then for the least senior person, something around $50 would be correct. The valuation of gifts is a tricky thing, and very much depends on the particular situation. Another important aspect is that, in Japanese eyes, brand names are important. Certain brands are most acceptable and appropriate in business gift giving among the Japanese. A typical gift currently (1983) being given is a Mark Cross pen-and-pencil set, with either the initials of the giver's company or the initials of the person to whom it is to be given. Another common gift is a Dunhill monogrammed lighter. Scotch is often given, but as of 1983 the only brands that the Japanese acknowledge as superior are Johnnie Walker Black Label, Old Parr, and Chivas Regal. Givenchy perfumes and colognes are also "in" this year; however, it is best to check on the latest brand preferences before meeting a Japanese guest. Another very acceptable gift is an item typical of your home country. Americans, for example, might give an item such as a pewter mug. A Western painting would be another good choice. Such gifts have the advantage of being somewhat more personal. Gifts are usually given during the social event, such as a luncheon, following a meeting.

It is helpful to keep a record of all gifts given, because a gift should *never* be repeated (with the obvious exception of Scotch). Unless a gift-giving record is maintained, one lands in difficulties quite quickly. After a few years of exchanging gifts, Western business people are often tempted to put their records in a computer file, because gift giving without duplication can become an intricate matter after several rounds of exchanges.

The sort of gift-giving competition implied in my comments regarding business gifts also occurs in gift giving among friends or acquaintances. The giver bestows a gift on the recipient who in turn has a deep sense of obligation and "burden of guilt" from having accepted the gift (although politeness makes it impossible to refuse). He or she then reacts by buying something better than the original gift in order to repay the favor with interest. The original giver is then put into the guilt situation and buys something even better, and so it goes. I can recall my wife throwing up her hands on more than one occasion when she wanted to give a small gift to a Japanese woman as a way of saying thank you for some kindness only to find a more elaborate return gift being delivered the next day. Our conclusion was that the only way to avoid this was not to respond after the first exchange of gifts takes place. It puts the Westerner in the role of having the guilt, but we can stand it better. The Westerner is less involved with the Japanese rules of etiquette with regard to gift giving, so it is possible and probably best to break the chain at this point, before it bankrupts both parties. Small thank-you gifts for hospitality are common in Japan, but Japanese are usually careful to limit their gifts to something on the order of a box of *sembe* (seaweed crackers).

As one might expect, business socializing in Japan has its own peculiar etiquette. To take just one example, a simple golf game becomes a ritual ceremony in Japan. Golf is a popular sport in Japan, but few can afford to play it. Merely to get a tee-off time, an office boy must be sent to the golf club three weeks in advance, and stand in line starting at 4:00 A.M. Tee-off times are arranged precisely and mathematically, with foursomes teeing off punctually every five minutes. For this reason, guests must never be late, but they must never be early either, because it is the host's duty to greet his guest at the front entrance to the golf club. The guest should leave his hotel or house early enough to be sure of arriving on time, but if he arrives too early he must park out of sight until the proper time. The host will escort his guest into the club, find him a locker, and present him with a small gift, usually a box of golf balls and some tees monogrammed with the name of the host's company. The guest is expected to use these balls and not his own.

The Japanese are very serious about golf, and agonize over putts, but it would be bad form for the foreign guest to fidget, no matter how many times the Japanese golfer recalculates distance, slope, and wind direction. Discussion of business is usually taboo on the golf course, and is seldom raised until all eighteen holes have been played —and then only at the host's initiative. Because of the need for precise control of tee-off times, it is usually the custom to have lunch (lasting from half an hour to ninety minutes) after nine holes, and protesting that one would prefer to keep playing is utterly useless.

At the end, after the *ofuro* (Japanese bath) ritual (scrub down *completely* before entering the tub, rinse every speck of soap, and watch out for that hot water if you have a heart condition!), players gather in the clubhouse. This is when one can present the host with a small gift (a silver tee or a golf watch, for example), if desired. The guest will probably receive a gift from his host of fruit for his wife and family.

Another Japanese social event that is subject to a code of etiquette is an office-group trip to a traditional Japanese inn, or *ryokan*. In order not to make the visit frivolous (and therefore unworthy in Japanese eyes), it is usually organized around a special event, such as a trip to a shrine, a game of golf, or a *go* competition (*go* is a game somewhat similar to chess and is very popular among Japanese salary men). I have had the pleasure of participating in a number of these *ryokan* outings, and have found it to be a time when the Japanese really feel that they can relax. In fact, I recommend a *ryokan* trip for anyone visiting Japan. There are many near Tokyo, and some famous ones located in the tourist centers of Kyoto, Nara, Beppu, Ama-no-hashidate, and Sendai. The Three Sisters Ryokan in Kyoto is a well-known establishment catering to foreigners.

The charm of Japanese-style group solidarity is well illustrated in a story about an incident at a *ryokan* that a nisei couple related to me. The couple were visiting a *ryokan* near Tokyo where there were two outdoor *ofuro* (hot baths). One was empty and the other jammed with men and women from a company in Tokyo. The couple asked why they were all packed together in the same bath and the reply came back: "Who would want to be alone in that *ofuro* when we can all just fit into this one and be together?" Unfortunately, these days there are few inns left with co-ed *ofuro,* one area where Western influence has had a definite negative effect on the culture.

The time to check into a *ryokan* is about 5:00 P.M. when the inn will usually be ready to receive guests. The etiquette is as follows. The guests first sign in, and then the maid accompanies them to their rooms. Shoes are left at the front door not to be used again until one leaves; guests are provided with slippers. Next, tea is served, together with traditional tea biscuits. After tea the guests are expected to change into a *yukata,* a traditional Japanese garment that we in the West sometimes mistakenly call a kimono. Next is the trip to the *ofuro,* which is one of the highlights of the visit. Many inns have natural hot-spring *ofuro* (especially in Beppu and the Japan Alps), and it is worth traveling to Japan just to experience the unique feeling of rejuvenation that comes from soaking in these baths, a feeling that lasts for hours afterwards. Following the *ofuro* the guest returns to the room where drinks (usually sake, beer, or whisky) are served by the maid. This is followed by a *sukiyaki* or other traditional Japanese evening meal cooked and served in the room by the maid. The meal is followed by more drinks and then sleep on a straw mat called a *tatami.* This isn't as uncomfortable as it sounds, since a type of cushioned sleeping bag called a *futon* will also be provided, which is extremely comfortable. Pillows are a problem, however. The Japanese traditionally prefer pillows that are rocklike, and the *ryokan* pillows are traditional in all respects.

Part of the charm of a visit to a traditional Japanese inn is the guest's sense of participation in a pleasant and antique ritual. Although a golf game and a stay at an inn are both subject to rules of etiquette, the inn has the added force of an ancient tradition on its side.

Perhaps because the Japanese are famous for courtesy and hospitality, Westerners often feel nervous when entertaining Japanese guests. The most important thing to remember is that most Japanese, especially those who have never traveled abroad before, feel uncomfortable and lonely in foreign lands unless accompanied by a group of their compatriots. So they greatly appreciate it when their hosts make a special effort to make them feel at home.

When receiving Japanese on business, before they arrive it is very important to find out as much as possible about their company. They will always thoroughly research the foreign company they are visiting, and they will be impressed if the foreign company returns the compliment. I used to provide my New York office with a complete analysis of the top fifteen to twenty Japanese pharmaceutical companies with complete data on their financial and marketing performance, including their R&D achievements, so that any Japanese visitor to my head office would always be impressed with our knowledge of his business. It may take a little effort, but it is well worth it. Such information can be obtained from various sources. One source might be the Japanese embassy; a second would be the Commercial Section of the U.S. embassy in Tokyo; a third would be the Japanese trading company (although security may be a factor here); and a very good fourth would be the office of Nomura Securities or any other Japanese stockbrokers who have local offices. There should always be two or three copies of the host company's annual report available to give the visitors. Further, the effect on a Japanese businessman would be extremely positive if he walked into an office in, say, Des Moines and saw a copy of the annual report of his own company lying on the table.

When the Japanese arrives, have him met by a secretary or receptionist and shown to an empty conference room. It is usually not a good idea to show him to his host's office, because offices in Japan are workplaces only, and are generally not considered formal enough for the civilities of a first meeting.

In Japan, visitors are immediately served Japanese tea. This will often be followed by hot coffee in winter, and ice-cold orange juice in summer—and that followed by Indian tea (or coffee again), or sometimes iced coffee with ice cream, depending on the weather. When the Japanese are visiting foreign offices, they will be pleased if they receive similar hospitality during their business meetings.

When the host executives enter the conference room to greet the Japanese, the meishi ritual should be gone through as described earlier, complete with bowing, if the hosts are sincere in wanting to make a good impression.

Many people are uncertain as to what the Japanese expect when it comes to business entertainment. Although it is true that the Japanese virtually never invite business guests, particularly foreigners, to their homes, that does not mean they will be offended if Western hosts invite them to their homes. On the contrary, they will be deeply honored, and for this reason it is wise to entertain Japanese business guests at one's home only when desirous of showing them particular attention. Inviting a Japanese on a first meeting would cause this gesture to lose its significance. To a Japanese, such an invitation is a mark of great esteem and proof of the seriousness of his host's interest in the business relationship being discussed.

One thing that foreigners are often perplexed about is what kind of food to serve their Japanese guests. But one needen't worry— when a Japanese leaves his home shores, he is resigned to eating Western food for the duration of his trip. He certainly will not be offended if he is served a Western meal or taken to a Western restaurant. Nevertheless, taking him to a good Japanese restaurant would make a positive impression. (Make sure it is frequented by Japanese, a sure sign that it is top class.) It is better not to take Japanese to chic French restaurants, because normally they don't know what to order and will not appreciate the food when they get it, although this, of course, depends on the individual. A better choice would be a steak house, a Chinese restaurant (Japanese are quite fond of Chinese food), or an impressive locale (in America the Sky Club in the Pan Am Building in New York or the "21" Club, and in London a London club such as the East India or the Carlton, are examples of such places). Tokyo is arguably one of the very best cities in the world for dining out, so it will be difficult to impress the Japanese businessman, but he will recognize quality and service when he sees it, and he will appreciate a famous place with a unique atmosphere.

Another question many Western businessmen ask is, "Should I bring my wife?" The attentive reader has probably noticed that the language in this book assumes that Japanese business executives are all men. For all practical purposes, this is true. There are very, very few Japanese businesswomen, although this situation may change in coming years. Generally, Japanese wives stay home. They do not participate except on rare occasions in business dinners, and will almost never travel from Japan with their husbands on a business trip. There is no hard-and-fast rule about what the Japanese businessman will expect in the West, but the best rule to remember is to include wives if the Japanese is bringing his, or if one wants to avoid discussion of business during the evening. The Japanese are very embarrassed when American men start discussing business in front of their wives. When wives are not present, as soon as the meal is over the Japanese will expect that business topics will be discussed.

For the female executive, entertaining Japanese businessmen—indeed dealing with them at all—will pose problems. Japanese society still adheres to a rigid division of labor by sex, and the Japanese guest of a female executive will probably feel somewhat at a loss. The idea of a woman doing what in Japan is done only by men may seem quite odd to him, especially if it is his first trip abroad. A female executive may find the issue further confused if her husband accompanies her to a business dinner with Japanese guests.

Japanese usually enjoy being taken to nightclubs and after-dinner entertainment. If it is at all practicable, taking a Japanese executive to a nightclub can be an excellent way of showing his distinction as an important guest. (London and Paris are better than New York for this kind of after-hours entertainment.)

THE JAPANESE LANGUAGE:
A KEY TO UNDERSTANDING

My old friend Larry Snowden, currently (1983) the president of the American Chamber of Commerce in Japan, has been in and out of Japan for at least the past twelve years. He has been both a successful military man (Chief of Staff of U.S. Forces Japan) and a successful businessman (vice president of Hughes Aircraft). Larry and I have always agreed on most things—except the Japanese language. Larry was fond of telling visiting American businessmen at our Chamber "briefing breakfasts" that there was no real need to learn Japanese and that he had been successful without ever mastering more than a few words of the language.

My reply was that for anyone who plans to have anything to do with the Japanese that is likely to be sustained and important, not learning the language was like trying to swim upstream with only one arm. Perhaps possible, but very difficult. Those who don't learn Japanese will find a barrier erected between themselves and real understanding of the Japanese. In Japanese it is not only *what* is said that is important—*how* it is said can be far more important. And what is *not* said can be the most significant of all. Understanding what is left unsaid is a vital skill in Japan. Japanese don't approve of the directness and frankness that Americans favor. Even those who don't learn Japanese will find that they must learn how Japanese prefer to express themselves, or they won't even be able to understand Japanese use of English. As Bill Dizer, another old friend, an expert speaker of Japanese and a close adviser during my entire stay in Japan, always says, "Don't let people give you any false ideas that you don't need Japanese. It is essential—as essential as needing command of English to be fully effective in America." Fortunately I listened to Bill and stuck with my Japanese lessons. They really paid off. Imagine a Japanese trying to work in Houston, New York, or London with no command of English. Westerners will be in almost the same boat in Tokyo or Osaka if they have no knowledge of Japanese. And remember that "it is more difficult for Japanese to learn English than it is for many other peoples, and language teaching in Japan is extraordinarily poor."[1] The visitor to Japan should not expect that "everyone will speak English." They don't.

Obviously most of my readers will not have the chance to live and work in Japan for a period of several years, as I did. Becoming fluent in the language is impractical for those who are not living in Japan. However, anyone lucky enough to be able to come to Japan and spend some time there should make the effort, and learn what they can of the language. They will be repaid for the effort many times over in their job performance, and it will be an extra bonus in that it will almost certainly increase satisfaction and pleasure in being in Japan.

For those who dread the thought of trying to learn a foreign language and work full time besides, let me stress that it isn't only knowing the language that will pay off. There is a tremendous amount that can be learned *about* the language which will be useful to a foreigner plotting his early steps in dealing with the Japanese.

Before beginning, let me briefly explain something about the origins of the language. I quote from one of America's leading experts on Japan, Edwin Reischauer:

> Japanese probably belongs to the Altaic family of languages named for a mountain range in Mongolia. The Altaic languages include Turkish, Mongolian, the Manchu of the last semi-nomadic conquerors of China, and Korean, and they bear resemblance in structure to other languages of Asian origin such as Hungarian and Finnish, and possibly the Dravidian tongues of South India.[2]

Because Japanese comes from such a small stream in the world river of languages, it is unlike any language that most Westerners are familiar with. However, a large number of English and Portuguese words have been borrowed and transformed into Japanese words.

"Television" becomes *terebi* (there's no *v* in Japanese); "bread" is *pan* (derived from *pão,* the Portuguese for "bread"); and a white-collar worker is referred to as a *sarariman*—a "salary man." One caution here: there is indeed a plethora of English words in Japanese, but as can be seen from the above examples, they are so distorted by Japanese phonetic rules and inflections that native English speakers will not be able to recognize most of them. Japanese often find it frustrating when the "English" words they do know are not under-stood by English speakers.

Perhaps the most significant difference between English and Japa-nese is that what can—and, indeed, must—be expressed in Japanese is not expressed in English. Japanese is situational, unlike modern European languages. By this I mean that the speaker's status versus the status of the addressee is expressed in the grammar of his or her sentences. In most European languages there are formal and familiar forms for "you": for example, *tu* and *usted,* and *tu* and *vous,* in Spanish and French, respectively. But Japanese is far more complex in its expression of hierarchy, almost feudal in its obsession with gradations in rank. A Japanese prefers to use the exactly correct form of address, but if he doesn't know his position relative to the person who is addressing him he will resort to the ordinary polite form.

One way of looking at this situation is to view Japanese not as one language but as a group of languages—they all have a common core, but nevertheless each one sounds very different from all the others. The most obvious example is the language used by women as op-posed to that employed by men. For example, the word *arimasu,* which means "to have," would be pronounced *arimasu* by women, with a *u* at the end of the word. A man talking to a superior or in a formal situation would normally say *arimas,* whereas a man talking to an inferior or someone of his own status in an informal setting would say *aru.* The same is true of every verb. One lesson that comes from this little example is that a man should usually avoid learning Japanese from a woman, and vice versa, unless the teacher in ques-tion is a trained and experienced Japanese teacher. Japanese women speak an entirely different style of Japanese than the men do, and there is considerable amusement when a foreign man starts showing off the newly acquired Japanese that he has learned from a woman. It is almost the equivalent of a Japanese businessman in a meeting with top American executives using the lisping, gushy style affected by some homosexuals.

It is not just the distinctions between male and female speech that reflect the situation of the speaker. There are distinct vocabularies and forms of pronunciation depending on whether one is addressing a superior, an equal, or an inferior. For example, when addressing a superior a Japanese employee might say *"Buchō,"* if the superior is a *buchō* (department head) in the firm. The superior would call his subordinate by his name followed by *kun* (meaning "follower") as in "Suzuki-*kun.*" (*Kun* is also sometimes used to indicate familiarity.) If two men are equal in rank, each would simply call the other by his last name, followed by *san,* when addressing him. To make a mistake in this formalized way of addressing one another is to give great offense. As one writer puts it:

> For every specific social relationship, there is a set pattern of what one
> is expected to say. This has brought about a certain inflexibility of lan-
> guage, resulting to some extent in social immobility. To a Japanese,
> trained subliminally from childhood in language usage and nuance, it
> is always possible and often necessary to be able to place oneself and the
> person to whom one is speaking in a relative position—whether it be
> superior, inferior, or equal—merely by listening to the way one says
> "How do you do?"[3]

In addition to social standing, another important factor influencing the language of the speaker is his age, based on the imperial era during which he was born. Older Japanese executives are likely to have been born during the reign of the Meiji or Taisho emperors. This means that they were born sometime between the turn of the century and 1925. The passing of time has blurred the distinctions between Meiji and Taisho. One can generalize and say that these men are generally very traditional in their outlooks and have stead-fastly refused to allow foreign influences to penetrate their lives. Their Japanese is quite formal, and they will refrain from using the kind of relaxed Japanese that characterizes the younger men who were born during the era of Showa (1925 onwards). These men, par-ticularly those born after the war, tend to be far more accepting of the use of English words and have a background of considerable exposure to foreign, and particularly American, influences.

For the Japanese of the Meiji and Taisho eras the events that have contributed most toward shaping their attitudes today are World War II and the Occupation, which made them reject the West and Western influence. They have usually refused to learn any foreign language, and although many can speak a little English, they would prefer not to let it be known that they do, and will insist on interpreters. The leadership of Keidanren, with the notable exception of Akio Morita of Sony and Norishige Hasegawa of Sumitomo Chemical, are all in this category.

The biggest influence on the people of the early Showa era has been the liberalization of Japan in the sixties followed by the oil crisis of the early seventies. Many Japanese felt after the oil shock that they had been caught off guard, and therefore their determination to avoid complacency was redoubled. For this reason their cultural predilection toward a survival syndrome has been reinforced, and they are always looking for ways to preserve and enhance Japanese power and influence while being ready and able to use the tools of the West. These men are quite willing to use English where necessary, and many can read and write the language even if they do not speak it. In the presence of their superiors who belong to the Meiji or Taisho era they may tend to play down their English capability, because they know that it offends the older men.

I remember when I was first studying Japanese that my teacher, Professor Nakanishi of the Aoyama School of Languages, would spend a considerable amount of time teaching me to recognize certain gestures and phrases in Japanese that would indicate the attitude the Japanese had toward me and my company. In this way I quickly came to realize that understanding the situational nature of Japanese could be a great help in my business dealings. I learned to sense these nuances long before I became fluent enough to understand everything that was being said. It was a useful skill. For example, if the Japanese businessman addressed me as "Zimmerman-*san,*" I knew I was being accorded normal respect and could anticipate that the conversation would be reasonably straightforward. If, on the other hand, I was referred to or addressed as "Zimmerman," I was either being demeaned by the Japanese (because he wanted to indicate to my Japanese associates that he would not be cowed by the presence of a foreigner) or he wished to indicate that there was some special familiarity between us, implying that we were on the same level. Conversely, if I was called "Zimmerman-*sama,*" then the speaker wanted me to know that he publicly held me (and/or my position) in the highest esteem.

One should always use the last name followed by *san* when addressing a Japanese. They do not expect foreigners to know the subtle difference between the name or title alone, the title followed by *san*, the name followed by *san* or *kun*, and the name followed by *sama*. Never use first names. The only exception might be in the United States with a very Americanized Japanese who has given up the struggle and allowed himself to be called by his first name or some easy-to-pronounce American equivalent like "Sam" (for Osamu) or "Ken" (for Kentaro). I recently met a senior executive with one of the pharmaceutical companies we deal with. He had just spent six years in Los Angeles and the staff there had taken to calling him Sam. He accepted it as long as he was there, but after returning to Japan he reverted to the normal Japanese practice of using his last name or title. (By the way, as in Chinese, the Japanese "last name," or family name, comes first, though nowadays they usually reverse the order when dealing with foreigners. Occasionally an executive will put the last name first even on the English side of his meishi, so it is well to be on guard.)

Here are a few easy-to-remember titles that could come in handy. They can help determine who is really calling the shots in a meeting with the Japanese. One of the most commonly used titles is *kachō*, meaning section chief. This is the lowest level that the Western business person is likely to meet. He is the equivalent of a project or function supervisor in the United States. The *kachō* really gets the work done, and is, for all intents and purposes, the first level of management in a Japanese company. When working with a *kachō*, one is dealing with a decision-maker/initiator and a workhorse of the company. The next level up is the *buchō*, or department head. He is the equivalent of a division chief or department manager in the United States. In a company of ten thousand employees there may be four hundred *kachō* and about one hundred *buchō*. Above the *buchō* is the *torishimariyaku*, or director. This is seldom used as a primary title, and the director is usually a *buchō* as well. The next level is *jōmu*, or managing director. He would be the equivalent of a group vice president in an American corporation and would hold executive power over an entire wing of the operation, such as marketing, finance, research, administration, or production. Above the *jomū* comes the *semmu*, or executive vice president. He is the third ranking officer in the company, and there is usually only one or two *semmu* in the average company. Above the *semmu* comes the *fuku-shachō*, or vice president, next the *shachō*, or president, and above him the *kaichō*, or chairman.

Let me destroy a few more shibboleths about the language before I go on to the use of interpreters (a practice that those who do not have sufficient command of the language are forced into). One piece of nonsense very often bandied about the American Club in Tokyo and other *gaijin* gathering places is that foreigners who learn too much Japanese are disliked by the Japanese because they feel threatened by a foreigner able to pierce the veil of language which they use as a screen to hide their real feelings. As with all such myths, there is a certain amount of truth and a certain amount of falsehood in this belief. The number of Americans who have reached such a level of proficiency in Japanese is under five hundred. If the academics are eliminated, who are not likely to be negotiating business deals with the Japanese, the number drops to below one hundred. Thus, no businessman who begins learning Japanese as an adult will ever become that proficient. Even if he did, it might even be an advantage, especially if he disclaimed his ability in the same way Japanese executives play down their ability in English.

What the Japanese don't like—and I have witnessed this firsthand —is to see Americans become so Japanese in their outlook and approach that they criticize their own countrymen and always try to react as the Japanese do in business situations. In other words, one can speak Japanese as well as one's linguistic ability and time to study will permit and never be so good that the Japanese will feel threatened by it, but anyone who begins to *behave* like a Japanese will be branded a *hen na* (peculiar) *gaijin,* and their American (or European) identity and credibility will be lost. They will never be taken seriously, and even their ability to represent their company will be in doubt. (The high value Japanese give to group solidarity explains why the Japanese don't like Japanified Americans any more than they like Americanized Japanese.)

Unlike Americans, the Japanese are not seeking to spread their culture around the world (although they do like their arts to be appreciated, and promote tours of kabuki performances, etc.). They resent foreigners who become Japanophiles to such an extent that they ape the Japanese. Americans don't like to see their fellow countrymen becoming Japanophiles, but for very different reasons, since the American cultural bias is to spread American values around the world, and we love to export our ideas and institutions. On the other hand, some Americans carry their respect for other cultures to the extreme of abandoning their own culture and adopting that of a foreign land. Europeans seem less prone to adopt this form of dealing with culture shock. I have known several European managers who have spent ten to twelve years in Japan but are as English, French or German as the day they arrived. The Japanese sense of uniqueness and vulnerability prompts such people to follow a course which is the opposite of that of most Americans, protecting themselves from outsiders by keeping aloof rather than by converting them to their way of life. In this sense the Japanese language does provide a screen around the culture, and the true feelings of the Japanese people collectively. However, once it is known that a foreigner can speak a fairly competent brand of Japanese, one can almost hear the sigh of relief around the room.

Another favorite myth about the Japanese language is that it is peculiarly difficult, to the point of being impossible for foreigners to learn. This is widely believed by the Japanese themselves. It certainly is very difficult, but it is not impenetrable. This belief has no doubt been fostered by two factors: first, only a small number of foreigners have made a real effort to learn Japanese, so only a small number, relatively speaking, have become fluent; second, the Japanese take pride in imagining their language to be more difficult to learn than any other. Prospective students of Japanese should not be scared away by this myth of insurmountable difficulty. Grammar is grammar, whether it is Greek or Hindustani or English—or Japanese.

Nevertheless, I must qualify the advice I have so far been giving about learning Japanese. I have been talking about *spoken* Japanese —written Japanese is an entirely different matter. For their written language the Japanese originally borrowed the Chinese system based on characters, or ideograms. Chinese characters involve one symbol per word, and are not based on phonetics as Western alphabets are. The Chinese characters borrowed into Japanese are called *kanji;* the minimum number of *kanji* that one must know in order to be able to read modern Japanese texts is around 1,850. It is a virtual impossibility to learn *kanji* without devoting years of full-time study to it. But Japanese is written not only with characters—there are also two phonetic alphabets used to transcribe foreign words, to write Japanese words that have no Chinese equivalent (such as place names, etc.), and to clarify the interpretation of *kanji* characters that have more than one meaning (some *kanji* have as many as seven different possible interpretations). These two alphabets, called *kana,* are possible for the foreigner with a limited amount of time to master, and it can be very useful to know them. *Katakana* is used for foreign words, *hiragana* for all other words not written in *kanji*. *Romaji*, which is what the Japanese call the Latin alphabet, is very little used in Japan. Most street and station signs will be in the Japanese *kanji* or *kana*. In the center of Tokyo, Kobe, or Osaka you will occasionally see *romaji* signs.

One of the most frustrating experiences for foreigners who have put in the time and effort to learn Japanese, and have started feeling comfortable in the language, is that often the Japanese still insist on addressing them in English. This is especially frustrating when the foreigner has reached the point where his Japanese is light years ahead of their English. Bill Dizer, my friend and adviser, points out that for the Japanese-speaking foreigner the best way to handle the language situation is to let the Japanese person pick the language in which he prefers to communicate. Often I will get a phone call from a Japanese executive who will begin the conversation in English only to find that he cannot get his message across. I will ask him for clarification in Japanese and usually he will thankfully go back to his own language and the conversation will proceed. Alternatively, he may feel that what he has to say needs to be communicated to me in English (that is, it is serious and important), and he will struggle on in that language and expect me to answer in English. In fact, he will be annoyed if I start answering in Japanese, so it is best to respect his wishes. Sometimes Japanese insist on English merely for an opportunity to practice. Then the polite foreigner must grin and bear it.

Now that I have given a fair idea of the obstacles foreigners face in trying to learn Japanese, it is my duty to give notice of the problems that he who refuses to learn Japanese will have with that necessary evil the interpreter. Ninety-nine percent of those who deal with the Japanese will need to use interpreters at one stage or another. Trying to communicate through two such disparate languages as Japanese and English is a Herculean task. Here are a few words of warning based on my personal experience and that of other old Japan hands.

To set the stage, let me quote again from former Ambassador Reischauer:

Even assuming a perfect knowledge of both languages on the part of the interpreter, which is rarely the case, English and Japanese both suffer a radical transformation in being converted into the other. Word order is in large part reversed; clear statements become obscure; polite phrases become insulting; and a remark, even though translated accurately in a literal sense, can take on an entirely different thrust. Simultaneous interpreters, for all their wizardry, can only cover about two thirds of what is said.[4]

Many well-known interpreters in Japan come from a firm called Simul International, which provides the best interpreters I have ever come across. To give an example of their dedication: in 1978 I attended a meeting of the U.S.–Japan Businessmen's Council in Dallas, where the hosts, led by Mark Shepherd of Texas Instruments, a Japan expert in his own right, had organized a rodeo for the Japanese businessmen guests. The problem was that the rodeo calls would be unintelligible to Mr. Iwasa, chairman of the Japanese delegation, and many of the other Meiji- or Taisho-era executives. Simul came up with the answer. They had one of their interpreters study Japanese explanations for words like "heifer," "lasso," "branding iron," and a host of other rodeo expressions, and thus the event went off smoothly, with the Japanese executives hugely enjoying not only the rodeo but also the steak-and-chili barbecue afterwards.

The best way to ensure that an interpreter effectively communicates what is intended is to have a one- to two-hour session with him or her prior to the meeting, reviewing any words or phrases of a technical or complicated nature with which the interpreter might not be familiar. This is also a good opportunity to explain to the interpreter the objective of the meeting, the desired atmosphere, and any special instructions that might enhance the quality of the interpretation and therefore the understanding of the Japanese hosts or delegation.

Even with the best preparation possible, unforeseen disasters can occur. I remember one incident, which occurred when I had been in Japan just over a year. I decided that the only way to improve our market share for a certain pharmaceutical product was to bring a European expert over to lecture to the Japanese doctors on how to use the drug most effectively. I had traveled to Holland to meet with the professor, who was one of the world's leading experts in the field. He agreed to spend two weeks in Japan lecturing on our product. The task I was faced with on returning to Japan was to find an interpreter who had a large English vocabulary in general and in-depth knowledge of psychiatric terms as well. My staff combed the universities, and finally came up with a thirty-two-year-old assistant professor of neuropsychiatry at Tokyo Women's College to work with us.

We called her into the office, and I spent an hour with her explaining what we hoped to accomplish during the visit, and gave her copies of all the works of the Dutch professor so that she could be thoroughly familiar with his style and terminology before he arrived. She had already read much of his work and seemed ideal for the assignment even though she had never done any interpreting before. Finally our Dutch professor arrived and we had another meeting with the interpreter so that she could get to know him and listen to his pronunciation. Finally the night of the first meeting arrived. It was held at a large auditorium in the Shinjuku skyscraper complex, and several hundred Japanese psychiatrists and neurologists showed up. Our professor started his presentation, and when he came to the end of the first two sentences, he waited expectantly for the interpreter to repeat his comments in Japanese. There was dead silence. The sweat poured off my forehead, and then finally the young lady managed to say in Japanese, "I don't know what he said," and fled from the interpreter's booth. After a moment I summoned my marketing manager and persuaded him to handle the chore of interpreting despite the loss of face that this entailed, since he was a *buchō*, and *buchō* don't do interpreting. Meanwhile, I ran after the professor/interpreter, and found her sobbing in the corridor.

I got her into a deserted area of the lobby and tried to calm her down, realizing that the considerable sum we had invested in bringing the Dutch expert to Japan with his wife for ten days might be a total loss if I failed to bring this woman around. She had stage fright. Eventually she regained her composure and told me that she had always been afraid of appearing in public but had regarded this as her chance to sink or swim, and unfortunately she had found that she could not do it. She apologized and started to get up to leave, but I made her sit down and explained to her that many people were depending on her. Finally she agreed to have one more try and I got her back to the auditorium, where she joined Saganuma-*san*, my marketing *buchō*, in the interpreter's box. After about five minutes I became conscious that she was now interpreting in a bold confident voice. During the course of the next ten days and eight cities, she became better and better, but I learned another lesson about depending on interpreters that day—one that I will never forget.

As mentioned in Chapter 2, when working with interpreters it is essential that they be allowed sufficient time to keep up with the speaker. Never forget that Japanese takes 30 percent more time than English to say the same thing. In other words, if it took five minutes to express a thought in English, it will take at least seven to eight minutes for the same concept to be communicated in Japanese. This is because the Japanese language is not used as concisely and directly as English. The interpreter has constantly to embellish the telling with honorifics and digressions in order to get the idea across. It is not that the grammatical structure of Japanese entails long sentences. Rather, cultural factors determine the way Japanese use their language. Bluntness and directness are possible, but nearly always avoided. Beware: if the interpreter takes less time to translate what was said than the speaker did to say it, then either he or she didn't understand or is paraphrasing, which is probably not what you want. Make sure that the interpreter does as much explaining as necessary.

My normal practice was to use interpreters when I knew that what was being discussed would be extremely important and I had to be able to understand every word and communicate it accurately to others. I never spoke more than two sentences at a time, and paused for the interpreter to translate, minimizing the chances for lapses of memory and inaccuracies. When a business is technical in nature— and most are nowadays—it pays to hire someone and train him or her in the terminology in order to be sure that the technical aspects are clearly understood and accurately translated.

So far I have discussed how I view the Japanese language as spoken and understood by foreigners. What about the English language as spoken and understood by Japanese? Let me quote from another excellent writer on Japan, Endymion Wilkinson:

> In Japan . . . fluency in speaking English is positively discouraged by the numerous examinations on written English and its grammar which students are forced to take in order to get in to the right schools and universities. . . . Those who for one reason or another do go abroad and become fluent in foreign languages often find themselves penalized in the job market when they return to Japan.[5]

The Japanese simply do not have an ear for English—or any other foreign languages, for that matter—despite the incredible number of English-language teachers in Tokyo and Osaka as well as the programs on Japanese television and NHK radio to encourage English fluency. To them English is a travesty because it requires them to unlearn everything they instinctively know to be "right" about a language. The Japanese translation of a Pan Am flight attendant's announcement is one illustration of this phenomenon. The American woman says, "Ladies and gentlemen, we will soon be landing in Narita. Please fasten your seat belts, bring your seats to an upright position, and stop smoking. Do not stand up until the aircraft comes to a complete halt." This comes out in Japanese as: "My esteemed customers, in about twenty minutes we will have the honor of bringing you to Narita Airport. It would be very much appreciated and considerate of you to now put out your tobacco and place your tables back in the upright position. We would also be very grateful if you would condescend, most respected customers, to put your chairs upright, and if you could also fasten your seat belts. This would be very much appreciated and we are deeply grateful that you have selected our humble airline to fly with today, you have done us a great honor. . . ." In short, the way in which we dispense with formal courtesies is considered quite barbarian by the Japanese.

If the average Japanese considers spoken English to be a barbarous tongue, it is no wonder that there are so few proficient in English, even in American companies with large numbers of Japanese employees. On top of everything else, English is difficult for Japanese to pronounce. The famous problem with *r* for *l* is only one of their many problems. The average American businessman finds out very quickly that he cannot rely on English to get his message across, and thus is thrown back on the interpreter or the fluent English-speaking executive, of which there are quite a few. Many of these men make an excellent contribution to their organization, but in too many cases they are promoted not because of their ability but because of their English. There is no easy answer, but beware of the *eigoyasan* (literally, English-speaking incompetents).

The nub of it is that there are no simple solutions to the language problem but language remains the key to understanding and dealing with the Japanese. My own solution to the problem was to learn the language. I worked at it for an hour a day for two years, averaging perhaps three lessons a week, and thanks to the patience and skill of Professor Nakanishi and the chance for daily practice (plus my previous experience in language study), I was able to attain a fluency that is still helpful even though I no longer live in Japan. My technique was to tape every lesson and play it back on the tape recorder in the car as I drove around in Tokyo's heavy traffic. I also practiced on my untiring and dedicated driver, who taught me how to express myself in the more casual style, which helped me to supplement the high-flown Japanese that the professor liked me to speak. By the time I left Japan, I could even tell the difference between Kansai *ben* and Tokyo or Edo *ben* (Western versus Eastern dialects).

THEY'RE ON A DIFFERENT WAVELENGTH

The Japanese often say and do things that seem totally illogical by
Western standards. The communication gap crops up in all areas, and
it often leads to unfortunate consequences. The chapter title I have
chosen to sum up the problem of noncommunication may be trite,
but it is quite accurate: they *are* on a different wavelength. The
Japanese mind is simply set on a different channel from the Western
mind. Unless a common frequency is actively sought, communication will not be achieved. Only by clearly realizing this fact, and
making a concerted effort to understand why they act the way they
do, can Westerners begin to deal with Japanese effectively. To use a
slightly different analogy, when someone turns on his television set,
he expects that even if he can't find a good program he will at least
be able to understand what is taking place. Suppose he finds instead
that he can't understand any of the programs and has to puzzle over
the hidden meaning of every word and gesture. After spending a
good deal of time flipping through the channels, only to find that
none of the shows make sense, he is likely in the end to shut off the
TV in total frustration.

The above scenario aptly describes the normal chain of events
when a Westerner first meets a Japanese in either a business or a
social context. The Westerner will try any number of standard con-
versational gambits, only to find that none of them meets the kind
of response experience has taught him to expect. In India, where I

live now, the Indians don't even try to figure out the Japanese. The Japanese in New Delhi are a little society unto themselves, and whether in the golf club or on the fairway (the only places where the Indians really see the Japanese) they are referred to as "those little Japs," and some Indians make remarks such as "They shouldn't be allowed on the course on Sundays," as if to imply that they don't have as much right to be there as people of any other nationality. The reason for this negativity is quite simply the inability of the Japanese to get on the same wavelength as the Indians, as well as the complete unwillingness of most Indians to even try to understand the Japanese. Fortunately or unfortunately, depending on one's point of view, we in the West cannot afford to adopt that attitude to the Japanese. We must get on their wavelength because they are too important to be ignored: they are our chief competitors and increasingly are also becoming our partners—and in some cases our employers.

The first and most important rule of golf is to keep your head down and your eye on the ball. The first and most important rule when trying to communicate with a Japanese is equally simple to state, and just as hard for the novice to put into practice. The rule is: Keep your mouth shut. A wise foreigner lets the Japanese do the talking, is extremely patient, and does not interrupt him. The Westerner who takes the trouble to draw a Japanese person out with expressions like "Yes," "That's right," and "Of course" will be absolutely amazed at the positive results. This approach will be very trying for most Americans particularly, since they have a national and natural tendency to use expressions like "Sorry to interrupt, but in America we . . ." or phrases like "That's not the way we do it in the States—let me tell you how we would handle that situation. . . ." After such interruptions, the Japanese will stop talking, listen politely and probably not say anything meaningful for the rest of the conversation. Therefore the cardinal rule in communicating with the Japanese is: "Don't grab the mike." Generally speaking, Europeans will have less trouble implementing this advice than Americans.

Many foreigners claim that to wait for a Japanese to get around to expressing what's on his mind demands effort beyond normal human powers, since the Japanese will just keep talking in circles. It may seem at times that if they are allowed to steer the conversation it will never get to the point. That is not true. They will bring the conversation very skillfully to (or around, at least) the point when they're ready. In the meantime, if the foreigner has been patient, the Japanese will be admiring him for his politeness, restraint, humility, and skill in conducting a conversation. When the time is ripe, they will expect the foreigner to talk, and they will ask for his opinion. That is the time to state one's case and not before—remembering to do it the Japanese way, beating around the bush a little *before* getting to the point. Let me emphasize that using this tactic does not mean one is playing into their hands; rather, it is a technique for getting them to say what is really on their minds. In a business context, from the way in which they discuss their business problems, it is possible to decipher how they see the person being addressed fitting into their plans (if at all). A typical Japanese conversation would take much the same course. One man (usually the senior of the two) does the talking, punctuated with a series of *"Ne?"* ("Don't you agree?") sounds at the end of each sentence, while the other man adds an occasional *"So desu ne!"* ("Yes, that's true!") or *"Totemo ii desu"* ("That's really good") to encourage the other speaker. Next the speaker will pause and look expectantly at the other person, waiting for the latter to express his opinion of the same subject. If the junior man disagrees with his superior, he will start out by agreeing profusely with everything said, and then after a slight pause he will apologetically look up at his superior and say hesitantly, *"Keredomo . . ."* ("However"), and tentatively explain that the opposite point of view, while totally wrong, must be examined in greater depth so that his superior can appreciate the arguments being used by its advocates just in case he has to counter them in a meeting. After listening, the superior might say that he has appreciated the information from his subordinate and change the subject. In the meantime his mind is digesting the input and is accepting or rejecting its implications. While these tactics are not unusual in the West, they are polished to a fine gloss in Japanese conversation.

The tactic of drawing out the Japanese by letting them do the talking is often very difficult when using an interpreter, but it should always be attempted. One must resist the temptation, no matter how strong, to explode and start lecturing. Among the Japanese *any uncontrolled display of emotion is regarded as a sign of weakness and is always in extremely bad taste.* To understand their attitude toward loss of control of any sort, compare it with the American attitude toward men who cry in public. Their reaction to an angry outburst from a foreigner would be similar to what a Westerner would feel if an executive with whom he was negotiating a business deal were to burst into tears if it fell through.

While anybody can see through the tactics described above of the junior who disagrees with his superior, the Japanese concern for saving face and maintaining harmony often manifests itself in less obvious ways. One must always be alert for signals that reveal that what is said is not what is meant. The difference between form and substance is summed up in the two Japanese words *tatemae* and *honne* (pronounced "honay"). Any American or European business person who cannot explain precisely what these two expressions mean will be in trouble if he tries to deal with the Japanese. Those who can sense the true meaning behind the words and expressions that the speaker uses are able to discern the *honne* in any conversation or business discussion. If, on the other hand, the foreigner's understanding is limited to the superficial aspects and the literal translation of what is being said, then all he or she is receiving is the *tatemae,* or window dressing of the conversation. *Honne* means true motives or intentions. *Tatemae* means what they think you want to hear or what they feel must be said in order to maintain a smooth surface.

On a trip to Japan in February 1983 I was visiting several Japanese companies in the pharmaceutical business to discuss possible licensing opportunities in South Asia. The objective was to persuade Japanese companies to license their new products to us in selected markets. The discussions were a perfect opportunity to observe and evaluate the depth and extent of my relationships with the Japanese. My task was to sense the *tatemae* and *honne* of Japanese licensing and marketing strategy and plans in South Asia and the rest of the world, especially with regard to licensing out to foreign companies. In one particular company I was greeted effusively and warmly by the senior managing director (jōmu) of the firm and all his colleagues with whom I had worked during my five years in Japan. Then I was taken out for a beautiful evening at a geisha house, and given the VIP treatment. This was *tatemae* in the sense that I immediately knew that my visit did not call for this kind of treatment; they were entertaining me so lavishly because the Japanese company had other plans for their compounds in South Asia but did not want to offend me because I was a valued friend (this was *honne,* or the true situation). I accepted the situation and gradually drew them out until they told me their strategy, and that information in itself was a useful result of the meeting. But if I had not had enough experience in reading the signs, I could well have been totally deceived by this all-out welcome into believing that the Japanese company was extremely eager to do business.

Early in my career in Japan I did once fall victim to *tatemae* before I had fully grasped its ramifications. In those days I was debating what to do about our new direct sales division. The sales were growing nicely and we were beginning to penetrate the Japanese market for over-the-counter pharmaceuticals, but we were forced to spend huge amounts of money on advertising, and on top of that we had to support a national sales force (each salesman in Japan costs a company $20,000 a year at the minimum) on a very small volume. I brought up the problem at a management meeting and asked each department head to think about the overhead problem and to come up with suggestions on how to overcome the red ink bleeding all over our P and L. Although New York had suggested that I should close down the division if profitability could not be attained soon, I did not believe that this was the answer, since we were on our way to a real niche in the market. I felt that closing the division would not be in the company's best interests. Finally the marketing group came back with a suggestion that we use our long-established relationship with a large Japanese diversified pharmaceutical company to persuade them to act as our distributor outside the main cities and supplement our field force in the large metropolitan centers like Tokyo, Nagoya, and Osaka.

After much debate this was felt to be the best strategy and I asked my marketing buchō (department head) to contact the Japanese company and sound them out on the proposal at the lower/middle levels of management. I did not want to bring it to top management until we had obtained preliminary *unofficial* consensus as to the acceptability of the idea from the "working level" in the Japanese company. (See Chapter 14 for more on this topic.) After a couple of weeks a positive signal came back from the Japanese side, and I organized a task force to begin the long and detailed market research required before we could officially suggest the idea to the top management of the Japanese company. Eventually we had a working-level meeting, and it still seemed as though all the basic signals were green. Finally I decided that it was time to take the proposal to the top management of the Japanese company and calculated that with all the discussion and presentations that we had been having at the working level there should be both no surprise and no problem with the concept or with the basic principles on which we would operate the collaboration. You can imagine my surprise when I began explaining the idea to the Japanese company and their president pretended that it was the first time he had ever heard about the proposal. He said that he could not comment on anything so major until his subordinates had every opportunity to investigate the proposal in detail. After fruitless attempts to get the project elevated to the president again, I gave up. It was months later that I was advised by a trusted friend in the Japanese company that the instructions had come from on high to assume a positive approach to the proposal in order not to offend me but to leave paper trails of *honne* signals to let me know that it was really not of interest to the Japanese company.

When I thought back, I began to appreciate those *honne* signals. For instance, why did I have to press for the meeting with the president? If they thought that the idea had merit, it would automatically have been elevated to the top by the Japanese company's subordinate staff and would not have required my direct intervention. Anxious not to offend me, the Japanese company had decided to maintain an appearance of interest, all the while hoping that they could subtly let me know that they really did not want to play ball. My own staff heard the signals but didn't want to tell me because I had enthusiastically told the New York office that our red-ink problems were over and that I had persuaded the Japanese company to act as our distributor. Nothing could have been further from the *honne* (truth). When foreigners understand the difference between *tatemae* and *honne,* they are well on their way to getting on the Japanese wavelength. These two examples should make it clear what happens when one fails to realize that there is a difference.

An extremely important aspect of communications in Japan is role playing. In a sense the custom of acting out a socially prescribed role is a manifestation of *tatemae* and *honne,* where what matters is to fill a role that will harmonize with the situation being created by the group, with each member's role clearly defined by rank in the hierarchy of the company or group. Role playing in Japan is much more highly developed and codified than in the West. Although individualistic Americans affect to despise "game playing," the truth is that it is not unknown in our culture. However, it is seldom carried to the lengths that it is in Japan. For example, in Japan the rule is that if you are going to get drunk, you must be a perfect drunk. Collapse on the street near your friends so that they can pick you up, and not in the subway on the way home because no one who matters will see you. I have been amazed to see a staggering drunk literally dumped onto a subway car and then, as soon as the train was out of the station, straighten up his tie, pull out a newspaper, and start reading as if he were the soberest man in town. His act was over. He had played it to perfection. His actions had created group harmony, and his staff or friends had appreciated his performance.

When meeting a Japanese, it is important to remember that he is—consciously or unconsciously—playing a role. If he is promoted to be managing director of a company, he is expected to speak and act in a totally different way than when he was a mere *buchō* or *kachō*. A relaxed and casual chief executive, who tries to be on buddy-buddy terms with his staff and prefers an informal open-collar corporate atmosphere, would be incomprehensible to the Japanese. They would consider him to be betraying his responsibilities in a manner that renders him beneath contempt. The concept of hierarchy I have referred to before is the determining factor in this aspect of Japanese relationships. One never goes to a meeting with a Japanese company of any standing at all in shirt sleeves or safari suit, no matter what the temperature might be outside. It is just not done and would spoil the atmosphere for everyone else. The businessman puts on the darkest suit he owns, a white shirt, and a sober tie, and *that is what he wears* in Japan. Edwin O. Reischauer has commented that it is amazing to go into a store in Japan and see how many varieties of drab necktie it is possible to make. During the hottest part of summer the government will sometimes announce that effective July 1 coats need not be worn. The next morning everyone (except the executives) will come to work in shirt sleeves and a tie. In 1978 the oil crisis was biting hard, and the government announced an "energy suit" (a sort of short-sleeved safari suit), which was designed to allow companies to save on air conditioning. The experiment was a failure because although a few ministers wore these suits for a week or two, no one felt they were "correct" clothes for the office. Many Japanese find such rigidity comforting because it eliminates the nerve-racking necessity of making choices. The influence of Zen austerity may also be a factor. Whatever the cause, doing what is expected is a virtue in Japan, and conformity does not have the negative overtones it carries in the West. In fact, it is considered virtuous to suppress one's individuality. Japanese teenagers are not admonished to "be themselves" and ignore peer pressure. On the contrary, they are expected to suppress their childish desire for an individual identity as they grow older.

One manifestation of the Japanese desire to blend in and submit to the will of the group is the emphasis placed on maintaining *wa,* or harmony. This is an important difference between the Japanese and Western styles of communication and group dynamics. In Japan the search for *wa* in all relationships and activities is of paramount importance. There is nothing a Japanese dislikes more than a Westerner who is insensitive to the atmosphere of a relationship, the unspoken understandings that lie behind the words, phrases and gestures, which are an integral part of any meeting with the Japanese.

It is not very difficult to develop a sense of *wa.* It comes naturally after working with the Japanese for a while, providing one is on the alert for it. Basically, *wa* is the sum total of the feelings *(kimochi)* pervading any gathering or business meeting that have all balanced out and been smoothed over. All the factors that have entered into the relations of those present, or all that has taken place before between two companies or between two individuals, enter into the intricate fabric of *wa.* The more complex the Japanese person, and the more "Japanese" (as opposed to Western) his outlook is, the more important it is to be sensitive to *wa.*

The Japanese will go to extremes to make amends if they feel that they are personally responsible for destroying *wa,* or harmony, within the enterprise. Foreigners who develop personal and corporate relationships with the Japanese must remember that willy-nilly they are involving a number of people in any proposed deal. These men become "responsible" to their company for making sure that the relationship with the foreigner is "harmonious" and does not cause any embarrassment to the Japanese enterprise or its executives. If things get out of hand, as they did in the Lockheed scandal (when millions of dollars in payoffs were exchanged for contracts to provide aircraft to all Nippon Airlines) or the Bucyrus-Erie/Komatsu joint venture (when Komatsu decided to contest the joint-venture agreement that prohibited exports to markets where Bucyrus-Erie has other agents), then certain people have to "take responsibility," which involves taking measures of one kind or another—ranging from resigning or transferring to a subsidiary to jumping out of the window.

So far in this chapter I have emphasized the difference between Japanese and Western outlooks. Perhaps I should close with a caveat against taking this advice too literally. Endymion Wilkinson in his book *Misunderstanding* has provided an amusing history of European views of Japan, which he calls the myth of "Upside-down Land." He warns against going to Japan thinking that everything is so topsy-turvy and Orientally mysterious that the Westerner stands no chance of ever really figuring it out. Westerners *can* learn to understand the Japanese, but I cannot emphasize too strongly that Westerners must continually analyze their assumptions about society and human nature when dealing with Japanese people. The trap of noncommunication can be avoided if one remains alert.

FOUR ESSENTIAL CONCEPTS:
NINTAI, KAO, GIRI, ON

Nintai (patience), *kao* (face), *giri* (duties), and *on* (obligations) are four important, complex, and interrelated Japanese concepts that have a strong influence on how the Japanese do business and conduct their personal lives. Much that seems mysterious and inexplicable in Japan can be more easily understood when one comprehends these ideas. *Kao, giri,* and *on* have a common link in dependency, a psychological phenomenon that psychologist Takeo Doi has theorized to be the most important factor in the Japanese psyche.

I have never seen the word *nintai* (patience) referred to by other writers on Japan, but it is an absolute essential in dealing with the Japanese. The Vaccari English-Japanese dictionary gives two words for "patience": *shimbō* (perseverance) and *gaman* (forbearance). *Nintai* is a more peculiarly Japanese concept, which is probably why the Vaccaris do not list it as a synonym for the English word. *Nintai* refers to the kind of patience a person contemplating a rock garden would need in order to perceive each nuance of light and shade, separately and collectively, and become completely aware of every aspect of the beauty surrounding him. In the business context it means having the endurance and intellectual fortitude to uncover methodically and carefully every factor that might have even the slightest bearing on a business decision or the outcome of a negotiation. It means having the patience and perseverance to make time in a busy schedule some weeks before meeting with the Japanese in order to thoroughly prepare for the negotiations.

When I was president of the American Chamber of Commerce in Japan, I was constantly amazed by the almost total lack of preparation that characterized the visits of many U.S. corporate negotiators. They expected their local Japanese staff to do all the preparation, and to quickly assimilate all the facets and complications in a matter of hours. It was frustrating for the local staff to see these "instant geniuses" from the States take over and ruin a carefully prepared negotiation just because the visitors lacked the *nintai* not only to immerse themselves in every detail before the negotiation but also to send all the relevant technical data and contract drafts well beforehand for prior review and evaluation by the Japanese party. There is nothing an American executive likes more than to pull a fresh contract out of his briefcase and with a flourish tell the Japanese: "Here it is, gentlemen, the complete draft of the contract—now, let's start the review!" One can almost hear the collective groan from the Japanese side. The Japanese decision-making process is long and tortuous. Anyone who expects to fly to Japan and fly out two weeks later with a signed contract must send the final draft over at least five weeks before he arrives. The Japanese will be appreciative, for with this gesture the foreign businessman will have won their esteem as a man of *nintai,* a character trait they greatly admire because they must show it every day.

A man who is utterly lacking in *nintai* would probably be continually in danger of losing *kao* (face). Eastern usage of the word "face" is familiar to many Westerners, but few clearly understand it. *Kao* is the most precious commodity a Japanese has. It is his badge of respectability and the source of his self-confidence. A spotless *kao* means that a Japanese is viewed by his peers, superiors, and subordinates as a man in tune with society. The worst mistake one can make with a Japanese is to say, do, or imply anything that might be construed to mean that one does not appreciate the other's work or his personality. This is the most horrible insult possible, and the unwary foreigner who utters such a remark will make an implacable enemy for life. In my five years in Tokyo I tried very hard not to make or even imply any criticism of any of my subordinates or Japanese associates in front of others, and when I did have some corrective suggestions to make, I used to spend at least ten minutes privately with the individual emphasizing the positive side of his work and character in order to fortify his face as much as possible before delivering one or two suggestions for improvement in vague, indirect, and diplomatic terms. Once or twice my irritation got the better of me and I was more direct in my criticism; the result was that the employee was shocked and angry—though he wouldn't show it—and the situation only deteriorated.

If you do not like the way you are treated in Japan, or if you disagree with a Japanese businessman, you should indicate this to him in the most subtle and discreet way possible so that he can understand what you are trying to convey but not suffer the slightest attack on his *kao*. *Kao* is such an important concept to the Japanese that the best-selling brand of soap is Kao Soap, and no one can criticize it because to do so would be an indirect slap at the Japanese sense of face. The Nagase family, who founded the Kao Soap Company, are among the most brilliant of the Japanese consumer-product pioneers, and naming their company "Kao" was one of their most astute maneuvers.

I learned my lesson about *kao* shortly after I arrived in Japan. Our organization was expanding, and I had a marketing manager who was looking after our main business (pharmaceuticals) and was also developing a new business area (consumer products). He was being run off his feet, and despite his obvious competence he was swamped by the work load. I didn't make things easier for him because I was intent on getting the consumer business going, and I rode him hard. I finally decided that I would have to separate the two responsibilities, and I thought long and hard about how to structure the marketing organization. My decision was to place the marketing manager in charge of the new consumer-products division, since he was beginning to show real results there, and to promote a new man from the field to take over the marketing of the pharmaceuticals division. This did not work, since the old marketing manager, instead of feeling thrilled at the challenge of the new high-priority division, felt that he had lost a tremendous amount of face with the company, and particularly with his subordinates, by losing control of the larger division. At the time I was too "Western" to realize what the man was going through, and when he eventually resigned I learned the hard way.

Moving from the fairly simple concept of *kao*, with its obvious implications for relationships with the Japanese, I turn now to the real substance of this chapter, and possibly one of the most important factors underlying Japanese behavior patterns. These are the allied concepts of *giri* (duties) and *on* (obligations).

The key to understanding these concepts is to comprehend one simple fact about the Japanese: they tend to take every debt and obligation incurred throughout life as a personal weight on their shoulders. The burden of these obligations can be lightened (but never eliminated entirely) by doing favors for and on behalf of the person or persons to whom they owe the debt. Ruth Benedict described this feeling in *The Chrysanthemum and the Sword:*

> Because Westerners pay such extremely slight attention to their debt to the world and what it has given them in care, education, well-being or even in the mere fact of their ever having been born at all, the Japanese feel that our motivations are inadequate. Virtuous men do not say, as they do in America, that they owe nothing to any man. They do not discount the past. Righteousness in Japan depends upon recognition of one's place in the great network of mutual indebtedness that embraces both one's forebears and one's contemporaries.[1]

Thus a sense of indebtedness pervades every action. Observing the behavior of a Japanese businessman, one notices that he is constantly expressing heartfelt gratitude for every kindness shown or special favor extended. This is because he is uncomfortably aware that he is on the receiving end of an obligation that he will be compelled to repay in the future. Thus the receipt even of small favors may make a Japanese uncomfortable, for the obligation incurred will begin inexorably to draw him into a complex web of duties. If he is overly effusive in his thanks, it is because he subconsciously feels that by so doing he is perhaps mitigating the depth of the obligation. He may be somewhat relieved by the sense that the obligation is only to a Westerner and need not therefore be taken quite as seriously as an obligation incurred to a Japanese, since the latter is likely to be fully aware of the nature of the favor bestowed and will expect the recipient to be ready to reciprocate in due course. But I should emphasize here that most Japanese treat their obligations very seriously, and the fact that a benefactor happens to be a Westerner will be incidental.

The Japanese word for the obligation incurred by the giving and granting of major favors (such as giving birth to someone or assuming responsibility for his or her education) is *on,* and the word for the duty or loyalty incurred by the recipient is *giri*. (*Gimu* is a more modern word, meaning duties in general.) Ruth Benedict explains as follows:

> The word for 'obligations' which covers a person's indebtedness from greatest to least is *on*. In Japanese usage it is translated into English by a whole series of words from 'obligations' and 'loyalty' to 'kindness' and 'love,' but these words distort its meaning. . . . *On* is in all its uses a load, an indebtedness, a burden, which one carries as best one may. A man receives *on* from a superior and the act of accepting an *on* from anyone not definitely one's superior or at least one's equal gives one an uncomfortable sense of inferiority. When they say, 'I wear an *on* to him' they are saying, 'I carry a load of obligations to him,' and they call this creditor, this benefactor, their *'on* man.'[2]

(I should mention that Ruth Benedict wrote her work on Japan more than thirty years ago, so some of the expressions she emphasizes may be out of date, though her general definitions are still accurate.) She goes on:

> One has particular *on* . . . to one's teacher and to one's master. . . . They have both helped bring one along the way and one wears an *on* to them which may at some future time make it necessary to accede to some request of theirs when they are in trouble or to give preference, perhaps to a young relative of theirs, after they are dead. One should go to great lengths to pay the obligation and time does not lessen the debt. It increases rather than decreases with the years. It accumulates a kind of interest. An *on* to anyone is a serious matter. As their common saying has it: 'One never returns one ten-thousandth of an *on.*' It is a heavy burden and 'the power of the *on*' is regarded as always rightly overriding one's mere personal preferences.[3]

We now come to *giri,* the less serious of the two sets of obligations. Every day the average Japanese will incur small debts and obligations that are called *giri.* He will also dispense kindnesses and receive *giri* from someone else. The Japanese businessman may find himself torn between *giri* to a friend or benefactor and his sense of right or wrong, and he is then, as Ruth Benedict has described it, "tangled with *giri.*" As she defines it:

> One all-Japanese dictionary renders *giri*—I translate:—'righteous way; the road human beings should follow; something one does unwillingly to forestall apology to the world.' . . . *Giri* has two quite distinct divisions. What I shall call '*giri* to the world'—literally 'repaying *giri*'—is

one's obligation to repay *on* to one's fellows, and what I shall call '*giri* to one's name' is the duty of keeping one's name and reputation unspotted by any imputation. . . . *Giri* to the world can roughly be described as the fulfilment of contractual obligations.[4]

In "*giri* to one's name" can be recognized the ramifications of face. There is a strong link between *giri* and *kao,* because maintaining face is a kind of duty. Thus it becomes difficult for a Japanese to admit failure because it would mean admitting that he has failed in his duty to maintain an unspotted reputation. The sometimes extreme acts of atonement for lapses are often attempts to discharge what Benedict calls "*giri* to one's name."

When Benedict defines "*giri* to the world" as "contractual obligations," "contract" should be taken in the abstract sense of "the social contract." Japanese feel the burden of mutual interdependence and commitment to maintaining social order more than most peoples. Reischauer emphasizes this aspect of *giri:*

> In earlier days [Japanese] talked about the heavy burdens incurred from the benevolence *(on)* of parents, rulers, and lords. Even today they are sharply aware of the need for great effort to live up to the rigid demands of society.
>
> Many Japanese seem overburdened by the demands of duty—to family, to associates, and to society at large. This sense of duty, usually called *gimu,* is so onerous as to have produced the underlying restiveness among the young, but it is a clear continuity from premodern times, when the word used was *giri. Giri* incurred in a thousand ways could not be allowed to be submerged by the personal human feelings, known as *ninjo,* that come spontaneously and can lead to social turmoil and disaster.[5]

The implications of *giri* (or *gimu*) pervade Japanese society, and the business world is no exception.

One can get a better idea of what the two terms mean in practice from examples of how *giri* can affect business relationships. The most obvious area where a foreigner may incur and receive *giri* is the giving and receiving of gifts. The Japanese are fanatic about gift giving, since they regard this as the most tangible and immediate way to discharge what they regard as a *giri.* Every restaurant waiter will scream "*Irasshaimase!*" (or, roughly, "Welcome!") when a customer walks into a small country restaurant, or, in the big cities, any traditional place like a sushi shop or bar. This cry of *Irasshaimase* acknowledges the *giri* that the staff and manager of the restaurant owe to you, the customer, for patronizing their humble establishment. From then on it is up to them to show, by the quality of their service and the present that they often give patrons as they leave, that they are repaying their *giri* as best they can and thereby relieving the burden slightly. Similarly, if a gift is given to a Japanese businessman, he will be forever grateful (obligated) to the giver, and can only live with the gift because he is fortified by the knowledge that one day he will repay the favor. A guest is also expected, although much is forgiven the stupid Westerner, to feel a deep sense of obligation, or *giri,* to a Japanese firm and its executives if it shows a visitor particular attention with a special gift or hospitality.

Sometimes Westerners find that a Japanese businessman of their acquaintance is gradually stepping up the value and frequency of his gifts and hospitality. This can mean that he is conscious of a perceived personal or corporate debt to the person so honored or to his firm, or, more cynically, that the Japanese is going to propose some new collaboration to the Westerner and wants him to have a heightened sense of *giri* so that he becomes more receptive to his proposal.

Even without deliberate intent to trap someone with *giri,* gift giving can become such a fetish that the stakes keep rising each time a Westerner revisits Japan and meets with the same company and its executives. We used to keep a card file in my office in Tokyo that recorded the present given to each of the Japanese businessmen met by each of our visiting executives. This file proved its usefulness again and again, and now our New York people keep their own parallel files. This cuts down on telexes such as "Gave Suzuki tie clasp last November, suggest cuff links this visit."

The basic thing to remember about giving and receiving gifts is that one can't escape the web of obligations that are thereby created, and that the worst offense (other than deliberate insults or an assault on a man's *kao*) is to refuse a gift. This manifestation of Western puritanism is a sure way to make a Japanese a bitter enemy. In the West a gift that seems inappropriately lavish can have overtones of an ulterior motive, and in certain situations might even be suspected of being in the nature of a bribe. This would be most improbable in Japan, where liberal gift giving has long been an honorable tradition. Western companies simply haven't adjusted to the Japanese practice of showering business friends with expensive presents, but even if the Westerner's small gift can't hope to compete with Japanese generosity, it is deeply appreciated by the Japanese because it demonstrates a willingness to acknowledge *giri* to him for past gifts and kindnesses.

To avoid the nightmare of the constant escalation of gift giving, where a frequent visitor to Japan must upgrade his gift every time he sees the same person, it is wise to make a serious effort to entertain the Japanese and make them feel completely welcome when they visit the United States or Europe. This hospitality, coupled with a modest gift, is roughly equivalent to the Nikon camera or $4,000 statue that a Western business person may be given on a visit to Japan. Consideration for the visiting Japanese, and sensitivity to their dislike of being alone in a Western city, is probably the best way to repay *giri* to them, even though it will mean missing the 5:15 to Westchester.

Gift giving is just one minor aspect of *giri*. *Giri* can also be expressed as overriding loyalty to an individual that transcends loyalty or obligation to the firm. The Japanese employees of foreign firms are particularly subject to this kind of *giri*, since they are regarded by other Japanese as *gairo*, meaning a lesser breed of worker who holds no *giri* for his company and is therefore free to change companies frequently. *Gairo* means "a roaming employee of a foreign firm" and is therefore somewhat contemptible in the eyes of the Mitsubishi or Mitsui man who owes his allegiance to one great employer for life. In this atmosphere the Japanese employee in a foreign company develops a whole network of *giri* obligations to his *oyabun* (bosses) in the various foreign companies where he has worked.

I recall, as if it happened yesterday, one frustrating incident involving *giri* that took place five years ago in Tokyo. A young and promising executive, the manager of one of our departments, had told his boss (my finance manager) that he was resigning and would like his resignation to take effect immediately, notwithstanding his contractual obligation to give a month's notice. He had a lot of leave due him and there was no way I could stop him, but I was determined to try, since he was an extremely able man. In fact, we had just given him a 20 percent increase in recognition of his achievements (three times the normal salary increase for that year, and most generous, even for a foreign company). His answer to my persistent questioning was that he had a *giri*, and despite his love for our company and his *giri* to me and to our finance manager, his prior *giri* to an old boss was stronger. It turned out that the old boss, now employed by an insurance company, had become ill and was not able to do his work as well as previously. The head of the insurance company, who was the sick man's direct boss, had subtly made his displeasure known and indicated that if the work was not to suffer, a trusted younger assistant would have to be hired. It was then that our man's former boss remembered that his ex-employee was now working for my firm, and that he could rehire him by forcing him through *giri.* I was furious and became even more so when I found out that the insurance company was underwriting some of our corporate policies. I called the general manager of the insurance company on the telephone and indicated that I would not be happy to lose my manager and would appreciate it if he would desist from forcing my man to leave his job. His response was to tell me that he could not stand in the way of *giri.* I canceled the insurance policies with the company, but I lost a good man because he was caught in the toils of *giri.*

John Roberts cites two classic examples of the workings of *giri* in his book on the history of the Mitsui *zaibatsu,* in the section dealing with the immediate postwar period. The president of Mitsui Bussan (Mitsui Trading) at the time was Yasutaro Niizeki. Many employees had left the company because it seemed to have reached the end. All the prewar *zaibatsu* were being systematically dismantled by the trust-busting Occupation administrators, and Niizeki's role as president was largely to supervise the liquidation of an empire that had been centuries in the making. As Roberts puts it:

> In the summer of 1947 there was a mass exodus of personnel, but Niizeki decided to remain with the sinking ship, mainly because of his *giri*—the peculiar sense of obligation that makes Japanese society so cohesive. "I was determined not to establish a new firm nor even think about my plans for the future until all employees of the firm had secured jobs," Niizeki told the author.[6]

A few pages later Roberts tells of how Mitsui Bussan managed to rise from its own ashes. At a critical point when Niizeki was ill a large promissory note had to be cashed:

> With money so tight, such a large note was difficult to negotiate, and Niizeki was in no condition to make the rounds of the banks. . . . he thought of a managing director of Mitsubishi Bank who was under

personal obligation to him. The ailing Niizeki drafted a letter to him.
. . . as expected, the director gave his approval, and the note was
discounted without delay. . . .

More than twenty years have passed since then, but . . . Mitsui Bussan
still deals with that branch of Mitsubishi Bank, despite the inconvenience of its location and the rivalry between the Mitsui and Mitsubishi
groups. . . . These incidents exemplify the power of *giri,* the rigid and
perpetual observance of mutual obligations that gives Japanese society
its stability and that enabled the shattered Japanese economy to recover
so rapidly after the war.[7]

This example shows that "calling in a *giri*" does not cancel a debt—
Niizeki made use of the fact that the bank director was under obligation to him to get the note honored, but the matter did not end there
—and has not ended yet. Moreover, Roberts's suggestion that *giri*
was a major force in reconstructing postwar Japan underlines the fact
that *giri* is a powerful force. Although these duties may assume the
form of a terrible burden, obligations are honored because that is
how society holds together in Japan.

The strong pull of duties and loyalties plays a large role in the
emotions and psychological attitudes that operate just beneath the
surface for most average Japanese. They are anxious to avoid any
situation where they might be insulted so that they can be spared the
agony of an affront to their *kao* (face). They also prefer to avoid
circumstances where they might incur an unwanted *giri.* For example, when a certain individual does not appear for a meeting and only
subordinates are present, it could mean that the executive in question wishes to avoid a possible insult to his *kao* that he fears may
result from the meeting. Perhaps he suspects that he will have to
hear that the proposed deal he has been supporting is to be called
off or postponed. He doesn't want to be the one to hear the bad news,
so he will send a subordinate. If, on the other hand, the meeting goes
well and his apprehension is unfounded, he may miraculously appear
later on in the meeting or at a social event apologizing profusely for
his tardiness or absence at the meeting. Similarly, one finds that the
senior executive (chairman or president) will be interested in visiting
the domestic operations of the foreign companies his company deals
with, but will usually send a discreet message via a subordinate that
he would appreciate it if any detailed discussion of business could be
avoided. It is not always true that the senior Japanese executive
doesn't know the details of the business his company has with other

companies. Often when such a request is made, it means that he is anxious to avoid an embarrassing situation where he may be called on to decide something without benefit of the consensus-building exercise of the Japanese decision-making process described in Chapter 9.

At the beginning of this chapter I mentioned that the psychological concept of dependency links *giri, on,* and *kao.* Psychologist Takeo Doi has a theory that all Japanese secretly yearn to be indulged and dependent in the kind of relationship they had as a child with their mothers. Thus the duties and obligations of a Japanese are the price paid for membership in a society where he can remain in a safely dependent position—that is, a position where what he must do is mapped out for him. His face is the measure of how successful he is in living up to the obligations imposed on him. Even *nintai* is an integral part of all this, since without it the typical salary man would be unable to discharge his office duties properly; for example, he might lose face if he makes an error of judgment as a result of not collecting all the facts.

The Westerner is often puzzled by the Japanese use of the word "sincerity," because to the Japanese sincerity is not openhearted truthfulness but a complex amalgam of ideas. The basic theme in this is that a "sincere" person is one who fulfills obligations no matter what and avoids giving offense unless he intends deliberate provocation, or, to put it another way, one who strives for harmony in all relationships and is always careful not to say or do anything without first taking into account all the possible consequences of action. Whether one calls it groupism and dependency, or *giri* and *on,* Westerners who have frequent contact with the Japanese will often find themselves coming up against situations in which these concepts play a part.

CHAPTER
6

THE NETWORK THAT BINDS: *NINGEN KANKEI*

My experience in Japan has convinced me that there is nothing from which a business person can derive more benefit in working with the Japanese than from learning how to develop *ningen kankei*. If Japanese society is seen as a network of interlocking relationships, hierarchically arranged, the strands of the net are formed by *ningen kankei*. The full sociological implications of this structure are beyond the scope of this book, but no one who does business with the Japanese can afford to ignore the impact the concept of *ningen kankei* has on business relations.

The literal translation of *ningen kankei* is "human relations," but to the Japanese the term conveys much more than that. Acting as a sort of barometer of friendship, *ningen kankei* is a measure of the amount of closeness and cooperation there is in a relationship. It is the expression used to describe the overall state of one person's relationship to another. For example, a Japanese salesman might say, "I got the order from that store because my *ningen kankei* with the buyer is excellent, and he couldn't refuse me." The expression can be heard in every business meeting. Japanese executives brief one another about their business activities always within the context of their *ningen kankei* with their colleagues, customers, superiors, or subordinates.

My purpose in devoting an entire chapter to this single concept is to provide readers with sufficient background to enable them to begin developing their own *ningen kankei* with Japanese people. Its importance cannot be overemphasized. Whatever success I achieved in Japan I attribute to the *ningen kankei* I was able to develop with the people I dealt with.

To have a true understanding of how *ningen kankei* operates, one must first comprehend what it means to the Japanese in their everyday lives. Between Japanese, *ningen kankei* arises in many different situations not applicable to most Westerners. For example, strong *ningen kankei* is instantly established if two Japanese discover that they have attended the same school—this is called being *dōkyūsei*, or classmates. This example shows how *ningen kankei* differs from such Western concepts as the Old Boy network or "having something in common." Such factors may or may not be useful in developing business relations between Westerners. It doesn't hurt to have attended the same school as a prospective employer or business partner, but in the United States it hardly constitutes a passport to success, for its relevance depends on the personalities of the people in question. The closer parallel might be the closeness between Old Boys of the pre–World War II British public school system. Graduates of Sherbourne School would be inclined to help fellow alumni, and old Etonians or Wykehamists would do likewise. This British Old Boy network still persists in the Hong Kong "hongs," but has become watered down in Britain itself. In Japan, having attended the same school, even the same high school or grade school, automatically establishes a relationship in which the *dōkyūsei* are honor bound to help one another. Other factors that produce *ningen kankei* include being from the same locality *(onaji umareta tokoro);* working for the same company *(onaji uchi);* or being neighbors *(tonari).*

The interconnecting web of social relationships summed up in the phrase *ningen kankei* is perhaps more important to a Japanese than any other aspect of life. To the average businessman, the way in which he is regarded by his superiors, subordinates, family, and neighbors is of vital concern. He must always have their respect, and the process of achieving that respect is to develop *ningen kankei*. Thus *ningen kankei* is a relationship designed to further the objectives of those involved, a relationship with definite motives and purposes behind it. Old school chums do not search one another out in order to become friends, but if they are brought together in circumstances where it would be mutually beneficial if they became friends, this would be an ideal setting for the formation of *ningen kankei*.

Ningen kankei seldom develops among employees of the same company if they are at the same level of seniority in the firm but in different sections or departments. Because Japanese society is vertical in structure, the significant relations in Japanese life are not those between equals but those between people of different status. Equals are often viewed suspiciously as competitors. Close personal relations develop most commonly with those who are either above or below you in status. Here the *ningen kankei* is reinforced by the working of *giri* and *on* (duty and responsibility), which were discussed in the previous chapter. The parameters of these hierarchical relationships are clearly defined, and close connections of this kind come much more naturally to the Japanese than friendship for the sake of friendship. One of the most important functions of a Japanese executive is to ensure that employees of the same level establish at least minimal *ningen kankei* so that they do not sabotage one another's work in the struggle for advancement.

In the light of what has been said above, one can more easily understand why the Japanese feel uncomfortable when they must deal with someone with whom they have no *ningen kankei*. Everyone in Japan occupies a place in the hierarchy, and ignorance of where the person one is dealing with fits in may lead to embarrassing blunders—and Japanese people dread embarrassment. A relationship without a context is discomfiting for all concerned. Thus, even when a meeting is merely brief and formal, Japanese prefer to establish some kind of makeshift *ningen kankei* by attempting to recall mutual friends, or finding some other grounds for acquaintance, no matter how minimal. A circumstance that to a Westerner would seem trivial and irrelevant may be magnified in the context of *ningen kankei* into an important factor in the success of a meeting.

Well-informed Westerners can, with some effort, turn the *ningen kankei* structure to their advantage. It translates itself in business situations in myriad ways. For example, the Western businessman who has established *ningen kankei* with a senior executive at a Japanese company can rely on his interests being promoted in that Japanese company. Similarly, the Westerner has an obligation to the Japanese executive to keep him advised of any business problems that might have an adverse effect on his company or career. Establishing such a relationship may take years, and the newcomer to

Japan or the Japanese has obvious handicaps. Nevertheless, *ningen kankei* starts the minute you meet a Japanese, and, properly nurtured, may continue for life.

In Japan everyone is always evaluating everyone else. The sizing up starts at the first encounter, and continues as long as there is a reason for personal contact. I was exposed to this process on my first night in Tokyo, when my boss and I were invited to dinner by three senior executives of a large Japanese pharmaceutical company with which my company had a long-standing business relationship.

I expected the conversation to gloss over social pleasantries quickly and get down to a detailed discussion of the clinical studies being performed on one product, the pricing of another, or the possibilities of my company licensing a third. Determined to impress my hosts with my knowledge both of our business and theirs, I came well prepared to display my grasp of these topics. But none of these matters were discussed. The Japanese executives had no intention of talking business. They wanted to establish *ningen kankei* with me.

The business that happens to be on hand at the moment when a Western businessman first meets a Japanese will almost never seem more important to the latter than the possibilities for developing a long-term, well-founded relationship of trust and mutual understanding. This is doubly true when the Westerner's company and the Japanese company already have a relationship, because the Japanese will perceive the newcomer as having a duty to understand the history of that relationship, and to promote and foster it in the future.

This is what the chairman of that Japanese pharmaceutical company wanted to convey to me that night. He began the evening with a ninety-minute monologue on the history of the *ningen kankei* between our two companies over more than twenty years. Although occasionally used to refer to the relations between companies, *ningen kankei* applies more accurately to relations between people, that between companies usually being described as *ware ware no kankei,* or "our relationship." He emphasized that it was my duty to memorize all the main events in the development of *ware ware no kankei,* since it would soon be my turn to recite them to employees of his company that I would meet in the course of business. I began to appreciate that here was a new and unfamiliar element in dealing with foreigners that I had not experienced in my assignments in Latin America but had seen glimmerings of in the Philippines. For the executives I met that night, the single most important thing to find out about me was whether or not I would fit in and be capable of fostering *ningen kankei* with the people of their company—in other words, whether I would be a help or a hindrance in the established business relations between our two companies.

Over the next week, my boss and I had many meetings and meals with each of the business partners important to us in Japan. Again and again the ritual recitation was repeated. I would first be requested to tell them all about myself—my education, including the name of my university and the subjects I had studied, my hobbies, whether I played golf (everyone asked about this), how long I had been with my company, my previous assignments, and so on. In turn I was expected to ask them questions about their experience and personal backgrounds.

The establishment and maintenance of good *ningen kankei* can be critically important. To underline this fact the example of a failure may be more useful than that of a success. I remember an incident with a large company, our closest partner in Japan, that could have been prevented if I had been more sensitive to my *ningen kankei* with the head of their research department. We had developed a new drug that seemed to be of great interest to a number of Japanese firms, and I was receiving letters and phone calls requesting meetings to discuss the possibility of licensing it. After discussion with my New York office, we decided to take the drug first to our oldest and largest partner for their review. After a few weeks they turned it down, and I then had to appoint our second most important partner to handle the drug. In the postmortem of why our most important partner had bowed out, I came to the conclusion that it was not the drug itself but my lack of *ningen kankei* with the research director that had been responsible. I had been spending too much time with the marketing department of his company and not enough with the research people. On one occasion I had turned down an invitation to play golf with the research director. Also, I had failed to handle his key subordinates well. They had been negative about my company's products for some years because of a bad experience with my predecessor, and I had let the situation deteriorate further instead of starting a *ningen kankei* program to gain their confidence and support. My only excuse was that at the time I was busy dealing with eighteen other companies and numerous other *ningen kankei* problems.

My senior Japanese manager had been warning me about this

problem, but I had failed to take remedial action. My New York office blamed the Japanese company rather than me; they looked at the problem as a failure of the Japanese to know a good thing when they saw it. I tried to explain to my colleagues in New York that it was a *ningen kankei* problem, but the concept was too alien for them to relate to. Thereafter I spent considerable time and effort, which involved many late nights and golf games, to win the confidence of the research director. Fortunately, one of his key subordinates who had been consistently against my company was transferred, and I was able to build up a good relationship with his replacement. Just before I left Japan we were able to negotiate a co-marketing arrangement on a far less exciting drug, and the New York office was amazed. They shouldn't have been; by that time my *ningen kankei* with the research department's key people was excellent.

First-time visitors to Japan on business may feel daunted by the prospect of trying to create *ningen kankei,* especially since failing to create it carries a high price. But it is important to remember that although the Westerner is called a *gaijin,* meaning an "outside person," the Japanese *want* to establish *ningen kankei;* they don't like feeling ill at ease any more than Westerners do. They are used to doing business in terms of human relations, and regard doing business with a *gaijin* who makes no effort to overcome the handicap of being an outsider—by definition, someone less than human—as an unpleasant experience. It is true, as noted earlier, that the Japanese tend to have a deep, underlying prejudice against foreigners, but they acknowledge that they have this prejudice, and are successful for the most part in concealing their dislike until it is replaced by a more positive emotion resulting from closer knowledge of the individual Westerner. It is important for a Westerner beginning to develop *ningen kankei* with the Japanese to be aware of this tendency. There is nothing to be done about it until the prejudice disappears naturally in the course of developing a genuine relationship, and it only means that one has to work all the harder to overcome it.

There are several routes open to foreigners for the development of *ningen kankei.* First of all, the visiting executive who is serious about success in Japan must thoroughly research the company he is to deal with and the people he will meet. A habit of obtaining background information is even more essential for those resident in Japan. What seems to the Westerner a waste of important time in personal trivia will seem to the Japanese the most essential part of a meeting. It is in the personal ties formed in the social events which inevitably accompany business meetings that the real business takes place. Meetings are usually formal events whose prime function is to solemnify the agreements already reached by the consensus method of decision-making that the Japanese employ. They will not be impressed by the American executive's eagerness to reach a decision or an agreement, but they *will* be impressed if he demonstrates during lunchtime conversation that he has taken the trouble to find out something about the people he is working with.

I remember one experience I had in my role as president of the Chamber of Commerce. I frequently had to call on bureaucrats and politicians as a matter of courtesy. Since it was mutually understood that the relationship would be unlikely to extend beyond a single courtesy call, one might think that *ningen kankei* would be irrelevant. Nevertheless, as discussed above. a relationship without context is distasteful to the Japanese, and they will cast around for something to establish a connection. Thus, when I went to meet such officials, I tried to find out something about them beforehand. At one meeting with an important Liberal Democratic party official, I began the conversation by commenting that he should be designated the American representative on the party's central council, since he had both a son and a daughter living in the States. He was so pleased that I had taken the trouble to find this out that what should have been a ten-minute courtesy call turned into a one-hour meeting. In the process of discussing several ideas on U.S.-Japan trade barriers, the concept evolved of having an ombudsman to arbitrate market-access disputes between the United States and Japanese business. This concept later became a reality.

Incidents such as the one just described, while highly rewarding —the just deserts of good preparation—might be regarded as extras. When dealing with Japanese subordinates, however, *ningen kankei* simply cannot be neglected. One of the best, if not the most convenient, ways of maintaining good relations with Japanese employees is to socialize with them after work. Socializing with people in the company is considered part of one's job in Japan. Japanese businessmen do not hang out in bars after work in order to "get away from it all"; in fact their reasons are just the opposite. They feel obliged to engage in these activities in order to maintain *ningen kankei* among themselves, for good *ningen kankei* among the people in a company is what makes the company successful.

After office hours I used to make it a habit to take one or two of my senior Japanese colleagues out for a drink at a local bar to see how things were going, and to help them understand what was on my mind. This became a ritual, and on several occasions I was asked by the employees association to spend an evening with them. The result was a significant decrease in office politics and rumor mongering, as well as in employee tension. My efforts led to *ningen kankei* being established one by one with each of the department heads.

Other ways of establishing *ningen kankei* can include performing some act of kindness or special consideration for a Japanese executive that makes him feel obligated to you in a way that binds him to you until he feels that the obligation has been repaid. (This is the principle of *giri* and *on,* discussed in Chapter 5.) I had an experience of this type, and the resulting *ningen kankei* has been perhaps the strongest among my many Japanese contacts. It was with the head of a large Japanese chemical and dyestuff company, with which my company has a joint venture. The business had been going from bad to worse in 1977, when I arrived in Tokyo, and I had been advised by my boss that the joint venture was doomed unless a way could be found to rejuvenate the sales effort.

My senior Japanese colleague and I spent about three months analyzing the business. We found that the problem was related to the difference in American and Japanese techniques for applying the product, and that changes were needed in the manufacturing method and quality control in our American factory. We then persuaded the American side to take a look at the problem, and after they agreed with our conclusion, we convinced the Japanese company to send a technician to our U.S. plant to explain the problem from the Japanese technical viewpoint. As a result of his visit, a quality-improvement program was worked out, and within six months we had recaptured the market share we had lost to a large Swiss company. Within one year we added over a million dollars in sales of that product line.

During all this time I had never had anything more than brief formal meetings with the president of the Japanese company, but one day I received a phone call from his office asking me to meet him at the third-floor lobby of the New Otani Hotel tower. I grabbed my briefcase, thinking to myself as I left the the office that it was about time he understood what we'd been trying to do for him all these months. When I arrived at the hotel I found it was not as I had expected. The only establishment on that particular floor of the hotel was a private health club called the Golden Spa. Assuming there must have been a mistake somewhere, I started looking for a telephone to call the office and get the right directions. Just then the health club door opened, and the managing director of the chemical company beckoned me inside. He showed me a cubicle and handed me a pair of shorts to put on. Then we went into the main part of the club, and there was the president of the Japanese company, sitting in a whirlpool bath and talking to one of the most beautiful Japanese women I have ever seen. It turned out that she was a movie star who was also a member of this exclusive club. The president introduced me to her, saying, "This is Zimmerman-*san*, who has done so much for my business that I am going to give him my thanks this evening." I spent an enjoyable afternoon and evening—there was swimming, sauna baths, massages, and finally a drink in the health bar. After dressing, the president invited me to join him for dinner at the health-club restaurant and from there the managing director took me on a tour of Tokyo night spots. As I left the restaurant the president said, "Zimmerman-*san*, this is a small way of thanking you for what you have done for my company." In other words, he was acknowledging the *giri* he owed me. *Ningen kankei* started from that day, and as time went on our friendship deepened. I was usually on the receiving end of his kindness, but in return I did my best to assist him in continuing to help improve the quality and delivery of our products, working with his staff on improving communications and preserving the flow of *ningen kankei*.

I was able to develop *ningen kankei* relationships with key individuals in nearly all of the twenty companies with which we did business regularly. In some cases it was because of a recognition of my contribution, but more often it was a logical outgrowth of an effort on my part to find areas of common interest that would bind me to the Japanese businessman no matter what his level or interest.

The Japanese use a number of techniques for developing *ningen kankei* among customers, clients, or colleagues. The most common and widely accepted way to develop this special binding relationship is golf, and the shared experience of a golf game. I have described the formalities of golf in Chapter 2, but now I will attempt to give the reader an idea of how personal ties can be formed from these structured social occasions.

The golf course has a very special place in the hearts of the Japanese. In their crowded islands, the green expanse of a golf course is sybaritic in the extreme. Millions of Japanese have a burning desire to play, but are restricted to a lifetime of practice on the multistory driving ranges that dot the urban landscape. They could never afford the cost of a membership certificate ($50,000 on average), the monthly dues ($100), or the cost of a round ($50 for a member, $150 for a guest, including caddie fees, lunch and a gift for the wife). Golf is not only expensive but also time-consuming. Most of the courses are located on the western and northeastern sides of Tokyo, and it can take up to two hours to get to a course, and then three hours to return in the evening! Add to that the six-hour duration of a round of eighteen holes, and it makes for a long day.

It is small wonder that the average Japanese businessman regards his expensive pilgrimage to a golf course as a ritual to be savored. The people who accompany the Japanese businessman to his golf course must also be fellow fanatics, and feel as he does about the extraordinary luck that made him a member of a golf club. My love of golf helped me to develop strong *ningen kankei* with dozens of men in positions of importance to my business in Japan.

One of the most satisfying *ningen kankei* relationships that I developed on the golf course was with a Japanese psychiatrist who shared my view that golf was not to be taken quite so seriously as other Japanese seemed to feel was vital to enjoyment of the game. We had been partners in a company-sponsored golf tournament for Keio University psychiatrists at my golf club, and Dr. Nishikawa and I won the tournament. Afterwards he decided to do me the honor of inviting me to his home in nearby Chiba City to celebrate. We were joined by the deputy branch manager of our Tokyo sales branch and three other doctors. My Japanese was still rudimentary, and no one except Dr. Nishikawa and I could speak English, but I struggled along and we had a marvelous evening. Mrs. Nishikawa had sent for *sushi,* we sang and drank Scotch until late, and *ningen kankei* was established. Dr. Nishikawa later set up a series of clinical studies that greatly assisted my company in the establishment of a new-dose therapy for one of our drugs, and he also encouraged other doctors to try our drug at the new dosage level.

I was able to reciprocate and assist him in a number of ways, and our friendship deepened. Suddenly, two years later, I was told that he had developed stomach cancer and was not expected to live. The bond of *ningen kankei* we had forged was strong, and I immediately called and requested permission to see him. My company and I did our best to assist the family after Dr. Nishikawa's death in 1981, and I still feel the emotional strain of the *ningen kankei* even now.

I may have given the impression that *ningen kankei* is just a relation of mutual exploitation, without genuine feeling, but it is not; without real goodwill behind it, *ningen kankei* is merely an empty exercise.

Some possibilities other than golf for establishing *ningen kankei* are a shared interest in art, Japanese culture, music, kabuki, baseball, or other hobbies. Oddly enough, shared war experience may be a passport to developing *ningen kankei*. The war is seldom discussed, but if both principals served in their respective armed forces, it is a constant reinforcement for *ningen kankei* between them. In my first meeting with the president of one of the companies with which we dealt, he figured out from conversation with one of my colleagues that he, the president, while flying his Zero during the Battle of Leyte had strafed the ship on which my colleague was a junior officer. That was the beginning of a developing relationship that has continued over the last five years.

Obviously, those who remain bitter about the war are not in a position to capitalize on such opportunities. We had one or two visitors come from abroad whose only knowledge of Japan was from the war. These people thought of Japan in World War II terms, and should never have been permitted to represent their company in meetings with the Japanese. Even a Westerner like myself could sense the resentment and dislike that radiated from such individuals. The Japanese, whose sensitivities in such matters tend to be far more acute than those of Westerners, were most uncomfortable. Nothing was ever accomplished during such visits.

How does one go about initiating a *ningen kankei* relationship? It definitely does not occur during the first meeting. The golf game with the doctor was the trigger for *ningen kankei* between us, but it took several further meetings before the acquaintanceship flowered into *ningen kankei*. The foreigner must be alert to opportunities. I have mentioned that if the Japanese businessman is your guest he will greatly appreciate it if you invite him home for dinner. For a Japanese, being invited to a home is a rare event, and it can shorten the *ningen kankei* time cycle dramatically.

When visiting Japanese in Tokyo or Osaka, an invitation from the hosts to go to a nightclub can be an excellent opportunity for *ningen kankei* to flourish. When giving gifts to Japanese business associates, one might perhaps select an extra special one for a *ningen kankei* target, but it should not be given in public unless he is the senior executive. Starting a *ningen kankei* relationship is not difficult, providing the Westerner uses common sense and indicates by his manner and thoughtfulness that he would welcome further deepening of the relationship.

In the examples so far presented, I may have given the impression that it is best to somehow zero in on one individual in a Japanese organization and devote all one's efforts to establishing *ningen kankei* with him. Nothing could court disaster more quickly. Business people must work at *ningen kankei* with everyone in the Japanese company with whom they have a reason to meet regularly. That would usually involve four or five people for a visiting Westerner who is negotiating a licensing or technology agreement with the Japanese. To the Westerner who is assigned to Japan, as I was, it could mean two to three hundred people.

By now it has probably become obvious to the reader that a woman executive trying to deal with the Japanese in Japan will have an extraordinarily difficult time. Leaving aside the fact that women are less likely to be golfers, they are usually banned on weekends at most clubs, and even if the golf game is midweek, the male clubhouse camaraderie of bathing and having saunas together, during which so many valuable business ties are formed, is closed to women. In fact, to the Japanese businessman, playing golf with a Western businesswoman would be strange and uncomfortable. The rounds of geisha houses and nightclubs would also be considered by the Japanese as inappropriate for a woman. On top of all this, Japanese society simply does not acknowledge that women can perform the same functions as men. To illustrate the difficulties of being a woman in business in Japan, I cite a bleak statistic: of the twelve hundred members of the American Chamber of Commerce in Japan in 1983, only thirteen were women. This figure is significantly higher than the five women who belonged to the Chamber in 1979, so at least there has been some progress.

In dealing with the Japanese in America, the situation is, naturally, somewhat better, since the woman executive is on home ground. The Japanese who comes to America is more or less obliged to take matters as he finds them. In this case, the advice given in this chapter is relevant for the woman executive as well.

I conclude with an account of my most personally satisfying experience with *ningen kankei*, which happened unexpectedly one morning. I was visiting the head office of a Japanese pharmaceutical company when the meeting was interrupted by the *jōmu-torishimariyaku* (managing director), who invited me to follow him. We proceeded to the tenth floor, and I was ushered into a large room, where all of the branch managers, deputy branch managers, and key staff from all over Japan were having their twice-yearly sales meeting. The *jōmu* introduced me by saying, "You all know Zimmerman-*san*. He has visited every one of you in your branch offices and worked with you in visiting hospitals and doctors to promote the products of his company. For the first time in the history of our company, I am inviting someone from outside the firm to address you." With those words he gave me the floor, and I was able to express my appreciation for their help, exhort them to strengthen their future efforts, tell them about our latest promotional programs and generally accomplish what otherwise would have taken me several months of hard traveling. That was *ningen kankei* on a national scale!

PART
TWO

NEGOTIATING WITH
THE JAPANESE

CHAPTER
7

THE JAPANESE AND CONTRACTS

Much of Part I of this book was devoted to the general characteristics of Japanese society because of their direct impact on Japanese business culture. Part II will deal with topics that are more specifically related to business, which the reader will be in a better position to understand now that he has a grasp of some of the basics. This chapter deals with one of the most pernicious problems confronting U.S.-Japan business relationships: the contract—what it means to the Japanese, and how to negotiate it successfully.

My company is involved with more than twenty pharmaceutical firms in Japan in various types of relationships, ranging from straight distribution agreements to complicated joint research and development agreements, as well as many other technical and licensing agreements of differing degrees of complexity. Thus, although I draw on some of the published literature on the subject of negotiating with the Japanese, my perspective is directly influenced by being personally involved in actual negotiations.

Contracts are foreign to the Japanese way of doing business, and Americans and Europeans would do well to keep this fact in mind at all times. Exposure to the West, which has resulted in the adoption of many aspects of the Western legal framework, has led to the use of written contracts, especially when negotiating deals with Western companies, of course. But the Japanese don't like contracts and tend to feel that if personal trust and integrity are absent the mere possession of a piece of paper will not salvage the situation. Many Japanese will not even bother to read a contract before signing it because they don't attach substantive importance to it. This is safe enough in Japan, but Japanese who are unaware of the Western fetish for legalistic wrangling and getting everything in writing sometimes find themselves in unfortunate situations when dealing with foreigners. Likewise, foreigners who think a deal has been carved in stone once the papers are signed are frequently shocked to discover just how cavalier the Japanese attitude toward a contract can be if circumstances make it "unfair" in their eyes.

Thus, because the Japanese prefer to place their trust in people rather than paper, it is essential that during the process of negotiations the Western negotiator take extreme care to make sure that mutual understanding has been reached.

> A complete understanding between parent companies with respect not only to their motives, but also to the agreements by which they are binding themselves at the outset is one of the most important prerequisites for long lasting success. . . . a foreign partner should realize that the Japanese are typically reluctant to document agreements. A Japanese may appreciate the need for a written contract only if careful explanations are made to him of the dangers of not having any.[1]

The foreign negotiator must understand that the Japanese dislike haggling over contracts. They put much more emphasis on establishing whether or not they can trust the foreign partner. In my own experience I found that if I succeeded in establishing that trust, in many cases I could virtually write the contract because the Japanese would sense that whatever was put before them would be fair and equitable and therefore would not be overconcerned about the fine print. This buildup of trust is well described in a recent book on Japanese business edited by Bradley M. Richardson and Taizo Ueda:

> . . . the fine points of a contract are rarely haggled over, and negotiations over a business project, while they may be prolonged, are often more a process of establishing mutual trust than working out the details of a contract that will protect each party from all foreseeable occurences. Once that trust is established, both parties put great emphasis on maintaining the relationship over the long term. That attitude often means forgoing short-term profits that could be gained by shifting to another buyer or supplier and being willing to be flexible about the terms of a contract when the other party is under pressure or short-term difficulties.[2]

One of the most common types of agreements that my company has in Japan is a sales-and-marketing agreement with a number of Japanese pharmaceutical companies. These agreements establish our mutual rights and responsibilities, including the raw-material-purchase obligations of the Japanese partners. Time and time again I have been pleased to see Japanese companies cooperate in buying from us despite fluctuations in world prices that in the short term might be prejudicial to the Japanese buyer. The underlying reason for this cooperation is the realization that in the long term the Japanese company will benefit by an enduring relationship with the foreign partner. There are numerous opportunities for future research collaboration and licensing that would disappear if the Japanese partner operated only on the basis of short-term gain. And the converse is also true—Western companies that gladly accept a Japanese company's loyalty but ignore the possibilities for reciprocating that trust will find that such opportunism works against them in the long run.

Part of the suspicion that the Japanese have toward contracts derives from the change in their situation over the past thirty years. The aftermath of war saw Japan with almost no basic research of any kind. They had to rely on the West for the technology needed to rebuild the nation. Today the tables have turned and the Japanese have the edge in applied technology in many key industries, from steel and anticancer drugs to consumer electronics. This about-face has resulted in the Japanese becoming suspicious that a foreign partner will try to insist on the same language and parameters used in contracts negotiated during the sixties and early seventies as the starting point for today's deals. In fact, Western companies would be well advised to reassure the Japanese partners on precisely this point, and clearly and openly acknowledge that circumstances have radically altered in the last ten years, that Japanese and Western companies now deal as equals, and that no agreement will stand the test of time unless it is mutually beneficial.

Another important change since the seventies is the liberalization of foreign investment in Japan (from 1976) and the change embodied in the Foreign Investment Law (Foreign Capital Control Law), as modified and amended in 1980, which states that contracts between Japanese and foreign companies are now considered to be approved in principle, the only stipulation being that the Bank of Japan must be notified and given thirty days to comment. Prior to 1980 Japanese companies were largely protected by the government in the sense that all foreign contracts had to be approved by the Bank of Japan and, in the pre-1976 period, by the Ministry of International Trade and Industry (MITI). The infamous preliberalization MITI guidelines were so severe that unless foreign companies were very skillful, technology found its way into Japanese hands at bargain-basement prices. That MITI protection is no longer as readily available as it once was, and Japanese companies that have no past history of negotiating detailed contracts with foreigners feel vulnerable without the constant reassurance that they are dealing with people whom they can trust. At the same time the foreign partner in a contract with the Japanese is no longer bound by the rigid percentages and time limits governing royalty arrangements prior to liberalization. Foreign companies can use this to their benefit, and should not give any technology to the Japanese today unless they get a fair price for it.

In the five years that I was involved with contract negotiations with the Japanese I rarely had to discuss a signed contract or its enforcement with our Japanese partners, and I do not remember one incident when they ever referred me to a contract in order to persuade me to take a certain action that they felt was necessary. On the other hand, I was frequently obliged to remind the Japanese side that through oversight they were acting in violation of a contract. They just don't read contracts after they are signed and filed!

The Japanese attitude toward law and lawyers in general is very different from that of Americans. Thus the different expectations of a contract are directly linked to how the legal system works in Japan, which is not at all like that in the United States or Western Europe. For although Japanese law was consciously patterned after European models in the early part of this century, and amended to conform to American ideas during the Occupation, in practice it does not operate at all like the models on which it is based.

To the American or European, a contract negotiation is a process of scoring points by means of clever maneuvering, nudging the other side into a position where they concede key points that will enable us to feel we have worked out a good deal in spite of our opponents. The American executive negotiating a contract with a foreign company is usually accompanied by a corporate counsel or legal adviser who keeps him straight on points of home-country law and watches assiduously for any intemperate remarks or clauses that may imply violations of either FCPA (Foreign Corrupt Practices Act) or the antitrust law. Once the contract is signed, it is considered immutable unless both parties agree to a formal change.

Japanese, on the other hand, almost never bring a lawyer into a contract discussion; they rely completely on the nonprofessional negotiating efforts of their own (usually international department) executives, backed by (unqualified) legal assistants who work in the general affairs department of most Japanese companies of any size. This is not surprising, considering that while there are more than five hundred thousand lawyers in the United States, there are less than eleven thousand in Japan. These legal assistants may know as much as, and usually more than, many lawyers about the aspects of law that affect their company. (This shortage of lawyers is no accident, it is a Japanese government policy. See the discussion in Richardson and Ueda's *Business and Society in Japan,* pp. 143–154.) In fact, the Japanese regard the introduction of an attorney or lawyer into a business negotiation as an unfriendly act implying that you, the foreign partner, do not trust them, and this bodes ill for the outcome of the negotiations. Furthermore, the government actively discourages its citizens from using litigation as a means of solving disputes. To illustrate how rarely the Japanese use lawyers or litigation to solve disputes, I quote again from Richardson and Ueda: ". . . a study of Tokyo taxicab companies showed that of a total of 2,567 accidents causing either physical injury or property damage, only two cases were filed."[3]

Thus the contract in Japan has traditionally been considered to be the mere formalization of a binding personal agreement, which loses its validity if circumstances change and make its conditions unfavorable to the company's interests. The Japanese company will sometimes even feel betrayed if a foreign company insists on the fine print in a contract, or if their Western partners are unwilling to be flexible about the terms after the contract has been signed.

The Japanese do not use the law as the basic point of departure in a contract draft. Normally they send the contract in draft form to the local Fair Trade Commission (which is the successor to MITI as the modern-day protector of the contract rights of Japanese companies) for an opinion as to the "fairness" of the agreement, but only when encouraged to do so by the Japanese party (in an international agreement) does the Fair Trade Commission ever write an official letter requesting changes in the contract "to conform with the law." (I have never heard of an instance where the FTC found that an agreement unfairly prejudiced the interests of the foreign partner and forced the Japanese company to make concessions.)

One of the most common points of contention in contracts is the restriction placed on the Japanese party as to where it can or cannot export. In practice the FTC will intervene in this area more than in any other. The famous case of Bucyrus-Erie and Komatsu is one that was broken up by the FTC on just these grounds. After fifteen years of working with Bucyrus-Erie of the United States in a joint venture in Japan, Komatsu decided that it wanted to export to China. The original contract had specified that the joint-venture territory was limited to Japan, Korea and Taiwan; it excluded China because it was not an important market at the time the agreement was signed. At the urging of Komatsu, the Japanese FTC entered the scene in 1980 to inform the American partner that the agreement was no longer acceptable, and had to be modified to include China. Since the American party had made other arrangements in China, they naturally refused, and the agreement was dissolved. A key point to remember about the FTC is that there is no statute of limitations governing its actions, and no right of appeal from its final decision.

If the reader is getting the impression that Japanese companies can use the law in Japan to good advantage in their dealings with foreign companies, he is on the right track. The Japanese "company lawyer" is actually the largest law firm in the world—namely, the government of Japan. Through a system that is loosely referred to as "administrative guidance" *(gyōsei shidō)*, each ministry is able to interpret the law in a manner that suits it, and there is almost no appeal against its interpretation. Japanese companies are very fond of getting administrative guidance from MITI, the FTC, and the Ministry of Finance, as well as other ministries, in the event that they feel a contract might be prejudicial to their interests, and, using the government as a shield, shrug their shoulders and point to the government when the foreign partner objects to changes in key sections of the contract. In the past two years there has been a gradual realization that this type of overtly xenophobic use of administrative guidance is not likely to be tolerated indefinitely, because foreign companies are using the U.S. embassy or the EEC legation to fight back. This is a recent phenomenon, however.

To quote from the *1980–81 Annual Report* of the Program on U.S.-Japan Relations:

... from the perspective of the Japanese, the extraordinary complexity of the American legal system and the propensity of Americans to rely on lawyers and legal processes to resolve problems contribute to a perception of the United States as a hazardous and, to a degree, hostile place to do business. Americans dealing with Japan ... are often frustrated by the absence of clear legal guideposts defining permissible activities and the broad, and frequently non-reviewable, discretionary powers wielded by the Japanese bureaucracy.[4]

Thus the Japanese find our system nearly as confusing and threatening as we find theirs. But the fact remains that an American court can almost always be relied on to decide on the merits of the case; at any rate, there is no system of institutionalized preference for local over foreign interests, as there is in the bureaucracy of Japan.

I turn now to the art of actual negotiation of contracts. Over the years I have developed a number of dos and don'ts that have stood me in good stead. As I see it, there are five basic rules (and a few corollaries) that will help the foreign businessman conclude a successful negotiation.

The first rule is to recognize from the outset that the Japanese side is going to be suspicious of foreigners, and doubly suspicious if they are accompanied by a lawyer. The only way for Western negotiators to overcome that suspicion is to create an atmosphere of trust. There is no simple way to do this, but one of the best tactics negotiators can employ is to keep more or less even with the pace set by the Japanese, and strive to reassure them as often as necessary that the Western side is aware of their interests. Some of the points made in Chapter 2 may be relevant to review before beginning to negotiate.

The second rule applies to the negotiating style that the Japanese prefer. It is essential to avoid a hard sell. The way to coax the Japanese into appreciating one's point of view, and the business concept that one is trying to sell to them, is to adopt a self-effacing and humble role while at the same time being quietly forceful whenever necessary or appropriate. As mentioned previously, the Japanese cannot stand the aggressive smooth talker who makes such a favorable impression in the West. No matter how slick he is, he will never succeed in establishing a durable relationship with the Japanese company, which is the only real guarantee that the deal will stick.

When Westerners are negotiating with a Japanese firm that they have never dealt with before, either personally or as a company, they must establish their credentials with the Japanese before beginning to discuss business. This can usually best be done by enlisting the support of reputable third parties who are well thought of by the Japanese firm. Once when I was looking for a Japanese company to distribute one of our products, I was able to establish my credentials through a well-known but retired member of the Japanese imperial family, a distant relative of the Emperor, who served as my go-between. An excellent way to establish credentials is to make use of the banks or trading companies that deal with the Japanese company in question. In fact, the use of a go-between is so common in Japan that it is quite normal for the first stages of the negotiation or contract to be conducted entirely by a go-between before the principals ever get involved in face-to-face discussion. The institution of the go-between arose in Japan as a face-saving device, which was particularly useful in arranging marriages so that neither party was embarrassed by the other's refusal. (In fact, in a Japanese marriage ceremony it is the go-between who has the seat of honor.) Thus a go-between can also be useful in business when one is anxious to know if the Japanese party is really interested or just being polite. (Recall the discussion of *tatemae* and *honne* in Chapter 4.) The go-between can usually tell whether the deal has a chance of proceeding to the next stage. Those who don't have any Japanese contacts or bank or trading-company connections (and even those who do), might contact one of the consultants listed in the directory of the American Chamber of Commerce in Japan (ACCJ) in Tokyo. There are a number of experienced American consulting firms and banks that can assist in making initial contact and soundings as well as helping throughout the negotiating process.

The third rule for successful negotiating is that negotiators must be sure that they really have the mandate of their headquarters to speak for the company. The Japanese have long memories, and they will never take someone seriously if they get the impression that he has to call the head office every time a problem comes up in negotiations. "Calling New York" can be a useful gambit in a real emergency, but it is not to be recommended more than once or twice in a long-drawn-out negotiation.

Some insecure CEO's in the States have a feeling that nobody can be trusted to finalize a negotiation and that all deals have to be signed by them. This is so alien to the Japanese way of thinking that it can threaten any chance of a contract. Of course, the ceremony of signing is often practiced in Japan, and the chairmen or presidents of the two companies may sign the agreement before photographers, but they never read the contracts and are almost never involved in any negotiating. This is left to the working management levels of the company.

A corollary to this rule is, "Don't send a boy to do a man's job." I can remember the case of one American pharmaceutical company based in the Midwest that didn't have much experience in Japan. They kept sending over a negotiating team of their "brightest people," which consisted of some whiz kids—one of them female—in their twenties and early thirties. After a series of frustrating failures they got in touch with me in my capacity as president of the local American Chamber of Commerce to ask my advice. They had visited Japan three times but couldn't even get their own joint-venture Japanese senior department heads to listen to them, let alone the principals of the Japanese company with whom they wished to negotiate. As tactfully as possible I suggested that they augment the team with a twenty-five-year veteran of the company who was at the very least a corporate vice president. They took my advice, and the change in attitude by the Japanese partner was immediate and positive. The Japanese dislike having to negotiate with young people, since a Japanese would never be allowed to act for his company unless he had been with it for at least fifteen to twenty years. Aside from the bias in favor of age in Japanese society, there is the added factor that they find it hard to believe that young executives have any real power, so they feel it is a waste of time, as well as an insult to their dignity, to be asked to negotiate with "youngsters." Another problem handicapping Western negotiating teams that include women is the male chauvinism of the typical Japanese executive, which, as mentioned before, is extreme. American companies with experience in Europe usually consider carefully before sending younger executives to negotiate with the British or French, yet some don't think twice about sending such people to deal with the Japanese. This is a trap to be avoided if a Western company's corporate relationships with the Japanese is not to be subjected to unnecessary strains.

Rule number four is that the minute a concession is made it will be regarded as immutable by the Japanese. Negotiations in Japan are not conducted in the horse-trading atmosphere that Westerners are used to, where the bidder can change his mind if he discovers that the horse is a bit longer in the tooth than he had bargained on. If a negotiator so much as nods his head to a suggestion that he should forgo a royalty or accept a reduced lump-sum payment, he will have a tough time convincing the Japanese that he really didn't mean it. As one writer puts it:

> At any meeting the foreign manager should comment with care since anyone within hearing range is certain to take note of his remarks. Statements which he did not mean seriously or which were made on the basis of insufficient facts, can be quite embarrassing when quoted. The Western tactic of talking to fill silence or referring to vague figures or facts when the speaker is unsure of himself is a very dangerous practice in Japan.[5]

In the American Chamber of Commerce in Japan (ACCJ) we used to be embarrassed (until we decided to do something about it) when the American delegates to the Joint U.S.-Japan Businessman's Council would arrive without the detailed preparation that is essential when confronting Japanese. The Japanese delegates would have every fact at their disposal and six assistants behind them in case there was one item that they might have forgotten to anticipate and prepare for. Many of the American delegates were busy frontline CEO's who regarded their participation in the council as a sort of patriotic duty, but they did not approach the meetings with the seriousness they reserved for their own business. The Japanese, on the other hand, were also senior people in their organizations but were no longer involved in day-to-day decision-making and therefore had both ample time and sufficient interest to have boned up. The Chamber finally decided that it should do the homework for our delegates, and now a committee of the ACCJ works directly with the U.S. delegates to ensure that they are as well prepared as the Japanese.

A fifth and final rule is to recall that to the Japanese a contract is more like a marriage document than a business agreement. To the American or European the deal is expressed in terms of the potential sales and profits that he will derive from the arrangement. Although profits are important to the Japanese, the effect of the deal on their relationships within the Japanese business community is for them a major concern. Indeed, it is just as important as potential profitability. The questions revolving in the mind of a Japanese contemplating a deal are how the industrial group (*zaibatsu**) with which he is

---

*I use the term *zaibatsu* because it is a familiar one, but the proper term is *zaikai*, meaning "financial circles." The holding companies that formed the core of the prewar *zaibatsu* were officially dissolved by the Occupation, and the modern industrial groups survive in uncodified forms, based on unwritten laws.

affiliated will view the new arrangement with a foreign company; what the association of his industry will have to say; and whether he will be taking unfair advantage, thus causing his competitors to react violently. In fact, the Japanese is as concerned with the impact of the agreement on his standing within the Japanese business community as he is with the direct monetary benefits that his firm will derive from the arrangement.

I should add to these five basic rules a couple of other obvious ones. Nonresident negotiators should avoid telling the Japanese when they plan to leave, or at least keep the date vague for as long as possible. Often the Japanese will orchestrate the negotiations in such a way that the foreigner is faced with a deal or no-deal situation with only a few hours left to catch his flight home. The weak American or European negotiator may be tempted to settle for much less than he expected to get, on the theory that any deal is better than none at all. Many American companies regard overseas trips as an exotic waste of the company's money rather than vital contacts that build tomorrow's business. When working for such companies, there is a double pressure to make a deal then and there. My advice is to hold out for the arrangement that is fair to both parties.

Few, if any, top Japanese company executives will have any idea of the details of contracts that are being negotiated with foreign companies. When Western executives meet these men, it will usually be on an *aisatsu* call (a call to pay one's respects), or in the evening at a geisha house or a good restaurant. This is not the time to discuss business. The higher-ups to whom one is introduced in this fashion will be briefed on the main elements of negotiations, and the Westerner's remarks should be confined to emphasizing the mutual benefits that the deal will bring and the consequent strengthening of the relationship between his company and theirs.

One final suggestion: it is a good idea to have a formal contract review every two or three years to be sure that it still represents a commonality of interests. Although I never had a chance to put this idea into practice when I was in Japan, in hindsight I am convinced that in the eyes of the Japanese it could be a positive indication of willingness to accept the reality of changing circumstances. Many contracts have been put in file cabinets for years, to be brought out into the light of day only when there is a serious problem. By reviewing them first, and then with the Japanese partner, on a regular basis, one can prevent this situation from ever occurring.

To put all these helpful hints into perspective, I draw here on the excellent research of Professor Rosalie L. Tung, of the Wharton School of Finance and Commerce, on Japanese-American contracts signed over the past thirty years. She surveyed 582 American firms in both Japan and the United States, and had replies from 114 of them. Tables 1, 2, and 3 below are taken from her book *Business Negotiations with the Japanese* (Lexington, Mass.: Lexington Books, 1984), and I am deeply grateful to her for allowing me to use the highlights of some of her findings.

To give the reader an idea of the scope of operations that these firms had with Japanese companies, her survey showed that licensing was still the most common type of relationship between American and Japanese companies. This was followed by U.S. equity manufacturing firms and joint ventures. Her survey also indicated that very few firms were engaged in turnkey operations or consortia, lease agreements or management contracts.

The average firm in Professor Tung's survey had four active contracts with Japanese companies. When asked to state whether they were satisfied with the arrangements that they had, 49 percent indicated that they were. About 10 percent were unhappy, and the reasons for their dissatisfaction were given as differences in negotiation styles, language barriers, and delay in Japanese decision-making,

TABLE 1

Types of Operations in Japan Preferred by American Companies

TYPE OF ARRANGEMENT PREFERRED	% OF COMPANIES ENGAGED IN ACTIVITY
Licensing of technology	61
Manufacturing in Japan with equity in local company	44
Joint-venture arrangements	37
Export to Japan	37
Technical assistance	34
Export from Japan to U.S.	25
Equity in local company but no manufacturing	23

NOTE: Total adds to more than 100% due to multiple responses.

TABLE 2

American versus Japanese Negotiating Styles

AMERICAN	JAPANESE	CITED BY
Direct style	Indirect style	61%
Faster	Slower	49%
Time horizon of agreement geared toward short term	Time horizon of agreement geared toward long term	37%
Flexible	Rigid	33%
Little emphasis on face-saving	Heavy emphasis on face-saving	32%

TABLE 3

Factors Responsible for Success or Failure of Negotiations

FACTOR	VERY IMPORTANT TO SUCCESS	IMPORTANT TO SUCCESS	MODERATELY IMPORTANT
Preparation of U.S. team	67%	23%	5%
Patience on part of U.S. team	59	30	8
U.S. team's sincerity	59	28	10
Unique U.S. product	40	37	16
Personal relationships	33	39	18
U.S. team familiar with Japanese business practices	31	38	26
Familiarity with social customs	22	31	33
Past technical assistance	29	39	19

all more or less equal in weight. This result seems to support my contention that it is worth spending time to learn to understand the Japanese and how to deal with them.

Another finding of Professor Tung's survey that supports some advice given in an earlier chapter is related to the composition of the negotiating teams. Most Japanese teams consist of members numbering between four and seven, while most American teams consist of one man and an interpreter. This is a double handicap for the American because not only is he operating in little-known territory, but he is also heavily outnumbered. Only 20 percent of the U.S. firms in the survey indicated that the bilingual member of the negotiating team was anything more than an interpreter.

The survey next looked at reasons for dissatisfaction and areas for improvement in negotiations. The largest percentage of firms (40 percent) indicated that the main area for improvement was the lack of effective communications with the Japanese partner. Other problems focused on the slowness of Japanese decision-making, and on the need for greater mutual trust between the two parties.

In analyzing the difference between the American and Japanese negotiating styles, the respondents cited many that have already been covered above.

The survey went on to cite the factors that were most responsible for the success or failure of negotiations.

Note that Table 3 above indicates that preparation ranks first, and patience and sincerity tie for second place.

CHAPTER
8

"HAI" MEANS *"I HEAR YOU"*

Entering a conference room in Japan to negotiate a complex technology transfer or joint-venture arrangement is not unlike entering a minefield blindfolded. The inexperienced Western negotiator is usually alone except for an interpreter. At most, he has two or three colleagues with him. The Japanese are on their home ground, and usually field a team of ten to fifteen, each with special expertise in every phase of the negotiation. The Westerner is jet-lagged; they are well rested. He cannot understand their Japanese while they pretend not to understand their guest's English—but watch them write down everything he says before the interpreter speaks one word! The Westerner's mind is tuned to London or New York, while they are completely focused on the matter at hand.

It is no wonder that many Westerners are reluctant to negotiate with the Japanese. Even more frustrating is the Japanese fondness for not saying what they really mean. They regard blunt, frank statements as the height of rudeness. In this chapter some guidelines are provided for recognizing the true meaning of the often confusing signals Westerners receive from Japanese negotiators. In order to overcome the advantages the Japanese gain by forcing most negotiations to be held on their home ground, the Western negotiator must prepare as thoroughly as possible.

The Japanese are reluctant to say no to anything because they feel that a flat rejection may offend the person being addressed or cause him to lose face. This confuses Western negotiators because they often conclude that the unwillingness to say no may mean that the Japanese can be persuaded if only they can be worn down, or if a particularly effective argument can be found to convince them. This illusion only compounds the problem. The Japanese will listen politely until the foreigner runs out of steam, and their response will usually be to say *"Hai."* Do not be deceived. Although the dictionary defines this word as "yes," it usually only means "I hear you"—in other words, "I'm listening, but I'm not convinced." Negotiators should never assume that they have agreement just because they hear a chorus of *hai*'s coming from the opposite side of the table.

Since "yes" often means "no" in Japanese, one may well wonder how it is possible to tell when agreement has been reached. This *is* a serious problem, but there are a number of verbal and nonverbal signals that can indicate whether progress is being made. Nevertheless, even when one has mastered the meaning of these clues, it is still advisable to repeat and reconfirm one's understanding of what has been established at each stage of the negotiations. The Japanese will enter and leave the conference room frequently and will not be surprised if you decide to repeat some key point when a negotiator returns to the conference table.

The fear of offending crops up in international relations, as well as in business. In recent years Japanese prime ministers seem to have been afflicted with foot-in-mouth disease. They come to the United States anxious to ward off continuing protectionist threats that would erect barriers against Japanese exports to America. Perhaps because this is uppermost in their minds, the U.S. concern with Japan's military role seems a useful side issue with which to please the Americans by *tatemae* statements about Japan's commitment to a strong defense.

When the late Prime Minister Ohira arrived in the United States in 1980, he was mostly concerned about persuading Congress and the President not to take any drastic action against Japanese car exports. In return, he was prepared to please his American hosts by making some positive statement on the importance of maintaining a strong defense against the Russian threat to northeast Asia. In this context he used the word *dōmei* (alliance) to describe the relationship between the United States and Japan. This turned out to be a major gaffe because the Japanese people were not ready for that word to describe their "security arrangement" with the United States (any hint of militarism has remained in bad odor ever since the war). As a result of using this strong word, he got a favorable press in America, but came under such pressure when he returned home that he was forced to retract.

Similarly, when Prime Minister Nakasone visited Washington in March, 1983, he used the phrase *ōkii na kōkū-bokan* to describe the role that Japan would play in the defense of Asia against the Russian threat. This was translated by the interpreter as "an unsinkable aircraft carrier," and the reaction in Washington was one of sheer joy. They were hearing exactly what they wanted to hear, and the favorable reaction ensured not only a successful visit but further patience on the trade front. The countries that Japan had occupied during World War II and the strong pacifist movement in Japan did not take so kindly to what appeared to them to be a revival of Japanese militarism. The actual translation of *ōkii na kōkū-bokan* is "a big aircraft carrier," which probably would not have aroused the same furor. This example shows not only that the Japanese are prepared to say what you want them to in order not to offend, but it also illustrates the problem with interpreters mentioned in Chapter 3.

One of the reasons Americans sometimes find it difficult to understand what Japanese are trying to communicate is that they often use nonverbal means to convey a message. Thus, the most important indicator of progress in negotiations is a nonverbal form of communication known as *haragei*. Literally this means "stomach language," and is described by Jane A. Corddry as "the process of feeling one another out on an issue." She goes on to say:

> The Japanese regard haragei as the highest form of interpersonal communication. A person with a problem or in need of a favor, unable or unwilling to confront a friend with it head on, will merely drop suggestions; and the greater the favor, the more allusive the suggestions. The friend, meanwhile, does not feel the need to press for a direct explanation, but relies on his powers of intuition. Having a common history, language, and culture, and a rather homogeneous society, the Japanese have developed into an art the act of communicating one's heartfelt desires in the fewest number of words.[1]

In the context of business negotiations, *haragei* takes on the connotation of a wordless battle of wills going on beneath the surface, behind the smiling faces and polite words that are the usual components of a developing negotiation.

A good negotiator must always be sensitive to the *haragei* in any meeting. It is more complex and vital than just sensing the mood or gauging the atmosphere as we do in the West. The facing off of two sumo wrestlers before they actually make contact is the closest analogy to *haragei* that comes to mind. These athletes spend at least five minutes prior to a bout just preparing themselves to fight. They glare at each other and throw salt into the ring to bring good luck. The audience says nothing, but one can feel them willing their favorite to victory. In fact, there is comparative quiet in the sumo ring before a fight begins. These silences can also be felt at the conference table before a round of negotiations. Both sides try to make clear through nonverbal means that they are the ones with a stronger position and that it would be foolish to think there is any way to persuade or cajole them into compromise. This does not mean that compromise is impossible; it merely means that it is going to be difficult. The best way to handle *haragei* is to realize that it exists, and that to the Japanese the negotiations are going on at the "stomach" level as well as the verbal one. Negotiators who indicate by their responsiveness to the mood of the meeting that they are well aware of *haragei* will gain the respect of the Japanese.

The more important the matter being discussed, the more indirect the Japanese manner of communication will be. They rely on the intuition of those they deal with to feel the *haragei* and deduce what they are really trying to say.

Of course, Japanese communication is not all based on *haragei*. Here are a few expressions that can also help indicate how they view the progress of the negotiations in general, or whether one has their agreement on specific points being raised. Among the most common phrases are:

Sō desu ne.	Literally translated, this means "Yes, that's right," but in practice it is used simply to encourage the speaker to continue.
Kekkō desu.	"Agreed." This is very promising, and can imply actual agreement with the point made. The best thing to do here is to verify the point.
Wakarimashita.	"Understood." This is used like *"Hai,"* but carries more emphasis.

Tabun.	"Maybe."
Mondai nai.	"No problem." This can be used by both sides in a negotiation to indicate agreement in principle by stating that they see no obstacle to the proposed course of action, clause, or portion of an agreement.
Mutsukashii.	"Difficult."
Dekimasen (or the informal *Dekinai*).	"It can't be done."
Mama.	"As it stands" is one of the ways this expression can be translated. The Japanese use it to mean that everything is going very well. A frequent answer to the question *Dō desuka?* ("How's business?" or "How is it going?") would be *"Mama desu"* ("Not bad").

Before every negotiating session of any importance the Japanese team will have held a series of internal meetings and discussions in which they have reached a consensus between the various factions in the company on the most important nonnegotiable elements of the proposed contract. The negotiator who hits one of these points will find an absolute lack of flexibility on the part of the Japanese. The process of arriving at consensus within a Japanese company is extremely long and complicated; therefore negotiators are unlikely to give away points already determined as fixed by this process.* At almost all costs, they will avoid the extreme inconvenience of trying to reach a fresh consensus. A Western negotiator who must get them to give way on one of these points has to be prepared for a long delay.

In a typical negotiation there is usually an introductory phase of pleasantries, followed by opening speeches given by the two senior negotiators. This is an important part of the meeting, since one may be able to discover what the fundamental points are on which the Japanese have already reached consensus within their company.

The Western side is expected to speak first if the negotiation is taking place in Japan. The ten-minute introduction by the senior

*Refer to Chapter 9, "The Decision-Making Process."

negotiator from each side outlines the purpose and objectives of the negotiation and should give some hint of each company's expectations as to the outcome and mutual benefits of the arrangement once completed. The meeting then moves on to what might be called the "technical phase." Here the Japanese are most comfortable because they are usually better prepared than Western negotiators on technical matters. Frequently, when negotiating the licensing of technology that the Japanese are anxious to acquire, the technical phase of negotiations will be largely taken up with discussion of the shortcomings of the foreigner's product. They will claim that if they were to license the technology they would have to spend millions of yen improving it before it can fulfill its claims.

Those who want to keep ahead of the Japanese during the technical phase of the discussion would do well to make a thorough investigation (using Nomura Research, Stanford Research Institute, or one of the other consultants in Tokyo or Osaka) of all the allied research that the Japanese company has been doing in your product area. It sometimes turns out that the Japanese company has been trying for years without success to develop a similar product; this information will help to determine the value of the product or process to the Japanese company. (If the situation were reversed, the Japanese would do the same kind of checking.) From a negotiating standpoint, it is essential to make a real effort to find out how much your company's technology is worth to them. Few American companies take the time (usually several months are involved) to investigate the Japanese company thoroughly, finding out about its research productivity and the significant benefits that the technology will give them in Japan and in export markets. One of the main reasons why such an investigation takes so long is that the information is not easily available, and is almost never found in English. It takes a lot of patient digging to get it.

One of the best ways to go about getting information on Japanese technology is to join the official Government of Japan Scientific and Technological Information Center in Nagato-cho, near the National Diet Library, in Tokyo. This is a computerized search facility, which has an entire body of information on current Japanese and foreign technology. It can be enormously useful, provided the user speaks and reads Japanese. Trade journals and other trade publications are another good source of information on a particular industry and the companies in it. Data is also available from the trade association, chambers of commerce, JETRO (the Japan External Trade Organization), and a host of other sources. A Western company would be well advised to use all these sources, and also to retain a specialized consultant in Tokyo to dig up information. There are a number of smart entrepreneurs in Tokyo, Americans who have settled there and run consulting businesses, as well as one or two Japanese consultants and research firms. They can help obtain needed information.

The knowledge that a Westerner brings to the negotiations will never be as complete and comprehensive as his Japanese counterpart's understanding of his business, but he will at least have a better idea of the value of his technology if he has done his homework. It may also save a lot of time, since he could be talking to a company about a product or process they have already spent millions of dollars on attempting to develop themselves. They may only want the foreign company's product as an insurance policy in case their own research fails. Another possible scenario is that the Japanese company will try to acquire Western technology merely to keep it from the marketplace for as long as possible while they further develop their own technology. Not surprisingly, they would rather have an inefficient mousetrap developed in-house than license a perfect one from a Western firm. In research this is sometimes called the NIH (Not Invented Here) syndrome.

In 1979 I was involved in discussing a new drug from our own research department with a particular Japanese company with which my company has had a long and important relationship for more than twenty years. We had a tacit "mutual first-refusal right" understanding with this company, and I could not understand why they were so cool about what looked like an outstanding new breakthrough in cardio-vascular medicine. I asked my people to find out if they had a similar product under development, and within a few days the answer came back that they had just begun trials of a new drug that was directly competitive with ours, though not as good. I used this information discreetly but effectively at a subsequent meeting with the R&D department of the Japanese company, and greatly strengthened my negotiating position as a result.

An additional benefit of knowing about the Japanese company's research is that one will be able to assess the capabilities of the research workers in the Japanese company and calculate how much time will be required to transfer the technology after the negotiations are completed.

The technical phase of the negotiations can take days. The Japanese company will bring in the heads of each of the technical departments to make a presentation on the technology under discussion. This is partly to examine its advantages, but the foreign negotiator can be sure they will dwell mainly on its drawbacks. They will ask questions in endless detail, and no negotiator can answer all of them. During this phase they will insist on receiving written details of all aspects of the technology, as well as written answers to every question that they have raised, to be provided within days after the meeting. My colleagues from New York used to be annoyed by what they considered to be immaterial, red-herring questions; nevertheless, until the Japanese had their answers there could be no further progress. Further, they demanded a certain *type* of answer to their questions. Often they would feel frustrated by the American technical experts' habit of offering opinion rather than hard data when confronted with such questions.

Whether this boundless thirst for information is simply a product of the Japanese decision-making process or a deliberate tactic employed by the research people, the delays give them a decided psychological advantage. The start of the business discussions has been delayed as long as possible while the Japanese demonstrate that they know more about the product or technology than the other side does. I have sat through many a two- or three-day negotiating session in which these tactics have been employed very effectively. When the New York VP who handles my company's negotiations with Japanese licensees and licensors started bringing top technical experts with him on his trips to Japan, the presence of these knowledgeable people helped to offset the Japanese psychological advantage. But it was always a struggle getting the corporation to spare any top scientific people for two weeks, which is the minimum length of time that you should allow for a trip to Japan.

The obvious advantage that the Japanese company derives from having the negotiations in Japan is that they can always make the foreigner feel uncomfortable and force him to go overboard in adapting to their style of negotiating. In addition, they are able to stall the discussions on technical grounds by raising minuscule points that force postponement of the meetings at the Western company's initiative instead of theirs. (Sometimes they do this because they are also holding discussions with another company and want to see who will give them the best deal.) To avoid all this, American and European companies should try to get the Japanese to agree to have at least part of the negotiations on the Western company's home ground, and to anticipate the areas where they may pose technical questions so that the relevant experts can be available, irrespective of where the negotiations take place. Often I have sat, along with three well-informed generalists and a top expert, opposite a Japanese fifteen-member negotiating team with experts on every discipline represented on their side of the table. We were always having to table matters of a minute technical nature because we did not have the answers at hand.

Another problem when negotiating technical matters with the Japanese is that Americans in particular have an unfortunate tendency to lecture. Being thus patronized naturally irritates the Japanese, and this is certain to cause further delay. Many American technical experts feel superior to the Japanese. Senior Western research and development and scientific people are nurtured in an atmosphere where they are flattered and deferred to by their subordinates. Even the more junior ones feel superior to the Japanese because of job mobility in the United States and the fact that they can always escape an unpleasant situation at work by taking a higher-paying job with a competitor. In stark contrast to them are the Japanese researchers, who are subject to tight discipline. They cannot resign and join another company because they would universally be regarded as disloyal and untrustworthy; no one would hire them. The lack of mobility and company loyalty of the Japanese technician are distinct assets in integrating him into the negotiating team. If he makes a mistake in dealing with a Western company, he could be "sent to the window," which is the Japanese way of getting rid of incompetents without firing them.* The American researcher usually feels nothing like the team spirit of his Japanese counterpart and thinks of himself first as a specialist in a given field before recognizing that he is a part of his company. Therefore it is important that technical experts sent to Japan know something about the Japanese style of doing things. No matter how competent the Western expert is, he must have at least some gift for diplomacy, or he will be of limited usefulness when dealing with the Japanese.

Mado no hito, "window people," are employees of Japanese companies who have failed—rather than being fired, they are given a desk by a window and never assigned any work. They just sit there until they retire, suffering the ultimate punishment for incompetence.

When the technical phase is completed, the Japanese will have most of the answers they want and be sufficiently convinced of the value of the technology in question. The next phase is the actual negotiation of the business terms of the agreement, which is what the Western negotiators consider the most important part of the negotiations. To the Japanese, on the other hand, this phase is the least enjoyable. As explained in the previous chapter, they actually dislike the give-and-take of bargaining.

My experience in discussing business terms with the Japanese has been varied, ranging from situations where the Japanese seem almost uninterested, apparently relying entirely on their trust and confidence in you to give them a fair deal, to the tough clause-by-clause negotiating style that one usually finds in the West. In the past two or three years, when negotiating financially significant contracts, I have found that the Japanese are becoming better and better at extracting the best possible terms. In the pharmaceutical industry, for example, there have been some large payments made by foreign companies to the Japanese for licenses on anticancer and antibiotic drugs, fields where the Japanese have equaled or surpassed Western technology. In fact, as their technology improves, it is becoming harder for Western companies to reach agreement on business arrangements acceptable to the Japanese.

Back in the 1970's it was possible for Western negotiators to use the "Take it or leave it" technique, and it often produced quick results, but nowadays this remains true only in the case of really outstanding technology that the Japanese have no hope of duplicating. Most contracts today must have provisions for first-refusal rights (each side has the right of first refusal on a product developed by the other) and cross-licensing provisions (each side commits itself to giving the other a license for an equivalent piece of technology either then or in the immediate future).

The business session will usually take several hours, unless there is a recently negotiated prior contract between the two companies that can serve as a model and reference standard. In fact, my experience has been that the point of departure for any contract discussion is the most recent and most similar in basic concept of the contracts that have been signed between the two companies. Japanese tend to be most sensitive about such contract items as the right to manufacture the product in Japan and minimum annual purchase or royalty clauses. The reason for the preoccupation with the manufacturing rights is that the Japanese always want to use their manufacturing facilities to maximum capacity. In some cases they will evaluate a new product or process as much in terms of its impact on their operations as on the intrinsic merit of the product.

I remember we once managed to overcome the Japanese dislike of royalty payments by announcing, to the surprise of the Japanese company with which we were negotiating, that we were not going to insist on a minimum royalty, and in fact were not going to ask for a royalty payment at all in the classic sense of the term. They were dumbfounded, since we were licensing them a process that would not only save them millions of dollars a year but also give them a higher-quality product. How, their vice president of manufacturing asked, were we expecting them to pay us for the technology? We explained that we were so sure of its intrinsic value and the savings that they would achieve that we merely wanted a third of their savings, using a very simple formula, which was, in turn, tied to the consumer price index so that the saving would reflect inflation over the lifetime of the contract. After some discussion they agreed to this approach and we concluded an agreement along these lines. We held our breath, because the technology was complicated, and we knew that only when the Japanese company had really mastered it would they achieve the full potential savings. After nine months of negative indices on the formula computation (indicating that their costs were higher with our process than with their own) they were suddenly able to repeat the manufacturing process at almost the same yield and quality that we had been teaching them. And, as you might expect, they went on to improve the technology further. For the past several years the result has been a much higher income for our company than if we had licensed the technology and charged the normal royalty fee.

The key to the negotiation described above was the confidence that our approach inspired in the Japanese, and since that time I have found that in almost every case this particular Japanese company has gone out of its way to favor us when they offer product or process licenses to foreign producers. Obviously such a gambit will not be possible or appropriate in most agreements, but this example illustrates that the best strategy is to evaluate the main concerns of the Japanese side and then try to meet them halfway. The Japanese put a great deal of trust *(shinyō)* in a Western negotiator who is tough and firm in defense of his own interests but who nevertheless makes a real effort to understand their concerns.

Western negotiators will know that they have basic agreement in the business phase when they no longer feel the *haragei* that characterizes the earlier sessions. One warning here: do not allow the meeting to end without making sure that all the business terms are clearly and precisely agreed to. At times I have left a meeting with the Japanese thinking that I had obtained an agreement on several points, when in fact they had merely agreed to consider my request. This vital difference can be expensive if an executive returns to the States or Europe and finds out days later that the main points of the agreement he telexed back to his head office were never actually accepted.

Before adjourning, make sure that there is agreement by comparing notes on every aspect of the discussions. This should include all the pending tasks that have been mutually agreed upon during the technical session and a restatement of the contract terms as finally agreed upon between the parties. It is at this point that one will usually get either agreement or the qualified statements that reveal what has actually been accepted and what needs further consensus building. It is also helpful to pin down dates for the final contract signing and for the interim steps leading to finalization.

In some Japanese companies the contract terms are discussed separately from the technical aspects by a different department within the Japanese company. Here the progress of the meeting can be measured by observing who is present. The head of the negotiating team will probably sit through all the sessions, but his *kachō* (section heads) and *jichō* (deputy department heads) are usually waiting in the wings to enter the room when the technical aspects have been completed. I found it useful to cultivate a separate relationship with the international department, because it usually has the responsibility for business terms in a contract negotiation. One quick and easy way to tell if there is a possibility of a deal is to count heads. If there is only one man, or possibly two, present, then there is no deal. The Japanese would allow one or two men to say no, but never to say yes to any proposition.

One ploy to watch out for is the way an important Japanese negotiator will occasionally disappear suddenly and inexplicably during a meeting. A young female employee will enter the conference room, distracting the Westerner, and, hesitating for a minute, hand a piece of paper to the junior man at the end of the table. The paper eventually will find its way to the key negotiator, who will read it, excuse himself and leave the meeting. The Westerner is baffled. My advice is to ignore such activities, but when the Japanese executive returns, all that has been agreed upon in his absence should be repeated. This will avoid future problems.

In summary, the key to a successful negotiation is the use of intuition rather than pure logic or intellect. From the nonverbal communication of *haragei* to the shades and nuances of meaning embodied in such words as *Hai* ("I hear you"), *Wakarimashta* ("I understand you"), and *Kekkō desu* ("I agree with you"), the common element required of the Western negotiator is the ability to sense what lies behind the words and expressions, the half-closed eyes, and the silences that intersperse the meeting. As former Ambassador Reischauer has said:

> To Americans the Japanese style of negotiation can be confusing and even maddening, just as our style can seem blunt and threatening to them. An American businessman may state his case clearly from the start and in maximal terms for bargaining purposes. The Japanese may be appalled at this as an opening gambit, wondering what more the American may really have in mind. And the American in turn may feel that the cautious indirection of the Japanese is not only unrevealing but smacks of deceit.[2]

It is up to the Western negotiator to develop the subtlety needed to ensure that the situation does not deteriorate to the point of noncommunication. If the Japanese think Westerners exaggerate or are too blunt, and we consider them devious and deceitful, our business relations will, obviously, not go smoothly. If I had to put into one word the most important quality for successfully negotiating with the Japanese, it would be *sensitivity*. By this I mean the ability to sense the atmosphere, the warmth or coldness in the gestures, eyes, and manner of those with whom one is dealing. The Japanese distrust words. When dealing with them we should share this distrust, and always monitor what is happening beneath the surface.

CHAPTER 9

THE DECISION-MAKING PROCESS

Understanding the Japanese decision-making process is vital for the
Western businessman who wants to be successful in business relationships with the Japanese. Their method of making decisions is almost
the polar opposite of our practices, and Westerners often become
confused and impatient when confronted with this alien system. This
chapter will explain how Japanese decision-making is integrally
related to the emphasis in Japanese society on the group at the
expense of the individual, a point that was stressed in Part I. But
decision-making in Japan is not simply group-think. Many other factors influence how decisions are made in Japanese companies—such
as the company's long-term goals, its philosophy, and corporate culture. Japanese decision-making is a favorite topic with writers on
Japan, but I approach it here from a unique perspective: I intend to
show how Western businessmen can influence the decision-making
process in the Japanese companies they deal with.

In comparing Western and Japanese decision-making, it might be
useful to differentiate between contemporary Western and Japanese
images of a successful decision-maker. The Western view is often
based on the personal experience of working with a charismatic
leader. Such personalities, who often seem larger than life, have a gift
for making swift, effective decisions and rallying the support needed
to make sure they are implemented. To the Japanese such an image
seems very strange. They may feel that their founder-president (in

the case of a young company founded by a single individual) is imbued with such traits, but to the average Japanese salary man there is no such thing as a decision-maker in the Western sense of the word. American and European advertisements for luxury items, such as expensive watches, are usually directed at eagle-eyed men surveying the alternatives in a game of high stakes with tangible rewards in power and money. The Japanese would dismiss such an individual with a proverb: "The pheasant that flies gets shot." Their image of a lone decision-maker is of someone in agony. They would never admire such an individual unless he was struggling with the decision to commit *seppuku* (or *hara kiri*) as a result of having failed his company.

In the Japanese business organization it is usually difficult to say who decides anything. Indeed, an outsider is often left wondering whether a decision was made at all. But decisions don't just happen; the Japanese make them in the same way that shadows shift in a rock garden—slowly, imperceptibly, but nonetheless dramatically. From our point of view, it seems incredible that the Japanese achieve such concrete success as a result of such an apparently amorphous process. But the system does work.

In a Japanese organization the start of any decision is a suggestion, proposal, or outside event that forces the company to react. A Japanese company tends to deal with the world in much the same way that a snail does. Initially the response to any outside threat is to retreat into the safe haven of the company shell and meditate on the threat's significance. As time passes, the snail emerges; if the situation remains threatening, it will act, moving to a more protected location where the outside threat is not as likely to be present. Indeed, one gets the feeling that everyone in a Japanese company is so busy worrying about internal affairs that an outside event is viewed primarily as a nuisance to be eliminated as soon as possible so that the company can concentrate on its internal problems.

To understand what goes on when the Japanese are forced to take a decision, it is necessary to shed some of the common illusions about their system. First of all, it is not democratic. The decision-making process in the typical business organization tends to be concentrated in middle management. My own experience supports the view expressed by Yoshi Tsurumi that decision-making is essentially middle-management activity.[1] This differs from the American system, where senior management makes most of the decisions. But only when the decision will have a major impact and involve a foreign company will the top management of the Japanese company be involved.

Decision-making is participative, and involves obtaining a consensus from all those who will be affected by the action. That does *not* mean that a collective decision is made; all it means is that everyone is required to voice his opinion about a problem so that it can be clearly identified. Peter F. Drucker defines the difference between Japanese and American styles of decision-making as the difference between attempting to find an answer and attempting to define a question.

> The Japanese process is focused on understanding the problem. The desired end result is action and behavior on the part of people. This almost guarantees that all the alternatives will be considered. It rivets management attention to essentials. It does not permit commitment until management has decided what the decision is all about. Japanese managers may come up with the wrong answer to the problem . . . but they rarely come up with the right answer to the wrong problem.[2]

The Japanese hate decisions. As Drucker goes on to say:

> . . . their system forces the Japanese to make big decisions. It is much too cumbersome to be put to work on minor matters. It takes far too many people far too long to be wasted on anything but truly important matters leading to real changes in policies and behavior. Small decisions, even when obviously needed, are very often not being made at all in Japan for that reason.[3]

Thus the Japanese prefer to avoid hard choices unless it is a matter of major import. Theirs is a decision-making based on *vulnerability* —What will happen to us if we don't do X?—while our system tends to be based on risk assessment—What is the ROI (Return on Investment) or short-term impact on our P and L if we do X, and will we continue to derive profits over the long run? All this sounds as if the Japanese were nervous Nellies while we Americans were intrepid risk-takers. In fact, the Japanese method of assessing business trends makes them more willing to take risks on such matters as new product ideas in order to avoid falling behind the competition, while our so-called risk-oriented approach makes Western companies more conservative and and sensitive about their quarterly-earnings statements.

A good example of the conservative approach favored by many

American companies is their less than enthusiastic response to the use of genetic engineering as a manufacturing technique in the pharmaceutical industry. Few American firms have been willing to invest the vast sums that entry into this field requires (Schering-Plough and G. D. Searle are notable exceptions), whereas all the major Japanese pharmaceutical companies have made a significant commitment from their R&D funds for this purpose. To the Japanese it is a case of "We can't afford not to," while the Americans are saying, "Let's not be hasty—earnings aren't so good this quarter, and maybe the whole thing will blow over," or "Let's appoint a study team at the research center, because that won't cost anything and we can tell the shareholders that we're involved in genetic engineering."

In November 1978 I attended a course in Tokyo given by the Stanford Research Institute (SRI) entitled "Executive-Level Strategic Decision and Risk Analysis Seminar." It was a two-day seminar in English, and both Westerners and Japanese were invited to attend the course. The lecturer began by using the analogy of the coin toss to explain the principles behind the use of a decision-analysis system designed to reduce the probabilities of failure by breaking down the decision into component parts and assessing risk at each stage of the project. Various critical points were identified and numerical values attached to the risk at each stage. Many managers are familiar with this technique and use it in their day-to-day analyses. The Japanese executives had a great deal of trouble understanding the whole concept, partly because of the language problem but mainly because the decision-making system being described was so alien to their own corporate situation and experience. Several participants confided to me during coffee breaks that the system would never work in Japan. They were hoping to hear about a system that would enable them, as middle mangers, to help their company react to changes in the environment around them, and to protect it from unexpected events that might impede growth. They wanted a "vulnerability" model rather than a risk-analysis mode. I am sure that SRI has since redirected its Tokyo course to satisfy this different view, but the conflicting philosophy that marred the original course for the Japanese is a perfect example of the difference between American and Japanese ideas about decisions.

There is an air of finality to an American decision. When word gets around that top management has settled on a plan, there is not much that the lower echelons can do about it. In a Japanese company, on the other hand, there is a tremendous reluctance to be definitive. Every effort is made to procrastinate and review and re-review the facts, particularly when a foreign (i.e., unpredictable) party is involved. It is important that everyone involved should have some input into the process. To quote Pascale and Athos in *The Art of Japanese Management:*

> . . . the Japanese recognize as much as we do that decisions must be made. However, when they have the time, they prefer to invest it in carefully building a foundation of support. They recognize that many elements of an organization will be more committed to a decision if they take part in it. . . . The Japanese feel that not only do consultative discussions result in better decisions but that it is their *obligation* to include people. . . . Frequently, we hear stories of perplexed American firms receiving and briefing a delegation from their Japanese business partner only to receive a follow-up delegation two weeks later which requires the same briefing as before.[4]

The advantage of this seemingly cumbersome system is that making a decision and implementing it amount to the same thing. There is no delay during which a new idea has to be sold to the organization, whereas a postdecision delay is built into the American system. For Westerners an abrupt termination of the present situation seems best. To Japanese a mere shift in direction, as minimal as possible, seems the right answer.

Because a Japanese decision is organizational rather than individual, the Japanese corporate social system has an important impact on its evolution. If one has some idea of the social factors that are at work, one may be able to guide or at least predict the way a decision will evolve in a Japanese company.

Part I described the interrelationships between groups and factions *(batsu)* in a Japanese company. These factions are extremely important when it comes to predicting how a given course of action will fare in the final consensus that usually emerges at the end of the process. Factions can crop up in many forms, but the most common ones are the *oyabun/kobun* groupings (cliques of subordinates linked to a powerful manager) within the company. If a license arrangement for a new research product is being proposed, how will the R&D *oyabun* (leader) react? Because the product or process is NIH (Not Invented Here), will his faction's resources be mobilized to kill a decision to license the new product? As the Western negotiator listens to comments at negotiating sessions, he may perceive that this faction is the one always putting spokes in the discussion, asking irrelevant technical questions and requesting answers in writing before the discussions on the actual agreement can proceed. This has happened to me, and only after much probing did I discover that there were two factions within the R&D group engaged in a "dispute over turf," and that our product was caught in the middle.

These *oyabun/kobun* groups are not the only factions to have a role in the final decision. There are also strong relationships between men of the same college or university and of the same age. On one occasion we negotiated a license for a new drug from a large Japanese pharmaceutical company strictly on the basis of the Old Boy relationship *(dōkyūsei)* between our operations director and the R&D director of the Japanese company.

There are also factors that can be stronger than the direct loyalty of subordinate to superior or old school friends to one another. These are the pressures that are created when it appears that one faction is coming out on top and the others have to somehow change their position to make it appear that they supported (or opposed) the decision all along. The reader may be wondering why the president of the company doesn't step in and straighten out this mess. In a Western context that is what usually happens, but in Japan the president will seldom be involved with the decision-making process, and would rather ratify the victor in the power struggle. There are exceptions to this, but rarely do Japanese companies follow the Western pattern of "what the boss says goes." It must also be remembered that frequently the chief executive officer may not have the competence to intervene in the decision-making process, since he is often selected by the company's bank to watch out for their investment. Actual day-to-day decision-making is left to the group known as the *jōmu-kai,* or members of the managing director's meeting, to make the final decision on a given problem.

The process of obtaining consensus and the main document for formalizing a decision is the *ringi seido.* This system is well explained by Yoshi Tsurumi as follows:

> The commitment of individual employees to the widely accepted goals of the firm has produced an often mentioned decision making system in Japanese firms that is called *ringi seido.* Observers of this decision making process will note that new proposals—marketing or investment

decisions, for example—are often initiated at the lower or middle echelons of the firm. These proposals are passed along the hierarchy, collecting seals of approval or undergoing minor revisions, on their way up to
the president. The initiators or collaborating parties of such proposals
are busily engaged on an informal basis in pinpointing key personalities
whose support is needed. Some proposals fade away or die on their
journey to the top echelon. But those proposals that do survive cannot
be attributed solely to the initiators. By the time a proposal is accepted
by top management there will be a corporate consensus concerning its
feasibility.[5]

Thus we can say that the direction is "middle–up," as opposed to
the American decision-making system of top–down. When the white-
haired man of seventy-five or eighty, in his role as president, officially
informs you that the decision has been taken to go ahead with the
venture, he is merely conveying what has been decided at the middle-management level of the company. To quote Professor Ballon of
Sophia University (Tokyo):

> It is well known that in Japanese business so-called decision makers
> often act simply as "formalizers" and that the real decisions are made
> by the younger department heads and section chiefs who usually stand
> in the back row while older superiors take the honour of "conveying"
> the decisions.[6]

An effective decision is virtually never made in Japan without
preliminary groundwork done by the proponents of a given course
of action in order to ensure the support of their superiors, peers, and,
occasionally, subordinates. Any farmer knows that you won't get a
good crop if you don't till the ground. Tilling the organizational soil
to ready it for the seeds of a new decision is called *nemawashi* in
Japanese, which means "preparing the ground"; the literal reference
is to the transplanting of a tree. Before one can move a tree, one must
carefully dig around the base, making sure that none of the roots are
severed. Only then can it be pulled out of its present location and
transplanted. This procedure is an exact analogy of the work involved in preparing all elements of the company for a major decision.

Nemawashi is not unknown in the West. Most of us will try to drum
up support before we go into a meeting where we expect questions
to be raised and opposition to develop to a pet proposal. The Japanese try to preclude any threat to *wa* (harmony) in the actual meeting by obtaining consensus informally before the more formal *ringi*

seido procedure described above begins. *Nemawashi* is undertaken in a very structured way. The proponents will first identify everybody who is likely to be affected by the decision and then methodically "consult" with each *kachō, jichō,* and *buchō,* asking them to commit themselves to support of the proposal.

Although I have continually been making generalizations about "the Japanese," do not make the mistake of thinking that all Japanese companies follow one pattern of decision-making—they don't, any more than all Western companies do. The "corporate culture" of a Japanese company has an important impact on how decisions are made. In their best seller, *The Art of Japanese Management,* Pascale and Athos use the example of Matshushita Electric under the leadership of Konosuke Matsushita to show corporate culture at work. There is a tremendous difference between the philosophy of a company like Matsushita Electric and that of its rival Sony, another giant in the home-appliance field. They differ in business style, corporate philosophy, and, more important for our present purposes, in decision-making systems. For a negotiator to reach the same wavelength as his Japanese counterparts in a negotiation, he must learn as much as he can about the corporate culture. An approach tailored to the individual style of the company he is negotiating with will be far more likely to succeed than a more general policy formulated for dealing with Japanese companies in the aggregate.

It is not difficult to get a feel for the philosophy of a Japanese company. The style of each organization, its biases and prejudices, are open secrets in Tokyo, Osaka, or Nagoya. Foreign businessmen can turn to several sources of information: bankers, accountants, consultants, and resident American businessmen in Japan who are in the same or related fields. Turning to my own field again, I could describe in fairly intimate detail the corporate culture and decision-making system in about fifteen Japanese pharmaceutical companies after five years of negotiating everything from licensing agreements to the implementation of product promotions. If one makes the effort to learn the company's approach to the market, it can save weeks of frustrating delays. Knowing how to package proposals is the key to triggering the responses one is looking for.

The Japanese decision-making apparatus places a great deal of importance not only on how a given decision will affect employees, but also how they will react to it. In my early days in Japan I was not aware of this aspect, and made several decisions which, while of direct benefit to the company, were not properly sold and explained to the staff, and as a result, morale problems were created. The *ringi seido* (the formal routing of the approval document) is a system that will avoid this problem to a certain extent, because decisions, even if not favored by all factions, are never a surprise. Those who are pushing a certain policy always spend a great deal of time selling it to ensure that it will be implemented effectively, using the *nemawashi* process described earlier.

A sudden shift in policy can create real problems when dealing with Japanese companies. Several examples from my own experience come to mind. When I decided to alter a relationship with a certain Japanese company from a joint venture to a royalty-bearing license agreement, or, in another case, from an exclusive to a semiexclusive agent or distributor, I ran into strong opposition. Even though the Japanese company involved would not have suffered financially and the proposed changes would have merely been in our formal relationship with the company, in effect I was asking it to accept a lesser status. Here is where I ran head on into the question of face and the impact of such a change on employee attitudes. In one case, when we wanted to close down a moribund joint venture, I was forced to retreat. The Japanese company concerned adamantly refused to cooperate because the employees would view such a change as a tremendous loss of face.

Since redundancies and the displacement of people are taboo in Japan, the personnel factor also comes into play whenever a new stage of automation is discussed. This is more understandable than the intricacies of "face," but employee protests over such matters will not be overridden even when the company union is not strong. New work must be found for displaced employees, if possible within the same group and in close geographical proximity to their present location. The complications arising from a commitment to maintain employees can extend even to supply contracts. Often a Japanese company will decide not to buy a less expensive raw material from a foreign supplier because of its relationship with its traditional Japanese supplier and the negative impact that buying from the foreign supplier (or a new Japanese supplier, for that matter) might have on the traditional supplier and his relationship with the company.

A Westerner should become involved in the Japanese decision-making process to further his own interests. He is outside the Japanese world, so probably does not have the Old Boy connections or other group links to people that a Japanese would have. However, there are many ways that an outsider can affect the decision-making process by identifying the right pressure points and exerting an indirect but highly effective influence on the decision-making process. It takes infinite patience and considerable tact, but it can be done.

The first step should be to analyze the Japanese firm. One must find out how decisions are made in that particular company, and what interrelationships and internal problems are likely to affect the decision as it moves through the system. Are there factions involved? Who is the key person *(oyabun)* at each stage of the process? If a foreigner has any Japanese associates or colleagues who know or have confidence in their ability to communicate with any of these key people, it will help. Diligent search may turn up a friendly Japanese who is persona grata at the company in question. He can be an excellent weapon for the foreign negotiator to prod and push and cajole people into deciding the way he wants them to. When we began to deal with a new company, I would usually have a management meeting and ask each of my *buchō* (department heads) and my trusted operations director to find out everything they could about the company and its key people. I would order a Dun and Bradstreet report on the target company that would tell me within forty-eight hours all the names of the key individual executives, shareholdings, financial results for the past five years, etc.. I would then ask my financial officer to contact an executive at the lead bank of the target company.

We had relationships with Mitsubishi, Fuji and Sanwa, and our own bank was Sumitomo. The likelihood that our Japanese target also had relationships with one of these banks was very high. Sometimes they also dealt with one of our American banks, and so we would have another ready-made source of information. Our financial officer would have lunch with the banker and probe until he had discovered everything possible about the target company. Usually we were dealing within our own industry, so there would nearly always be numerous links within our industry associations. Other general-interest business organizations also provided us with connections, and within a week we would have a list of relationships. A typical survey would turn up one man who was a Rotarian, another who went to Keio University, and a third who was a graduate of Tokyo University. We would then produce a sort of composite commercial intelligence report on the target, and begin the process of developing links both formally and informally.

Those based in the United States who have no Japanese associations and are dealing with a Japanese trading company instead of a manufacturer can still make inquiries. They might find, for example, that the *buchō* in charge of, say, soybean purchases, is an exceedingly powerful man within his company and that his advice is sought on every new venture. He then would be a key target to cultivate.

By keeping an ear close to the ground one can usually find out when the key meetings on a particular project are due to take place. We used to plot the course of the decision-making process in the firms we worked with as an integral part of our own plan development. For example, every year we would have to convince each of our sales and marketing partners that they should not only maintain but actually increase the level of marketing muscle and advertising support that they were giving to each of our products. To do this we had our team prepare a draft marketing plan in which relative levels and types of support in our organization and theirs were clearly set forth. Strategy and tactics were presented in detail, and year-end share, sales, and profit targets were projected. I would expect the Japanese company to make changes, suggestions and refinements, but I made sure that my marketing and liaison people worked behind the scenes to ensure that these plans were not emasculated. We were working against the natural inclination of the Japanese company to promote its own products rather than ours. Many joint ventures have been dissolved or modified by the foreign party because of such difficulties as persuading the Japanese partner to support the foreign product as actively as it does its own products. My company seldom had that problem. Our relationships with our partners in Japan were excellent, because we understood and appreciated their decision-making system and knew how to harmonize our plans and goals with theirs.

Although I have been stressing the fact that there are means available to enable outsiders to have an impact on the Japanese decision-making system, it is important to remember that the single most important factor is intangible. As has been emphasized throughout this book, *patience* is vital if Western businessmen intend to achieve their aims. In fact, a businessman's own personality is critical to the success of any effort. If he is by nature cold, assertive and forceful, and one who does not suffer fools gladly, he should be wary of working with the Japanese. (I'm not saying the Japanese are fools—quite the opposite. But for those who are locked into a certain outlook, the Japanese way of doing things may seem foolish.) The very traits that may have contributed most to an executive's success in an American firm may be an actual handicap in working with Japanese organizations. On the other hand, if the Westerner is warm, affectionate, and, above all, patient, and if he sincerely likes the Japanese, he can intercede very effectively in the decision-making system. To quote Reischauer:

> A personality type which in the United States might seem merely bluff and forceful but still normal is defined in Japan as a neurotic state. Cooperativeness, reasonableness, and understanding of others are the virtues most admired, not personal drive, forcefulness and individual self-assertion.[7]

In Japan, what you are like is as important as what you can do, and these two aspects of a personality tend to intertwine in the Japanese view. Interpersonal skills are critical. I hope I have not left readers with the illusion that a devious spy network is all that is needed to have an impact on the inner workings of a Japanese company. It is the way one uses the information gained by the methods outlined above that will matter most.

PART
THREE

COMPETING WITH
THE JAPANESE

CHAPTER
10

JAPANESE BUSINESS STRATEGY IN JAPAN

The purpose of this chapter is to convey the point that to compete with the Japanese we must understand not only how they approach foreign markets, but also how they do business in their own country, because the two aspects of their business are intimately linked. Recently American and European managers have become interested in Japanese management systems and their decision-making process (as witness the popularity of such books as *Theory Z* and *The Art of Japanese Management*). These books focus on an important part of Japanese business strategy, examining how they arrive at strategic decisions and why the corporate philosophy of their companies is a significant factor in their success. But the emphasis in both books is on how to adapt Japanese techniques to the needs of Western, particularly American, business.

This chapter, however, examines how the Japanese operate in their own market, because such knowledge is essential if we are to compete with them in Japan, the United States, Europe, or any other markets. Western firms and Western executives cannot remold their thought patterns and working philosophies overnight, but that does not mean that we are doomed to fail in our efforts to confront Japanese competition. On the contrary, I believe that we *can* confront the Japanese challenge successfully. It is the biggest challenge that Western business has ever faced, and although improved management skills will help us, they are not the only tools we need. We must analyze Japan's domestic situation as thoroughly as they have investigated our own.

The hallmark of Japanese business is an overriding sense of vulnerability and competitiveness. Japanese companies struggle for first place in a do-or-die atmosphere. Each firm fights for market share with all the tenacity of a beleaguered garrison, and the goal of each company is to achieve the highest ranking not only in its industry but in the eyes of the business community as a whole. Despite this ferocious atmosphere, American business has been more successful than one might think in penetrating the Japanese market, and the firms that have been able to establish themselves in Japan have usually done so by adopting many of the Japanese business strategies discussed here. The Japanese have studied us for decades, whereas we are just beginning to realize the benefits of studying them.

The Japanese distribution system is one of the most complicated jigsaw puzzles ever contrived by human beings, and is the most dramatic difference between our way and their way of doing business. The system is tightly controlled. A product ends up in the consumer's hands only after it has passed through a distribution chain consisting of at least two and sometimes as many as five layers of wholesalers before landing on the retailer's shelf. Each layer (primary, secondary, tertiary wholesalers, etc.) adds a margin. A typical flowchart of a distribution channel for a product from a Japanese consumer-products company would look like the one shown opposite. The product moves from the factory to the sales company, which is a wholly owned subsidiary of the company that manufactures the product, but has usually been kept separate, since until recently Japanese corporations were not required to consolidate all their holdings for financial reporting and tax purposes. Toyota recently (1982) merged their manufacturing sales companies because the advantage in keeping them separate was eliminated once this tax loophole had been plugged.

The next layer (Layer One) is the large wholesaler or institutional customer and the small wholesaler who will take the product out to the secondary wholesalers and the hundreds of thousands of mom-and-pop shops throughout Japan. The large general wholesalers will be the most efficient channel, as they usually sell directly to large retailers, such as the Daei and Seiyu Supermarket chains, who in turn sell to the consumer at a much lower price than can be found in the corner stores that have to buy their products from a secondary

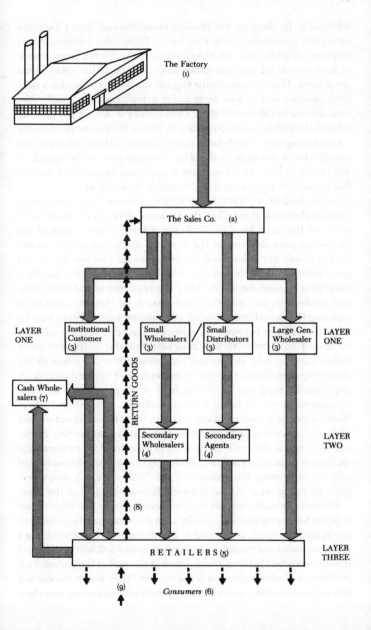

wholesaler. By the time the product passes through Layer Two (the secondary wholesalers) and into Layer Three (the retailers) it has acquired an additional cost of 50 to 60 percent. With a factory price of $1.00 a product will cost about $1.50 to $1.60 at the retail (small shop) level. This compares with $1.30 in the United States for a non-food product and as low as $1.10 for a food product. Finally the product reaches the retail shelf. Occasionally it doesn't sell and the retailer decides he wants to return it. Unless the Japanese company is very strong and has a definite policy against it, the shopkeeper can usually return the item to the sales company and get full credit. It will then pass back up through the system, and eventually return to the factory for repackaging and resale or destruction.

In the field of nondurable consumer products (over-the-counter drugs, toiletries and the like), the Japanese strive to maintain retail prices at the same level in all classes of trade. The concept of *wa* (harmony) prevails even in the arena of marketing policy. In the United States the Robinson-Patman Act would prevent this covert price fixing, but in Japan retailers who break the price line are often boycotted by manufacturers. They are regarded as untrustworthy, and wholesalers and manufacturers alike treat them as pariahs for violating the sacred code of retail-price maintenance. There may be minor differences between the prices of toiletries in pharmacies as compared with those in supermarkets, but this is the exception rather than the rule. In England the difference in the prices in the large drugstore chain of Boots, for example, and the local mom-and-pop chemist shop can be as much as 30 to 40 percent on some fast-moving items. In Japan you can walk into a Health and Clean (HAC) super drugstore in Yokohama with three thousand square feet of display space and find almost the same price as in the tiny chemist's shop across the road. To be sure, price control for cameras and electronic consumer goods has broken down, but this has occurred only recently, since the pressure of the discounters in Tokyo's low-price shopping areas (Akihabara and Shinjuku) has forced the issue.

Whenever a manufacturer makes a seasonal offer, the pharmacies in Japan buy vast quantities, usually with the understanding that they can return the goods at the end of the season if the product doesn't sell. Sometimes the manufacturer or wholesaler will balk at this, and the retailer is left holding a large stock at the end of the season. This is where cash wholesalers enter the picture. They watch the market like vultures, waiting to exploit any opportunity where the price line is broken, and where retailers have excess stock. They move in, buy it up and wait. When prices are stable again, they dump the goods on the market, and presto—chaos. Many of these cash wholesalers are Koreans, and this makes them doubly unpopular with the established trade. They do perform a necessary service, however, given the nature of the Japanese trade, where sales are made not only on the basis of consumer demand but also on *giri* and *on* relationships between buyers and sellers.

Another key aspect of the Japanese distribution system is the use of exclusive distributors and the way credit is used (the infamous "P note," or promissory note) to make it even easier for each level to buy, and even more expensive for the consumer in the long run. Essentially, the system cannot adjust to serving two masters. A large general wholesaler of consumer goods usually has a showroom on the ground floor decked out like a model store, and there one can see the merchandise beautifully displayed. There may be more than one brand on display, and the casual observer may assume that the situation is the same as in the West, where multibrand distributors are the norm. In fact, each distributor is a dedicated and exclusive wholesaler for one manufacturer in each product category, and he will not push (even though he may carry) any brand other than the exclusive one that he is contractually committed to sell aggressively. Japanese businessmen are amazed by the American or British system of grocery wholesalers who carry all the brands of each product that is selling well. In Japan such a practice would be a violation of the loyalty *(giri)* that the wholesaler has to the manufacturer. This is also true of the appliance shop. The customer who walks into a Curry's in England, for example, or a J. C. Penney's in the United States, will find every major brand of appliance displayed, and there will usually be sales people to explain and demonstrate any brand of merchandise. Not so in Japan, where the consumer must visit ten shops to see ten brands. It is possible to see different brands displayed in department stores, but they can't compete with the one-brand shops in certain product categories (for example, electronic goods), where the manufacturers have built up chains of exclusive distributors. The department stores will not even have people trained to demonstrate such merchandise, since the manufacturers refuse to cooperate with nonexclusive distributors. The Japanese think the Western way of selling very strange. They find it difficult to accept the fact that a Toyota dealer can give equal emphasis to Volkswagen or Chevrolet.

To them a distributor is worth working with only if he is totally committed to their company's line of products.

In addition to being exclusive, the Japanese wholesaler acts as a sort of finance company for the retailers that buy from him. Similarly, the manufacturer is expected to finance the wholesaler. Normal terms between a Japanese manufacturer and his key wholesalers are six months, with a promissory note exchanged at an interval of forty-five to ninety days after the sale has taken place. This "P note" can be discounted at the bank and the manufacturer will have the cash flow after ninety days, but discounting is usually an additional five to six percent off the invoice (factory price) value.

The key lesson about how the distribution system operates is that the Japanese manufacturer is conditioned to a market situation where he has a network of some fifty to five hundred primary wholesalers who are exclusively his. Their livelihood depends on his ability to continue to provide products that will compete successfully against rival chains of distributors. The distribution network is therefore an extension of the company itself, and is of primary concern to the Japanese manufacturing company. As a courtesy, senior executives are obligated to visit each distributor at least once a year in order to reaffirm their commitment. Similarly, the distributor will visit the head office, rest houses, factories, and branches of the Japanese company, knowing that he will be treated like an honored family member. Manufacturers are frequently equity partners of their key distributors, and the branch manager in each major town will almost always sit on the board of his local distributor. As a director he is privy to all the plans and strategies of the distributor, and can thus guide events in the way that is most favorable to the objectives of his own manufacturing company.

It would be difficult for any company, domestic or foreign, to ignore or bypass any layer in the Japanese distribution system. Procter & Gamble made a major commitment to the Japanese market in the mid-seventies, and it took them years to build a solid and cooperative network of primary wholesalers and distributors. They were not used to paying so much attention to the distribution network because in the United States and most other markets it is expected that the multiproduct distributor will go where the action is. In short, the marketplace will dictate the behavior of a distributor in other countries. In Japan the marketplace is important and decisive in the long run, but in the short run—and this can be five to ten years

—the importance of the exclusive network is even greater.

The name given to a distribution network is *kai*, or group, and one will often hear a Japanese executive talk about his company's *kai*. He assumes that the extreme importance of the distribution system to his company will automatically be understood. The name of the manufacturer usually precedes the term *kai*, and people use the terms "Lion-*kai*" or "Sunstar-*kai*" to describe the exclusive network of the Lion Company or the Sunstar Company. These distributors are also vital if the manufacturer wants to increase sales at certain times of the year, and distributors cooperate fully with the manufacturers in this exercise. As a result, they have the right to return goods at any time, and the manufacturer is forced to accept the returned goods, sometimes years later. There are, however, one or two large Japanese consumer-product companies, such as Kao Soap, that still sell directly to their large retail customers.

With this kind of vertical control of the marketplace, sometimes extending down to exclusive retailers in the case of electrical appliances, it becomes extremely difficult for the Japanese company to diversify into new fields, since it faces the formidable task of building a new distribution network, or *kai*, for the area that it wishes to enter. The existing distribution network is restricted to current manufacturers, and it is unlikely to be susceptible to an offer to switch to a new, untried manufacturer. Building a distribution network from scratch can take many years, which is one of the main reasons why foreign companies have trouble expanding in Japan unless they can piggyback on the already existing network of a joint-venture partner.

Although it looks as though exclusivity is here to stay, some aspects of the traditional distribution system in Japan are under attack. For example, the traditional corner grocery stores are threatened by the rapid growth of supermarkets. To meet the new demands created by the steep rise in quantity and variety of consumer products being sold, many innovative ideas have found a place in the system. It is important to remember, therefore, that the distribution system is, in the words of a study put out by McKinsey & Co. for the United States–Japan Trade Study Group, "undergoing a major evolution. Opportunities to participate and accelerate are available to both entrepreneurial Japanese and American corporations."[1] The Japanese government has recently been putting obstacles in the way of the expansion of supermarket chains, precisely because the politically powerful small traditional retailers are threatened by such growth.

The highly controlled distribution system is worth a book in its own right, but space limitations dictate turning now to another characteristic of the Japanese market that affects how the Japanese company develops its domestic business strategy: the emphasis on market share and rank within an industry as the primary factors in strategic planning. When the Japanese company begins its fiscal-year planning for either a new or existing product, its primary concern is how it stands against the competition in terms of market share and position. It will then develop a strategy that focuses on market-share improvement as the primary goal of the year's application of the five P's (product, packaging, pricing, promotion, and profit). Of course the Japanese value sales and profit performance, but if a company finds that despite a healthy increase in sales and a highly profitable year, it has slipped from fifth to sixth in its industry ranking, and its share of its main market has gone down, then the word on the street is that the company is in decline.

The competitiveness of the Japanese market, as exemplified by the desire to retain corporate face by not allowing the company's standing in the industry to decline, is a primary motivation for Japanese companies. In the bars where *buchō* and *kachō* congregate to review the office day, the conversation will inevitably turn to an anxious review of how their company stands. If a firm announces its intention to expand into a new foreign market, modernize its computer system, or take any other competitive step that appears likely to improve its business, it is published in trade journals and discussed in industry circles ad nauseam for the next week. In many cases, its competitors will all follow suit, since if one company has gone through the decision process with all the *ringi. seido* (chain of approval) and *nemawashi* (convincing everyone the decision is right) involved, then its rivals will consider it must surely be a necessary step and thus a matter of survival for the competition to take the same action. This lemminglike approach is one reason why a number of Japanese companies seem to do the same thing at more or less the same time. It goes back to their sense of vulnerability, and their feeling that the loss of even one market-share point could be the beginning of the end. This phenomenon also manifests itself in cartel situations, because Japanese companies sometimes get tired of the constantly accelerating competitive crises, and prefer to freeze the market share and shut out newcomers in order to avoid escalating conflict.

The Japanese company's fondest dream is to be thought of as an *ichi-ryū gaisha*, or "number one company." Once it has achieved that pinnacle, it can attract the finest talent of the Japanese universities, as well as become involved in the many government-sponsored projects that tend to be restricted to *ichi-ryū gaisha*. Chie Nakane discusses this preoccupation with being first in her book *Japanese Society*, and relates the Japanese corporate preoccupation with market share and ranking to the old rivalry between households in the villages of rural Japan. She claims that the obsession with corporate rank shows that "Japanese values are orientated rather to sociological than economic goals."[2] That is, the profit motive is subordinated to the need for prestige. She notes that even clerical workers in an *ichi-ryū* company feel superior to their counterparts in a third-ranking *(san-ryū)* firm, even though they are paid the same. It is easy to see why Ezra Vogel had such a success in Japan with his book *Japan as Number One,* for he chose a title that struck a deep chord in the Japanese people. The goal of nearly every student in the country is to gain entrance into an *ichi-ryū* company after graduating from an *ichi-ryū* university, largely because social status tends to be defined by company affiliation. The unspoken goal of every Japanese businessman, no matter what his position, is to have his company achieve world preeminence, and, collectively, for Japan to become the world's most important economic power.

Perhaps more than any other single factor, the Japanese preoccupation with quality control and after-sales service has been responsible for Japan's phenomenal economic growth in the last few decades. The story of quality circles and worker involvement in the pursuit of zero defects in factory production is a phenomenon noted by nearly every writer on Japan in recent years. What is less well known is that this important component of Japan's economic success is not only a postwar phenomenon but also of American origin. The father of Japanese quality control is a distinguished American by the name of W. Edwards Demming. Every year Japanese industry honors him by competing fiercely for the annual Demming Award, which goes to the company considered to have made the greatest improvement in quality. Nearly all Japanese companies have now implemented Dr. Demming's method of using statistical analysis to monitor quality control. (Here we see the positive side of the lemming factor.) The Demming philosophy as a factor in Japanese business strategy had its beginning at the Industry Club of Japan in Tokyo in July 1950, when Dr. Demming, a guest of the Occupation forces, was invited to speak on the use of statistics in quality control. I can remember that when I was in college in the mid-1950's it was still difficult to find a Japanese appliance (particularly transistor radios) that would work for more than a few months. Nowadays Japanese transistor radios are preeminent in the world. The goal of zero defects when the product leaves the factory is ever present in the minds of workers and management alike in every Japanese company of any reputation. The achievement of the goal, as the authors of *Theory Z* and *The Art of Japanese Management* have pointed out, can be attributed not only to a statistical methodology but to superior Japanese management techniques in the vital area of motivating people.

After the product leaves the factory, the next logical step is to make sure that the consumer will never have to complain about the service either from the store where the item was bought or from the manufacturer (if the problem requires the manufacturer's involvement). In Japan the consumer can return any item with a minimum of bother, since the store will be anxious to know if the item is being returned because of some perceived defect. Stores are required to make a detailed report to the manufacturer on any defects, and to send the offending item back to the manufacturer's quality-control center for careful analysis. Proportionately fewer American and European firms have invested in the same level of after-sales service. The preoccupation with such service is a major element in Japanese business strategy, because capturing market share depends not only on the ability of the manufacturer to provide a captive distribution network, but also on the kind of quality control and after-sales service that will ensure his success in penetrating the market.

Japan, Inc. is a much disputed concept. Many believe that government support for business is the reason why Japan has achieved such unprecedented levels of penetration in markets the world over. There is a degree of truth in the accusation that government, business, and labor work hand in glove to ensure that Japanese business continues to expand worldwide, spurred on by their belief in the vulnerability of their resource-poor country. It is also true that the Japanese government is a gentle and understanding regulator, and the philosophy governing the way such laws as the Anti-Monopoly Act and the Banking Act are administered is to do nothing that might work against the long-term interests of Japanese business. The government is seldom a litigant against Japanese business; it prefers to exercise "administrative guidance" in advising companies how to comply with the law. This means that it can be relied on to work with business and not against it. Japan has a very strong and powerful Economic Planning Agency, which maps out industrial strategy for the nation. The national strategy is carefully weighed and considered when companies develop their corporate strategies. This is quite unlike the United States, where the very thought of Big Brother prescribing how and when American business should invest smacks of Orwell's nightmare vision of total government control. But the role of the government is not perceived as adversarial to that of business in Japan. Instead, government is seen as a friend, adviser, and counselor, and will turn nasty only when a company ignores its advice. Business is generally happy with government because there is a genuine spirit of cooperation between the two, a feeling that all are ultimately working for the good of Japan.

Nevertheless, government and business do not always agree. There are areas where the government's policy can have a negative effect on the expansion of business. These areas deserve mention because they show that the notion of Japan, Inc., is a distorted picture of how Japanese business strategy actually develops. The clampdown on the growth of supermarkets, a move that favors one sector at the expense of another, has already been mentioned. Another example is tax policy. There are a number of areas where government tax policy has a negative effect on entrepreneurial business. The first is in the area of deductability of business expenses. Venture capitalists in the United States can take advantage of the tax law to help them through the difficult first years, and can write off losses today by carrying them forward to the next year or the one following. This is not so in Japan. In a recent interview in the *Stanford Magazine*, Norihiku Shimizu, now a vice president of the Boston Consulting Group, comments:

> Our tax system is a major deterrent. If you lose money in an investment, it is not deductible. You lose 100 per cent of that money. And if you succeed, you get heavily taxed. In the U.S., if you lose on an investment, you may lose only 30 per cent, depending on your bracket, the kind of

investment, etc., and if you succeed you may get 70 per cent—so it averages out to perhaps a plus 20–25 per cent gain. The risk in the U.S. is not nearly as great as that in Japan, and the potential financial return provides a very attractive incentive to investors.[3]

The role of the government is to stimulate tax collection, and tax inspectors are rewarded in direct relation to how much tax they have successfully assessed in comparison with the gains of prior years. The reader will recall that entertainment is a very important method of achieving consensus and communication in Japanese business, but entertainment expenses are now disallowed for large companies (they used to be limited to 2 percent of sales). Government does provide tax incentives to business indirectly by encouraging personal savings. The first $15,000 (3 million yen) of personal savings are tax-exempt in Japan, and by using the post-office savings system wisely (and legally) it is possible to have several accounts and obtain tax-free interest for a theoretically infinite amount of savings. This provides the banks and the economy with a liquid core that helps stimulate bank-supported investment in large corporate undertakings (as opposed to venture capital). (See Chapter 12 for more details on the role of Japanese banks.)

In the main the government does act in the interests of business. It would be unusual for an American businessman who has approached a federal regulatory agency and received an informal opinion on the legal acceptability of a given course of action to have complete confidence that the official concerned will stand by his word when the transaction actually takes place. Yet my own experience in Japan has been that I have been able to sit down with government officials and get administrative guidance that has helped me to overcome problems.

The other key role of government in the development of Japanese business strategy is to act as organizer for breakthrough efforts involving multicompany research and development, and to provide tax and fiscal incentives for companies to invest heavily in R&D. The following comments by Hideo Oda of McKenzie & Company illustrate the organizing role of government in strategy relating to Research and Development:

> The government plays more the role of organizer than of doer. MITI [Ministry of International Trade and Industry] and the Ministry of Finance will say to Hitachi or Toshiba or Fujitsu that our country needs

to cooperate to move ahead in a certain industry, and these companies respond. The attitude in our country is to work together—at every level —as kids, within departments in companies, between major corporations. So it is not the direct amount of money that MITI provides in its specific policies but just the government's suggestion about priorities. Of course, they might provide subsidies.[4]

As implied by the above quote, government support can be a vital factor in new technology. When MITI decided that Japan should attempt to overcome the lead of IBM and other U.S. computer manufacturers in the area of computer chips, the ministry acted as the catalyst, spending almost a billion dollars over a five-year period in organizing and controlling the research effort. This is why Japanese companies all seemed to come up simultaneously with such advances as the 64K and 256K RAM computer chips. Thus Japan's lead in the production of chips and computer ceramics can be attributed not only to industry expertise and perseverance, but also to government support and encouragement.

Cutthroat competition and cozy joint R&D arrangements may seem a contradiction in terms. In fact, they *are* antithetical. The corporations hate working together, and will seldom confer directly. The government must act as go-between to overcome the mutual suspicion and distrust of rival companies in order to ensure the success of such efforts. It is only when there is something like a national consensus on the necessity for pushing a certain sector that joint R&D is undertaken. It's like getting Republicans and Democrats together—only something as momentous as a declaration of war can make the parties truly work together. Similarly, the perceived vulnerability of Japan and its national interest can and does force archrivals to cooperate.

One factor controlling business strategy in Japan is often overlooked: the influence on business practices of fastidious and demanding Japanese consumers. They can be fiercely loyal to corporate names, but once let down they will turn away from a product in droves. Japanese manufacturers have still not fully understood the value of consumer research in the American sense, and they don't put together advertising campaigns that to our way of thinking sell a product, but what they *do* do well is design products with functionality in mind, make them of the very best quality that they can within financial limitations, and then make sure that everyone knows about them by spending more money on advertising than any other country in the world, including the United States (which is number two). The Japanese consumer is an avid TV watcher (averaging five hours a day) and newspaper reader, with over 34 million newspapers sold daily. Radio is another important medium. The Japanese are also the world's greatest users of mass transit, and are exposed to many advertisements going to and from work. It might be said that of all the peoples in the world the Japanese are the most widely read and also the most exposed to advertising. Japan has over twenty-seven thousand bookstores (the same as the United States) in a land area the size of California. When formulating strategy, Japanese business simply cannot afford to ignore its highly educated and well-informed consumers.

Japanese advertising strategy is built around the principles of reach and frequency. In other words, they try to bombard the consumer with so many messages that he or she is almost forced into trying the product. The commercials vary from hard to soft sell, but the vast majority of TV spots are what Americans would call "mood commercials" designed to make the consumer feel good about the product. The American "slice of life" or "ashcan" commercials (direct comparison with the competition) are almost never used in Japan. It is taboo for a company to acknowledge the existence of its rivals.

Another important factor related to the consumer is the strategy that Japanese companies use in pricing their products. In general it can be said that even when the consumer is satisfied with the quality of a product and the biggest ad campaign in history is mounted, a company is then only halfway to its goal of large sales. A vital component of strategy is pricing. Japanese marketing people spend as much time discussing the right price for an article as they do on the product or its promotion. The price has to be *what the consumer would expect to pay.* Another essential is that it must not change. Price adjustments in Japan may be easier than surviving a leap from the Golden Gate Bridge—but only just.

If you have to pick a price that you will be bound to for many years and you know that inflation, while modest, is still likely to be a problem in the future, you select a high price. But if a potential competitor has a low price, and the quality of the products is the same, it will be tough to fool the Japanese housewife. In general, however, prices of toiletries and most other consumer products are two to three times those of the United States. Part of the difference lies in the expensive distribution system. To take just one case, in the pharmaceutical business it is quite common for wholesalers to take up to 14 percent, and the doctor, who functions as the dispenser of prescription pharmaceuticals in Japan, to make between 30 and 100 percent profit on drugs. In the case of pharmaceuticals the customer is the Japanese government, which reimburses the doctor for the drugs he has prescribed to patients at a fixed (national health insurance) price.

Having to import the raw materials also drives costs up. The expense of providing many extra sales personnel to give the customer personal attention is another extra cost. (Japanese department stores hire women whose only job is to wipe off escalator hand rails and bow to customers as they get off.) Another significant factor in the higher price is packaging. The Japanese consumer will not buy a product that is not beautifully and luxuriously packaged. From shampoo to eye lotion, from lettuce to meat, you will never see merchandise as aesthetically perfect and as artistically displayed as in a Japanese supermarket or department store. Utilitarian packaging (functional, large packs designed to give the impression of economy) is practically never used unless the product is going to an institutional customer.

Although Chapter 12 will be devoted to Japanese banks and trading companies, a chapter on Japanese business strategy would not be complete without mentioning debt financing, which reflects the unique relationship that exists between manufacturers and their banks. The big manufacturers almost always have a large commercial bank as their largest equity holder. This bank is usually one of the Big Four (Daiichi Kangyo, Mitsui, Mitsubishi, or Sumitomo), and will have its tentacles into half of Japanese business in one form or another. Since, as Chie Nakane has noted, the purpose of business in Japan is largely sociological, rather than solely economic, it is vital for the company to continue expanding indefinitely and thus give its present employees a better *kao* (face) with their friends and neighbors. In addition, a company that is expanding hires new employees, and this also increases corporate *kao*. Mitsubishi group employees, for example, are proud of the huge numbers of people that work for their company. Corporately, bigger is definitely better in Japan. The banks flourish in this atmosphere because the very nature of expansion requires the cooperation of a friendly bank, which in turn benefits from the huge interest payments on its loans. Thus, the banks play a vital role in business expansion or diversification.

The fear of obsolescence or the loss of cost competitiveness on a world as well as local scale is another important factor in strategy development. As mentioned earlier, the prime factor behind many corporate actions in Japan is the feeling of "vulnerability" to the loss of market share due to a competitor's new technology or the emergence of newly industrialized countries.

An example of this factor at work is the entry by Brother Industries, Japan's leading producer of sewing machines and typewriters, into the office automation field in mid-1983. The statement of the president of Brother, Katsuji Kawashima, explaining why his company suddenly expanded into computer printers and electronic typewriters, points up the rationale for many strategic decisions. He was quoted by the *New York Times* as saying that Brother is "being forced into office automation" because its traditional business is no longer a growth industry. What had happened was that Brother had made such a massive penetration into the markets for home sewing machines and regular electric typewriters in Japan that no further significant growth was possible. New microelectronics technology forced the company to upgrade its product or face stagnation, the nightmare of every Japanese company.

The threat of a lower-priced, high-quality mid-technology challenge from newly industrialized countries has led many Japanese appliance companies to set up manufacturing facilities in those countries so that even if they develop competitive products, there will be Japanese labels on them.

The impact of Japanese business strategy at home on Japanese competitiveness overseas is very strong. Companies that face intense competition at home tend to be the ones that go into overseas markets largely because of the herd instinct. If one goes, they all go. To the Japanese, competition from the local companies in the foreign markets they have penetrated is usually tame and fairly easy to handle. To quote from the United States–Japan Trade Study Group Report:

> Japan . . . is probably one of the most fiercely competitive markets in the world . . . the number of bankruptcies of registered corporations in Japan in 1980 was about 14,000. . . . this is 12.5% higher than those in the United States, although Japan's corporate population of 1.2 million is less than half (40 percent) that of America's.[5]

These statistics may provide a clue to why the Japanese seem to bulldoze their way into any open market with such ease. They are trained in a tough school. However, it should be added that, as explained earlier, this fierce competitiveness has led to the formation of cartels so that the companies don't end up cutting one another's throat.

Just one indication of how seriously the Japanese take drive and aggression in business is the current popularity of training managers in schools that resemble a mixture of U.S. Marine boot camp, Outward Bound, and a Zen monastery. There is a training school for managers at the foot of Mount Fuji where five thousand trainees a year are put through a thirteen-day course that combines grueling physical ordeals with assertiveness training, Japanese style. Such companies as Nissan, N.E.C., Matsushita, Toyota, and N.T.T. pay over $1,000 a head for their brightest potential managers to execute forced marches (including a night march of twenty-five miles), undergo martial arts training, sing morale-building songs in public places at the top of their lungs, and participate in numerous other activities and workshops, many of them humiliating. In a recent article describing these executive training camps, a British reporter commented:

> For most of the trainees, their careers hang on their success in enduring the torments and hardships of the course. The sponsor companies send reports on the character and weak points of the employee sent for training. . . . if the trainees decide to quit the school, they quit their company.[6]

This paramilitary attitude toward business management is just one more indicator of the seriousness of the Japanese commitment. It may appear ludicrous to Westerners, but to the Japanese it is deadly serious.

Unless Western business begins to comprehend not only the seriousness with which the Japanese view their economic struggle but the pressures that have driven them to the top in so many fields, the West may well end up as a supplier of raw materials and agricultural products to their industrial machine while Western growth is confined to the service sector, where we still have a competitive edge.

As Kenichi Ohmae, the head of McKenzie & Company's office in

Tokyo, has pointed out in a speech entitled "Beyond the Myths . . . Explaining Japanese Business," the Japanese advantage is not unilateral. His most significant points are:

1. Japan is less widely based than the United States in its export industries. The Japanese are competitive where manufacturing expertise is the secret, in fields such as steel, consumer electronics, and some textiles.

2. Japan has been successful where it has very intense domestic competition (autos, paper copiers, etc.).

3. Japan pays its labor about what we pay ours (except for the automobile industry), but has worked hard to reduce labor content. Automation, coupled with a friendly supplier network, is the key to Japanese success, not low wages.

These facts make it obvious that it is not too late to learn from our mistakes, but until now American and European indifference to events inside Japan has been in stark contrast to Japan's continuing high-powered intelligence effort centered on what is going on in our markets. Japanese corporations analyze and reanalyze every facet of their business, constantly scrutinizing performance to avoid lagging behind, and continually searching for signs of vulnerability or barriers to growth.

The pressures exerted by the driving expansionism of Japanese business produce a hothouse atmosphere of ferment and growth in Japan. When I recall my time in Japan I remember most vividly the sensation of commercial excitement and stimulation—a twenty-four-hour-a-day, seven-day-a-week desire to make my company and business grow. This atmosphere provides the fuel for the energy and commitment of the Japanese workingman. To compete with the Japanese, we must never forget that their system provides the worker with such a high level of encouragement that we must be prepared to undergo nothing less than a revolution in attitudes if Western industry is not to become obsolescent.

CHAPTER
11

JAPANESE BUSINESS STRATEGY
IN FOREIGN MARKETS

In the previous chapter it was shown how the Japanese business structure has evolved in an atmosphere of fierce domestic competition characterized by a desire for sales growth as a means of achieving prestige and rank within the business community. The restraining influence on unbridled competition in Japan has been the respect for *wa,* or inner harmony, and as a result cartels have been formed in many of the large industries where each company pursues the market but tries not to encroach on the areas of special strength of a competitor and respects the market-share balance. The cooperation between established companies that would normally be competitors also has the desirable effect of shutting out unwanted competitors, whether foreign or Japanese.

Thus, although there is an armed truce in the domestic market, Japanese companies view overseas opportunities for their products as open territory for no-holds-barred competition. When Toyota or Nissan is frustrated in its drive to increase sales in Japan, it turns to exports to achieve the growth it feels is essential if the company is to survive. The same is true of Matsushita (National-Panasonic), Sony, and other major competitors in every field. When these companies look at the overseas markets for their products, they evaluate the local companies and the multinationals already operating there, but most important, they worry about what their Japanese competitors will do in response to their new venture.

The darkest fear haunting a Japanese middle manager is to discover suddenly that his leading Japanese competitor has begun sales activities in a new market. The usual response will be to follow suit. When more than one or two companies are involved in such a foray, the price of the product or commodity in question will drop, and local manufacturers will be overwhelmed, caught in a pitched battle fought between Japanese companies trying to capture the greatest market share. The Japanese entry is usually totally unexpected, and the motives for its unprecedentedly bitter competitive struggles too alien, for Western or local companies affected to realize what has happened in time to react. As was emphasized throughout the previous chapter, to a Japanese company what really matters is what happens at home, and it is the struggle for maximum prestige, maximum face—the burning desire to be the *ichi-ryū gaisha* (number one company)—that motivates overseas strategy. Being number one in Japan is crucial. If that means being number one in the world as well, that is what they will strive to be.

The desire to keep the name of the Japanese manufacturer in the forefront, and not to sell products to others for resale under their own brand names, dates back to the fifties. The man who symbolized this approach was Akio Morita, now as then the president of Sony. Morita is fond of telling the story of his sojourn in the United States back in the fifties when he tried to develop the Sony brand name in America. At first he was fighting the prevalent low-quality image of Japanese goods. Later, as he managed to convince department-store buyers of the high quality of Sony's products, they accepted both the products and the price. The problem was that no one wanted the name Sony. Department-store chains were willing to order by the thousands, providing the radios carried their own name. Other retailers were willing to buy if the name was changed to something associated with one of the then dominant American brand names. But Morita refused to compromise, and held out until finally he was able to get some orders with the Sony brand name proudly displayed on the radio set. Back in Japan his achievement was saluted by all the employees of the then small company. Those years had a deep impact on Morita's attitude to overseas marketing, and his understanding of the American market, gained over that period, has been responsible for his enlightened approach to Japanese investment overseas.

One Japanese company, Nissan, is so proud of its name that it is now prepared to ignore twenty-five years of advertising and marketing investment in building up another name, Datsun, which they had originally thought would be easier for foreigners to pronounce and remember. Nissan spent billions on developing the Datsun name overseas, but eventually the top executives of the company decided to push for a change back to Nissan so that all the company's employees in Japan could rejoice in the Nissan name the world over. The reaction of everyone in the auto industry outside Japan was incredulity. It seemed as strange—and as counterproductive—as Coca-Cola changing its name. Datsun dealers in both the United States and Britain were up in arms. The only concessions that Nissan made to all the uproar over their decision was to slow the speed of the change, and to place advertisements that showed both names side by side. By 1983 the effort was in high gear, and within five years Americans and Europeans will undoubtedly be comfortable with the switch.

Before turning to examine the modern strategies used by Japanese companies to expand overseas, it is worthwhile to look at the origins of the Japanese trade "miracle." Commentators often overlook the fact that Japanese industry did not start entirely from scratch after World War II. The real beginnings of the postwar "miracle" lie in the 1920's and 1930's (and the roots of industrialization go back even further). This was the time when the Japanese began their first big expansion into international markets in order to buy raw materials and sell manufactured goods. By cutting prices through the use of the low-cost labor provided by small family-owned subcontractors, and by capitalizing on Japanese dedication and efficiency—the effort was promoted as crucial to the survival of the country, and sacrifices were demanded of working people—the Japanese were able to seize control of a number of important international markets, and by 1936 its share of the total international trade had reached a level of 4 percent (compared with 10 percent today). Under the flags of large trading firms like Mitsui Bussan and Mitsubishi Shoji, Japan was able to overtake Britain's lead in textiles in 1932. This period was known as the Japanese Trade Crusade. Goods were copied from leading Western brands and sold at rock-bottom prices, often below cost, just to gain foreign exchange in order to buy armaments and raw materials essential for the military buildup. At the time, the Japanese were committed to a militarist policy, and economic goals were set with military objectives in mind. The slogan "Export or die" had its real roots in the thirties, when millions of Japanese in small and medium-sized companies were inspired to work under sweatshop conditions for the glory and survival of Japan. The specter of a "yellow peril," in the shape of powerful young Japanese industry underselling Western industry and taking over its markets, was the subject of a *Fortune* article in 1936, and French and Italian newspapers of the day were full of attacks on the Japanese silk industry that were much like those of today by the Western auto, machine-tool, and electronics industries.

The big difference between the Japanese trade expansion of the thirties and that of the seventies and eighties has been the change in the country's attitude to quality and the development of pride in Japan's own brand names. In those days the quality of Japanese goods was generally regarded as the lowest among the major industrialized nations, and the pirating of trademarks and manufacture of counterfeit merchandise was a common practice. Today the Japanese are regarded as having no equal in the quality of their products. Another difference between then and now was the close link between the military expansion of Japan onto the Asian continent and the resultant growth in her trade. Manufactured goods were exchanged for raw materials from conquered territories, and the "manifest destiny" of Japan to lead Asia away from Western colonialists to a harmonious Japanese-dominated Greater East Asia Co-Prosperity Sphere was the ruling concept of the decade. This zeal to conquer the East was expressed by Japanese industrialist Ginjiro Fujihara, one of the founders of Oji Paper, in his book *The Spirit of Japanese Industry:*

> Money spent on armaments is capital which promotes the advance of us businessmen. From the people's point of view it is a kind of investment. They invest and develop the nation's power. Using this power, producers advance steadily in the world. . . .
> We have a splendid opportunity to expand abroad. It is the manifest destiny of the Japanese people.[1]

The Japanese have long left such attitudes behind them, and the economic expansion of the last two decades has had no military overtones. (Only recently has the defense industry in Japan become a factor in the trade process.)

Nonetheless, one of the major reasons for Japanese success remains the same now as it was then: the devotion of Japanese workers and salary men to the success of the enterprises they work for. Toward the end of World War II, official government propaganda tried to convince the Japanese people that dedication and willpower alone were enough to win the war. Even though the country learned to its tremendous cost that this belief was tragically false, the experience did not destroy the will to succeed.

The traders of the thirties are gone now, the men who desperately sought a place for Japan among the industrialized nations, carrying their sample bags all over the globe in search of markets that would buy their goods, selling products that were half-priced imitations of Western goods (sometimes complete with logos such as "made in U.S.A."). The old traders have been replaced by the smooth multilingual jet traveler of today, who no longer needs to resort to imitation and gimmickry to gain entrance to any market. Such men may not have the desperation and burning desire to catch up with the West that characterized the traders of earlier decades, but certain factors remain constant. Chief among these is an intense pride in Japan, along with a continuing fervent belief that the Japanese people have no choice but to "export or die." It is this mentality that has given the Japanese the edge over its major rival, for the sheer size of the United States, together with its abundant natural resources, has always tended to reinforce a certain complacency and sustained the illusion that if worst comes to worst, we can draw in our tentacles and survive comfortably in isolation. The Japanese suffer from no such illusions.

Because the Japanese always have to worry about the lack of essential natural resources, a vital component in their business strategy is to gain control of the raw materials their industries need. The economy works by exporting processed goods made from imported raw materials, and using the value added thereby to pay for the raw materials necessary for domestic consumption. If some catastrophe or political upheaval cut Japan off from its vital supplies, this system would collapse. This weakness is ever present in the minds of Japanese businessmen, and the fear of losing access to raw materials was a direct cause of the Pacific war. In the thirties the Japanese had expanded rapidly in Southeast Asia, and by the outbreak of war they had established control over rubber assets in Malaya and the Dutch East Indies, bauxite in the Dutch East Indies, and a number of other key raw materials, such as sugar, raw cotton, lumber, and coal. Their terrible defeat convinced them that mercantilism was no longer a viable economic policy in the modern world, but they have not relinquished the idea of gaining control of the sources of needed raw materials through overseas investment. The prewar drive to control raw materials is being repeated today, but by means of economic rather than military force. The Japanese have invested heavily in everything from U.S. farmland to Australian uranium and coal. Wherever there is a raw material that the country needs, you can be sure that someone back in Japan is figuring out how to gain permanent access to it.

Next to a guaranteed supply of raw materials, the most vital factor in the economic success of an island nation is the maintenance of shipping lines. Thus, the Japanese have taken the logical step of expanding into the manufacture of ships and management of the world's shipping industry. Most Japanese shipping lines today are controlled by competing *zaibatsu*. When it comes time to vote at the International Shipping Conference, the Japanese companies insist on having six votes, since there are six companies—but, of course, the six companies never fail to vote as a block, and the power they gain from this solidarity, along with other advantages, has made them dominant in the world. It hardly needs to be pointed out that the Japanese ship-manufacturing industry has long since outdistanced any other. Moreover, a Japanese merchant-marine sailor works for twice the hours and half the pay that an American sailor does—and the Japanese have compounded this advantage with advances in shipboard automation that eliminate the need for many sailors.

Japanese dominance in the shipping industry is only one small component in their overall success. A much more important factor has been their continuing dedication to maintaining networks for formidably detailed information gathering. Led by the intelligence networks set up in the early thirties by the Japanese government, Japan was able to launch surprise attacks on island after island in the early days of the Pacific war. Manila is a good example of a place where the Japanese infiltrated everywhere, from MacArthur's headquarters to the local tailor or barbershop, and were able to feed back information to Japan that was vitally useful. In fact, Japanese trading companies often cooperated with the government to provide intelligence on the countries where they were trading. The same kind of zealous information gathering goes on today, except that now it is market, rather than military, intelligence data that are sought most eagerly. The huge intelligence networks that are run by the large Japanese trading companies feed essential information into the offices of Japanese firms so that they can outmaneuver their Japanese, American, and European competitors. In 1970 Mitsui formed the Mitsui Knowledge Industry Corporation, which provides a data bank, information network, and survey of developing-country opportunities, plus numerous other intelligence-related services, to the hundreds of corporations of the Mitsui Group. A Singaporean government official once commented that "Mitsui is better at information gathering than the CIA."[2] Other *zaibatsu* have similar information networks.

After quality products, access to raw materials, control of shipping lines, and adequate information networks, the one remaining element essential for success in penetrating overseas markets is money, and the way the Japanese have organized their banking system is so impressive that it is the subject of a separate chapter. The banks work together with the Japanese trading companies in assisting the rather narrow and insular medium-sized Japanese manufacturers in many industries to expand abroad, for otherwise such manufacturers would be unable to do so.

Another important factor aiding Japanese businesses in their overseas ventures is the support system that the Japanese government provides. Just to cite one example, the Japanese government's aid to developing countries (ODA) is linked to the purchase of goods from Japan, and thus creates an early market-share lead for Japan in the countries that receive the aid. In this way the government actively encourages the expansion of Japanese business into markets in developing countries that would not merit the efforts of individual companies. The policy also helps to forestall protectionist legislation.

Perhaps the most important aid given to Japanese business by the government is what it receives from JETRO, the Japan External Trade Organization. I have long been an admirer of JETRO, which operates as a sort of trainer or coach on the sidelines, cheering on Japanese business as it tackles the daily frustrations of doing business in countries around the world. JETRO helps by providing trade leads and monitoring the activities of competitors such as American and European companies in all the major markets of the world, and in all major product categories. The sole objective of JETRO is to help Japanese business expand, and to work with any Japanese company that requests its assistance. (It is my hope that the Foreign Commercial Service of the United States will one day have the same objectives, and be given the employees and resources to carry them out.)

JETRO, which has over ten thousand employees, is a significant support to Japanese industry overseas.

Just one of JETRO's many activities is to lobby actively on behalf of Japanese interests in the corridors of power of target markets, such as the United States and the EEC. Top law firms are retained to monitor legislation and influence it when practical. Top figures of out-of-power administrations are given handsome retainers to drop hints in the right places. Thomas E. Dewey was on the JETRO payroll, and he later introduced Richard Nixon to Mitsui (he was retained by Mitsui as a lawyer during the sixties after his defeat by John F. Kennedy in the 1960 presidential election). Combining accurate intelligence with lobbying and the "retaining" of selected individuals to ensure that the right people will be listening provides Japanese businesses with a powerful weapon for advancing their interests. The companies do not rely entirely on JETRO for this service, however. For example, Toyota alone had twenty-six law firms in Washington under retainer in 1981 (it has since reduced this number to eighteen, after the "voluntary restraint" on exports was signed that year).

I turn now from detailing the reasons for Japan's success—and I have named only the major ones—to examining the consumer electronics and watch industries, recent examples of successful attacks by Japanese firms on markets that had been dominated by European or American corporations.

The unprecedented success of Japanese manufacturing firms in capturing the world market for consumer appliances and electronics is probably the best rags-to-riches story of this century. To cite a personal example involving the early days of Japanese transistor radios, when I was a freshman at Stanford in 1956, I was always trying to find part-time jobs that would supplement the meager resources that were available to me because my father had died shortly after we returned from the Far East in 1950. From the few years I spent in Asia as a boy, I had an image of Japanese goods as cheap junk. But this did not deter me from taking the job of salesman for a Japanese trading company. The product was one of the first Japanese transistor radios. It turned out to be a dud, and I had to take back the two or three hundred that I had managed to sell around the Palo Alto area and apologize to the radio shops that had been unwary enough to buy them from me. When Japanese companies began introducing high-quality products, it was not easy to buck their previous reputation. Thus Akio Morita of Sony, and his rivals at Matsushita, faced a tough situation when Sony and Panasonic began their assault on the American market in the early sixties. But this time they came with a difference, which was the result of the lessons learned from Dr. Demming, the aforementioned American quality-control expert who was sent to help in the reconstruction of Japanese industry after the war. Both Sony and Matsushita, as well as other major firms in the same business —such as Toshiba (a member of the Mitsui group) and Hitachi—had taken Demming's advice and invested in quality. The rest of the story is history. America is practically finished as far as competing with the Japanese in televisions and radios are concerned, and never even got started in the video-recorder field. Only Philips of Holland has been able to put up a fight. Many U.S. firms are now making Japanese products under license and putting their brand names on them. The major reason for this success is not Japanese government subsidizing, or a fanatically dedicated work force; Japanese goods have captured the Western markets because of superior quality. It is a bitter truth to face, but it is the reality. As a business strategy it is the oldest and simplest of them all: good value for the consumer's money.

Nevertheless, it would be far from the truth to imply that Japanese companies don't use every means at their disposal to capture market share. A good product is a necessary, but not a sufficient, condition for success. A device used today by many Japanese firms in the consumer business is to spend on advertising and promotion purely to build corporate image. Few European or American firms are prepared to do this—except perhaps the oil companies, which resorted to this practice during the rise in oil prices when they didn't know what else to do with their money. For example, India is a closed market to imports of Japanese (or any foreign) consumer electronics. Duties range from 100 to 500 percent, and there are so many restrictions on resale that it is a nightmare. Undeterred, Matsushita has been taking out full-page ads in the largest-circulation newspapers reassuring Indians that National and Panasonic are two brand names they can always trust (see illustration). The lemming effect ensured that other Japanese companies followed suit. These companies know that many Indians work in and commute from the Middle East, where Japanese products are sold, and they also hope that one day the huge Indian market will open up to imports of consumer goods, or that the investment climate will improve to the point that direct investment in manufacturing in India can be justified.

Another highly successful Japanese industry in the overseas expansion of Japanese business has been the watch industry, led by Seiko. The Seiko company philosophy has been a commitment to quality and modernity. The Seiko miracle was to introduce modern technology and merchandising techniques into an industry that had been known for its traditional approach. The famous Swiss makers are reduced to selling watches to a limited market at $500 and up, and has virtually conceded the mass market to Seiko and its Japanese rival Citizen.

The crucial difference between Seiko or Citizen and its Swiss rivals came about when the manufacture of quartz and digital watches became feasible. The Swiss invented the quartz and self-winding watches, but, unlike the Japanese companies, were not equipped with the financial and management resources to develop the world opportunities for inexpensive high-quality timepieces. Now a new revolution in timekeeping is taking place, by combining it with such other functions as message taking, television, radio, and pocket paging features. This new technology is also being developed in Japan by Seiko. It will be interesting to see how popular these new multipurpose wristwatches will become. I would imagine that, thanks to Seiko, by the end of the 1980's many Westerners will be wearing television sets on their wrists. That is, providing the Japanese haven't irrevocably weakened the West by displacing all its manufacturing industries, so that no Westerner can afford a TV watch.

Japanese companies tend to enter a foreign market one after the other in quick succession, using low price, high quality, heavy advertising, and shrewd knowledge of customers and competitors gathered prior to penetrating the market. First they open a type of "forward listening post" and call it a "liaison office." This office will usually consist of two to three men, and will be responsible for communicating details of the market culture and its dynamics back to their headquarters in Japan. (The liaison offices are usually established in a given export industry at about the same time for the reasons given earlier. Entry is therefore likely to be simultaneous.) The rapid successive entries of Japanese companies all suddenly vying for one particular market sector has been called the "laser-beam effect."

A laser beam focuses light waves along a very narrow pathway so that light can be intensified to the point where it can cauterize or burn out anything in its way. This method is analogous to that used

Full-page advertisement in the *Times of India*, June 5, 1983.
(Note in lower left-hand corner reads: "For information only.")

by Japanese companies when entering a market. I have compared Japanese companies to lemmings, all deciding to leap off a cliff into the same patch of ocean at the same time. This is not entirely fair, for when a Japanese company moves into a market, it is seldom a suicidal move. The market intelligence forces of a trading company will transmit back to headquarters that such and such a segment in Country X looks promising. The JETRO office sends a similar report. Perhaps American or European companies are moving in, and the opportunity for Japan will be lost unless the market is analyzed and exploited quickly. These same signals will be received by several Japanese firms concurrently, and if the risk is not overlarge, you can be sure that they will all enter at more or less the same time in order not to let a competitor get an advantage. This "laser beam" strategy has affected a number of Western industries, and is currently operating in the U.S. semiconductor field. Unless beleaguered local industries are determined and willing to fight it out over the long term, they are bound to be burned out under this concentrated onslaught.

One example of this phenomenon occurred in the dye-manufacturing industry. Five Japanese companies making a commonly used dye all decided at the same time that the only way to expand their business was to begin exporting. The reason they decided concurrently was quite simple. The fierce fight for market share in Japan had given way in the natural course of affairs to an informal agreement that maintained the market share of each company at a steady level. This was followed by a drop in domestic consumption. Having divvied up the domestic market in this comfortable fashion, in the face of a declining market, the companies' desire for growth inevitably turned outward. Which is why the American dye industry suddenly found five Japanese companies selling the dye to American customers at half the price it had been going for, effectively putting the U.S. manufacturers out of competition. It would be unfair to label such incidents deliberate plots to destroy American industry. But it is true that these Japanese companies were trampling the U.S. industry without paying the slightest attention to the fact that they were doing so—they were too busy trying to win in their war against one another.

The marshaling of Japanese forces for a larger and higher-risk market entry than the one described above is usually undertaken by the Japanese government or by the large *zaibatsu* working in close partnership with the government. Many a large venture has been started through the initiative of the government, ranging from the classic case of the petrochemical industry—when the government urged the *zaibatsu* to build their own facilities for naptha cracking and refining in order to reduce dependence on imported petrochemicals—to the current $400 billion program led by MITI to build fifth-generation computer equipment.

This type of government involvement is an element of Japanese export strategy that is completely unlike what prevails in the West. It is called "industrial targeting." The concerned ministries constantly scrutinize the business scene in their attempt to anticipate which industries can be expected to grow both domestically and overseas. The result of the most current analysis is that a shift in emphasis is taking place in Japan, away from the traditional Japanese industries—automobiles, textiles, shipbuilding, and steel and aluminum smelting—toward the high value-added arena of high technology. Lionel Olmer, the former Motorola executive who spearheaded his company's expansion in Japan and is now Under Secretary of Commerce for International Trade, said in a recent speech:

> Japanese high technology industries are advancing rapidly—due largely, but not exclusively, to government direction and support. The [Japanese] government has chosen to promote high technology because they believe the benefits which flow thereby to the entire Japanese economy are greater than the benefits that would accrue from promotion of industry generally. The government's role is to select target industries, to reduce risks, and to facilitate large-scale economies in research, development and production. The process for achieving these goals is for MITI [the Ministry of International Trade and Industry] to work closely with industries to identify promising technologies, to establish cooperative research programs, to select a leading foreign company as a model, and then to foster protection of the domestic market. This kind of support develops a strong base from which the chosen firms can launch aggressive export drives.[3]

Even though "Japan, Inc." is, as stated earlier, a myth, industrial targeting is a grain of truth behind that myth. No other free-market country has been as successful in combining competition and government planning.

The "financial circles," called *zaikai* but better known to the West as *zaibatsu*, also give Japanese business a powerful advantage. Most of the *zaibatsu* have their Monday Clubs or Fifth of the Month Clubs, where they assemble the top men in the various companies within the group, ostensibly so that they can get to know each other. But in practice such meetings often lead the companies to combine forces in an effort to make the most of an opportunity that has opened up in either the overseas or domestic markets. Government is usually brought in as an ally once strategy has been decided on by the industry concerned.

In the long run the laser-beam phenomenon, accompanied by predatory pricing and unmatchable sales terms, will wear out Japan's welcome in even the most tolerant of markets. Many Japanese companies, particularly those that have been most successful in wiping out local industry in the markets they penetrate, have begun to sense that protectionism is a growing threat, and that Japan will be forced to manufacture in the countries it wants to export to, or those markets will be closed to it. It was to alert Japanese industry to this threat and urge them to consider different tactics that I wrote my first book, *Japan's Choice: Conflict or Cooperation* (published in Japanese in 1981).

One company that early on realized which way the winds were likely to blow was Sony, as mentioned earlier. Akio Morita had observed the pressure on Japanese textiles that culminated in the multinational fiber agreement and the demise of Japan's fastest-growing industry through the creation of quotas. He was determined to prevent any such protectionist measures being taken against Sony, and unlike most other Japanese CEO's, he knew, understood, and liked Westerners. For these reasons he was one of the first of a number of farsighted Japanese executives to recognize the importance of placing Japanese manufacturing investment in the major markets, rather than relying exclusively on exporting to each market from the controlled manufacturing environment at home in Japan.

Sony's experience parallels that of a number of other Japanese manufacturers who operate plants in Europe or the United States. The existence of the overseas production base provides both the incentive and the means for placing a broader range of the company's products into the overseas market. A significant benefit to Sony has been the positive labor-relations record at its San Diego plant, as well as the fact that the very existence of Sony America's manufacturing facilities gives the company a strong argument in countering protectionist agitation in the United States. Sony's plants in the United Kingdom and other major overseas markets provide similar convincing evidence that Sony is not responsible for unemployment in the host countries.

Two other examples of overseas Japanese manufacturing investment are the cases of Nippon Miniature Bearing Company (NMB) and Green Cross Corporation. Both illustrate the mutual benefits that can derive from persuading the Japanese to move out of their controlled home-base environment. These examples also serve to highlight the strategy of the more enlightened Japanese manufacturers who are no longer content to feel the pulse of an overseas market only through an indirect presence (trading company or liaison office). In one case the manufacturer was forced to produce overseas, and in the other it chose to do so.

The first case is that of Nippon Miniature Bearing. NMB makes a specialized precision product for applications that impose demanding product specifications. In most bearing markets, close rapport between sales engineer and factory is essential. In 1971 the U.S. Department of Defense prohibited further use of imported ball bearings in military equipment. NMB quickly purchased a bearings plant in California to protect its existing U.S. market. Soon the ability to provide close technical-service support from its California production base to its customers in the United States opened new U.S. markets to NMB. Its local staff—Americans familiar with U.S. business needs and requirements—tied NMB still more firmly into the U.S. market. Today NMB supplies more than 30 percent of the total demand for U.S. precision bearings.

Another example of Japanese manufacturing investment in the United States with excellent results was the brainchild of Roy Naito, the founder of the Green Cross Corporation, a $350 million annual sales manufacturer of pharmaceuticals. Naito needed plasma for his blood-fractionation products in Japan. Unfortunately, blood donation is not a Japanese habit, and it was difficult to meet demand from local resources. He went to America and bought the Scientific Products Division of Abbott Laboratories in 1978. At that time Abbott was grossing about $30 million a year through this California-based subsidiary. Under the watchful eyes of Naito and his American colleague Tom Dress, the sales of Alpha Therapeutics (the new name of the U.S. company) have trebled since the acquisition, and the subsidiary has provided Green Cross with not only a source of plasma but also a springboard into the U.S. market for its highly sophisticated product line, which includes the first commercially produced artificial blood, Fluosol.

The concept of direct manufacturing investment in the target markets of Europe and the United States is good business in many industries. It has the added advantage of being generally welcomed by countries that are otherwise inclined to ban or strictly limit the export of Japanese manufactured products to their markets. Despite these advantages, Japanese firms still have about the same investment in the United States in manufacturing as American firms do in Japan (about $3 billion each). The main reasons for the reluctance of many Japanese firms to invest overseas are their concern over the quality and dependability of foreign labor, and the fear that costs will escalate as a result of not having captive suppliers that owe their existence to the patronage of a large Japanese manufacturer (thus resulting in lower inventories and more efficiency for the manufacturer). Japanese firms continue their foot-dragging over direct investment even though they have the added advantage (not shared by foreign companies coming into Japan) of being able to acquire a company overnight in many countries. The acquisition of a Japanese firm by a foreign company remains extremely difficult for many reasons, but no such bias exists for Japanese firms coming into Western markets.

Despite all this, investment overseas remains a strategy preferred by only a few Japanese firms. Most would prefer to strive for ever-improving efficiency at home, hoping to weather passing squalls, such as the French decisions not to unload Japanese cars and to refer all video recorders for inspection at a small town (Poitiers) located hundreds of miles from the entry ports. The usual response to such threats is to divert exports to other less aggressively protectionist countries until the rules are relaxed again. My good friend Ambassador Bruce Rankin, the Canadian ambassador in Tokyo, once told me that his main concern about the decision by the Japanese car manufacturers to "voluntarily" limit exports to the United States to 1.6 million automobiles was that the avalanche of Japanese cars would be diverted to Canada.

It has often been observed that those who know exactly what they want and have the will to strive for it usually succeed in realizing their desires. The operation of this old maxim is the reason why Japan has left other nations so far behind in commercial activity. The consensus in Japan has been that success in trade is essential for survival. Thus they have been struggling to achieve this goal, while other nations have been caught in the throes of debate over what their national purpose should be. This is the Japanese advantage, and it is a formidable one.

CHAPTER
12

JAPANESE TRADING COMPANIES
AND JAPANESE BANKS

Japanese trading companies and banks are two important corner-stones of Japanese success. The role of the trading company is the more dynamic of the two in building business for Japanese compa-nies, but the banks provide the essential financial support that has made it possible for Japan to lead the United States in the expansion and growth of multinational business across the globe. Behind the trading company and the bank are the financially interconnected companies known as *zaikai,* many of which descended from the prewar *zaibatsu* oligopolists. The modern *zaikai* has remained every bit as strong as its *zaibatsu* predecessors, achieving this result by linking companies (through interlocking directorships and equity participation) whose operations comprehend most of the major areas of Japanese industrial activity.

The *zaikai* industrial operations are further supported by a num-ber of service companies that act synergistically to ensure that the manufacturers in the group prosper. These service arms include not only the trading companies and the banks but also shipping compa-nies and insurance firms, as well as trust banks and information/data concerns, all contributing strands of the spider web that forms a *zaikai.* The *zaikai* are one of the greatest strengths of the modern Japanese business machine, because even though companies are not always formally related, the strong force of history and personal ties causes them to act in concert and to assist each other whenever possible.

Trading companies in Japan are divided into two major groups. The more important are the *sōgōshōsha*, or general trading companies. These companies, now nine in number (since the demise of the Ataka Trading Company in 1978), are each linked to large *zaikai* groups, and they typically handle twenty thousand to twenty-five thousand items each. The *semmonshōsha*, the other group, are specialized trading firms. They are, as the name suggests, much smaller organizations, and they handle trading in selected commodities and products.

The role of the approximately eight thousand *semmonshōsha* is of great importance in domestic Japanese marketing, but less so in the world market, which is largely the province of the general trading companies. The specialized trading companies are not very different from import-export companies in the West, whereas the *sōgōshōsha* are a different breed altogether. To give you some idea of the size and power of the *sōgōshōsha*, the nine companies combined employ over eighty thousand people, with an average sale per employee of from $2 million to $6 million. The total turnover of the *sōgōshōsha* in 1981 was just under $400 billion, or over 30 percent of the Japanese national GNP. Despite their enormous sales volumes the *sōgōshōsha* are also characterized by razor-thin margins of profit, with the average *sōgōshōsha* operating at a 1.5 percent to 2 percent ratio of profit to sales (pretax), which helps explain how a company like Ataka with a turnover of $5 billion went belly up so easily and spectacularly.

Japanese trading companies originally evolved during the post–Meiji Restoration period. They were the natural offshoot of the major industrial groups, such as Mitsui and Mitsubishi, providing invaluable service as the marketing arm of the manufacturing firms that formed the major part of the groups. The member manufacturers relied on the trading companies with which they were affiliated not only to identify markets (both domestically and internationally) but also to buy goods from them and to take on all the risks and financial responsibilities inherent in this role. In Japan, marketing has traditionally been considered to be a function somewhat separate from the really important role of a Japanese company, which is to provide employment in the manufacturing sector.

I was always amazed when the production manager and plant

officers of my company in Japan expressed indignation at the marketing department for not selling everything they produced. The accusation was based on their feeling that under no circumstances should they be asked to produce goods that were not already presold. In retrospect, I see this as a holdover from their schooling and previous experience in purely Japanese companies, where the trading companies are expected to forecast sales and then take the responsibility for buying any overproduction. Generally speaking, manufacturers, from the post-Meiji period up until quite recently, entrusted all their marketing to the trading company. It solved a number of problems for them. They did not have to concern themselves with the peculiarities of foreign markets; this was left to the trading companies. Nor did they have to worry about taking a financial risk on a foreign customer who might or might not be reliable and creditworthy. That was also the responsibility of the *sōgōshōsha.* The trading company was invaluable to the vast majority of Japanese manufacturing firms in the period of fast growth during the fifties and sixties.

The trading companies attract a certain type of man, and, because of their size and prestige, have been able to draw on the top university-educated talent in Japan. The recruit for the general trading company is a different breed from the civil servant, banker or even trainee salary men in the manufacturing firms. He is usually a thoroughly well rounded and well educated individual, with the kind of flair that will give him the flexibility to move freely in the many different environments where trading companies operate, in both the developed and the developing world. They are generalists rather than specialists. Many are sent for additional training, mainly to the United States, in order to give them a better understanding of their customers and to help them to develop a global rather than a parochially Japanese way of viewing world markets. Some recruits not only are exposed to a multinational training but are also expected to develop expertise in the trading requirements associated with several critical industries in which the trading company is involved. The trading-company executive is the frontline soldier of Japanese industry. His experience and expertise should never be underestimated when dealing with a *sōgōshōsha,* since his versatility and loyalty are a formidable asset to his company.

The various traditional functions of the *sōgōshōsha* can be grouped as follows: information/data gathering; market-potential analysis; detailed market investigations; financial risk analysis and risk-taking; after-sales service and quality assurance in international markets; guarantor of risk to new projects involving Japanese companies overseas (particularly for fellow members of the same *zaikai*); as well as a number of other functions to support the efforts of the *zaikai* group that it represents. In short, the *zaikai sōgōshōsha* has become the outward face of Japanese industry abroad.

But not all of the major nine *sōgōshōsha* have descended from prewar *zaibatsu*. Five of them have evolved from prewar cotton industries known as *kansei gomen* (although one of these, Toyo Menka, was formed in 1919 as a splinter organization that broke away from Mitsui, and was charged with handling cotton trading for the group. Toyo Menka is closely linked with the modern-day Mitsui Bussan or Mitsui Trading Company).

The traditional roles of the trading companies as described above have been declining in importance in recent years because many large manufacturers who had traditionally left their overseas marketing to the trading companies are finding that to grow they must do their own overseas marketing. This is especially true of manufacturers who have either technologically advanced product lines requiring specialized marketing and servicing capabilities beyond the capacity of the trading company, or consumer-goods companies who feel that the advertising and promotion investments required to be successful in countries like the United States or Britain need direct company control. The generalist orientation of the trading company makes it difficult for them to exploit market opportunities in such cases as efficiently as the manufacturers themselves. This has led the trading companies to diversify their roles, a move that augurs well for their continued financial viability and usefulness within the Japanese business structure. The *sōgōshōsha* have responded well to changing circumstances, and seem unlikely soon to wither away, despite predictions to the contrary that were current a few years ago, when it first became clear that the traditional functions of the traders were being superseded in part by the manufacturers.

One of the new roles that the trading companies have taken on is the burden of assuming some of the risks inherent in equity investment by Japanese *zaikai* and other interests in natural-resource development, particularly in the developing world. Throughout the first half of the twentieth century, Japan was plagued by a shortage of foreign exchange reserves, which seriously hampered her ability to invest overseas. But those days are gone, and Japan has now taken the lead in new investment to develop natural resources overseas, particularly those that are of vital interest to Japan. For example, C. Itoh, the fourth largest of the *sōgōshōsha,* took the lead in establishing a Japanese foothold in the development of Zaire's copper resources.

Similarly, the trading companies have become involved in a number of natural-resource infrastructure projects, such as the development of iron-ore resources in Australia by Mitsui and the exploitation of Brunei's copper and natural gas resources by Mitsubishi. Japanese trading-company men are to be found in every location where the raw materials and natural resources needed to sustain Japan's industrial machine can be found.

Another comparatively new role for trading companies is in manufacturing investment overseas. As mentioned in the previous chapter, Japanese industry resisted becoming involved in overseas manufacturing investment until after the 1973 oil crisis. From that time on, there was a growing recognition that for Japan to free itself from dependence on distant sources of raw materials, it would be better to manufacture products overseas, or, at the very least, to control the raw materials themselves. This is the strategy now being followed, and Japanese trading companies are buying up American agricultural land, Canadian oil refineries, and coal and uranium deposits in Australia and the United States. The risks are enormous in such ventures, and the great Ataka Trading Company, formerly the tenth *sōgōshōsha,* went broke largely because of an ill-advised investment in a Canadian oil refinery. *Sōgōshōsha* are setting up small and medium-sized companies to look after Japanese interests in all parts of the world. In this sense the trading companies are once again in the vanguard of Japanese expansion around the world. They are fulfilling their traditional risk-taking role by doing so. As circumstances change to force Japanese manufacturers to take the plunge and invest overseas, they look to the trading companies' experience in international commerce to take some of the burden off their shoulders.

According to the Japanese embassy in New Delhi, there are over three hundred Japanese businessmen in that city. Two hundred of them work for *sōgōshōsha.* By comparison, there are now (1983) fifteen American businessmen in New Delhi, which in itself is a 50 percent increase over 1982. This small example is duplicated in other

Indian cities and all over the developing world. Even in tiny Goa the Japanese trading companies have stationed people to be sure that Japanese interests are looked after in the growing iron-ore trade from that Indian territory to Japan.

In addition to their increasing role as natural-resource developers and risk-takers for new Japanese investments overseas, trading companies are now acting as catalysts for new Japanese multicompany ventures abroad. These are the so-called third country ventures. In this capacity, Mitsubishi Trading has taken over the management of a large salt-production complex in Mexico, and has organized the entire infrastructure from mining to marketing in Japan, the United States, and Canada. The salt from Mitsubishi's Mexican venture is even used on American highways in winter. Mitsui took the lead in setting up the petrochemical investments of the Mitsui Group in Iran. Unfortunately, the political situation there changed suddenly, and Mitsui's $3 billion investment has been the cause of severe concern back in Tokyo, although it now appears that some arrangement with the government in Iran may be possible.

Another area of trading-company involvement that is quite recent is investment in downstream activities, such as fast-food franchises. Mitsubishi has taken the lead by becoming partners in the Kentucky Fried Chicken business in Japan and in setting up a Japanese fast-food chain in the United States (Dosanko Larmen).

Yojei Mimura, the president of the Mitsubishi Corporation (Mitsubishi Trading Company) has summed up the functions of a *sōgōshōsha* in this way: "The *shosha* locates, buys, ships, insures, finances and helps coordinate all the steps required to bring everything together."[1] He could add that nowadays the *sōgōshōsha* sometimes even ends up retailing the product, given Mitsubishi's entry into the fast-food business.

About half of the *sōgōshōsha*'s business can typically be found in Japan, with the other half overseas. According to statistics compiled by the Keizai Koho Centre (Japan Institute for Social and Economic Affairs), in fiscal year 1981, 13.4 percent of the sales of the nine general traders was in offshore trade. Thus we can estimate that at least 10 percent of the trading company's business has nothing whatsoever to do with Japan. The company makes or otherwise acquires goods in one country, usually a developing one, and then arranges for it to be shipped to a developed country. Promoting the expansion of such trading is one way the trading companies are diversifying their roles in order to avoid becoming obsolete. They have a hundred years of expertise in most of the markets of the world, and are just beginning to use that formidable headstart to their advantage. One example of such trading is currently taking place with China. The Japanese have a long experience of trading with China, while many European and American companies are novices in this area. Because the Chinese seem to be going ahead with their industrial-modernization program, the prospects appear good that China will continue to buy many kinds of industrial machinery. The Japanese trading companies are cashing in on this situation not only by selling their own groups' products but also by selling those of European or American companies that would otherwise be reluctant or unable to enter the market.[2]

Despite change and innovation, the greatest asset of the Japanese trading company remains its close affiliation with a *zaikai*. From this integrated position in a large industrial grouping it can serve the manufacturers of the group in a type of *giri/on* (duty/obligation) role. Often I have had discussions with manufacturers that were *zaikai* members on the subject of chemical exports to the United States and other countries (ex-Japan), only to be told in the end that the trading company had to be involved, and that it would not be possible for the manufacturer to deal directly with us. This killed the deal in a couple of cases, since there was no room in the pricing arrangements for a middleman. The Japanese manufacturer cannot go against the *giri* it holds to the trading company that has been promoting its business abroad. Eventually the trading company relinquishes its control over the overseas business of the *zaikai* member as the latter matures, but it does so reluctantly, and only after the Monday Club or other *zaikai* policy body decides that Company X is now mature enough to handle its own overseas business. Until then every company in the *zaikai* is obliged to work through the trading company, even though by the time it gives up its hold it may only be handling sales, with all the marketing, technical, and negotiating details being worked out by the manufacturer itself. This tenacious clinging to outmoded privileges is one device the *sōgōshōsha* have employed in order to buy time to expand and diversify their operations. Also, continued close cooperation has many benefits. For example, despite a worldwide downturn in the oil-refining and petrochemical industries, Mitsubishi is going ahead with an enormous complex being built in Saudi Arabia. One of the reasons it can afford to do so is the fact that 60 percent of the general trader's business is done for members of its *zaikai* group.[3]

Western business people may well envy the Japanese. Even a smallish Japanese manufacturer can profitably begin exporting with no previous experience by drawing on the support that a *sōgōshōsha* can give. All the Japanese manufacturer has to do is to meet with his trading-company representative and explain what he wants to sell. The trader then takes on the task of finding out if there is a market, and then lines up customers. It will buy the product and pay the manufacturer in yen. These days many deals struck with Third World countries come with unpleasant strings attached, in the shape of counter-purchase requirements. The often nearly unsalable products thus foisted on a company that wishes to invest in an LDC (lesser developed country) are frequently turned over to the trading company to handle. This is just one example of the headaches a Japanese trading company can take over from a manufacturer. (In fact, some Western companies are employing the *sōgōshōsha* to get rid of commodities acquired because of counter-purchase requirements. This is a potentially lucrative field for the ever-versatile *sōgōshōsha*.)

There is no precise modern equivalent of the Japanese general trading company in either Europe or the United States. There are many reasons for this. In the United States the antitrust laws have been one factor inhibiting their development, but probably more significant has been America's lingering isolationism and the general disinclination of medium-sized companies to go into exporting. England, on the other hand, has long been a trading nation, and there is a lengthy tradition of British trading companies, ranging from the grandfather of them all, the East India Company, to the great British hongs of the China trade, such as Jardines, Swires, Dodwells, Hutchisons, Watsons, and a number of others, which have carried British goods to Asia and other parts of the developing world. But the halycon days of British trading declined with the passing of the empire.

The Hong Kong–based trading firms are still active, however, and have created entries for British goods throughout the Far East. But they lack the power and versatility of the *sōgōshōsha,* and fulfill a more narrow trading and import-export role that is comparable with that of a *semmonshōsha.*

Several countries have become interested in establishing Japanese-style *sōgōshōsha.* Korea has been trying to develop trading companies, and more recently President Reagan signed the Export Trading Company Act, which permits the formation of American trading companies with functions somewhat similar to those of the Japanese ones, but which are restricted in their ability to participate in the U.S. domestic market and to import as well as export. (It should be noted that the Japanese trading companies are authorized and encouraged to work both in and outside of Japan.)

If the Western businessman is interested in using the Japanese trading company as a vehicle to buy from Japan, or to arrange a trading-related deal involving Japanese companies, the *sōgōshōsha* can be very useful and effective. I have found that there is no more professional organization than a Japanese trading company when it comes to buying from Japan, although often, in my capacity as president of the American Chamber of Commerce in Japan, I was contacted by American firms anxious to avoid going through the trading company in the belief that they would get a better price by working directly with the manufacturer. The manufacturers themselves are often willing to work out a deal, but it usually means that the export will have to be made to a country where the trading company has already surrendered its exclusive rights, and where the manufacturer has its own direct-sales organization. Otherwise, it is almost pointless to try to buy directly from the manufacturer, since they always refer overseas customers back to the trading company. The trading companies themselves take a similar approach when dealing with Western companies wishing to buy directly from Japan, rather than through a local agent or distributor who has been appointed to handle their products.

The trading company is likely to be the first Japanese organization that many Western companies will ever deal with. The power and capabilities of these organizations are awesome, and they are superb at organizing the kinds of business that involve commodity trading or simple imports from Japan. They can also provide the Western company with a way of selling in the Japanese market, although this can only be viewed as a short-term method of entry, since most trading companies will try to determine if one of the manufacturing companies in their own *zaikai* group is capable of duplicating the Western product. *Zaikai* strategy is to attain an initial volume using the Western product, and then the trading company introduces a Japanese me-too product into the picture and pushes the Western product into a more specialized market segment. For this reason it may not always be a good idea to rely for too long or solely on a Japanese trading company to represent the Western manufacturer in Japan.

Few informed observers are currently predicting the impending decline of the Japanese general trading company. While these companies are not relying on any single strategy to see them through, the critical factor in their continued success is their ability to take the long-term view, whether it is a question of diversifying products and services, or using financial innovations to beat the world credit squeeze. Of course, they are always seeking to improve their information-gathering techniques and scope. Like all Japanese companies, when they analyze risk they think in terms of years and not quarters. The success of the Japanese *sōgōshōsha* illustrates, perhaps better than any other example, that companies whose goals are directed toward many factors rather than solely the bottom line, will be the long-term victors in any prolonged trade conflict.

If the *sōgōshōsha* is a business institution unique to Japan in modern times, Japanese banks are also extremely different from anything we have in the West. The difference lies not so much in function as in style. The relationship of a Japanese bank to its customers, both Japanese and foreign, is unlike what prevails among Western banking institutions. The Japanese bank is the center of the *zaikai* spider web, and through its investments in group companies it can control the assets and influence the boards of each *zaikai* member company. The local bank manager *(shitenchō)* of the Japanese bank is one of the most important individuals in the community. His is a position quite similar to the traditional British bank manager's. He is involved with and interested in every aspect of the companies who have accounts with his branch. Just one indication of the extremely close relationships a Japanese bank has with its chief customers is that it is common practice for a bank to appoint one of its trusted lifetime executives to take over the management of a company that is in trouble in order to protect the bank's investment in that company.

One key difference between the American and the Japanese bank is that in Japan the customer feels that the bank is putting service ahead of profits. One sometimes gets the impression in America that the bank feels that it is doing you a favor by taking your money. When I worked in Japan, my company dealt with three U.S. and three Japanese banks; in comparing my experience with American banks in Japan with the Japanese ones—with the notable exception of the Irving Trust Company, which is an outstanding service-oriented American bank—I must conclude that Japanese banks are dedicated to a much higher standard of service than most American banks. The service that my company received from Sumitomo, Fuji, and Mitsubishi, our three Japanese banks, was of such excellence that I feel obliged to mention them by name.

The first impression that I received of a Japanese bank was on my first day in the office in Tokyo. Among the calls and messages was one from the local manager of the Sumitomo Bank to the effect that he wished to welcome me personally to Japan. I was astonished by this, and asked my controller why the bank was so quick off the mark. How did they know that it was my first day on the job? The controller explained to me how important the bank was to our business, their interest in us as good customers, and the concessions and assistance that it had already rendered. I began then to appreciate the essential role of the bank in Japanese business strategy. When the Sumitomo Bank manager eventually came to the office, he reemphasized the bank's commitment to serve the company. Every day, he explained, the bank would send a messenger to our office. All our banking affairs would receive top priority. He would be very pleased if I would do his bank the honor of opening a personal account at his branch. In the course of the next five years I was privileged to become acquainted with a number of top Sumitomo men, from the executive vice president of the bank to the head cashier in Kojimachi, our neighborhood branch. They were all outstanding in providing service. Some of their services included helping us to locate a new office (through Sumitomo Real Estate), leasing a computer (through Sumitomo Leasing), researching an acquisition possibility (through the head office of Sumitomo Bank in Tokyo and an old friend who was the former branch manager of our Kojimachi Sumitomo branch), and accompanying me as a go-between to introduce me to potential business partners. One of the assistant managers at Sumitomo Bank was so excited about my company and its growth prospects in Japan that on his daily rounds for the bank he would help line up sales opportunities for our industrial chemicals. Thanks to him we were able to get several important contracts. The same pattern also held true for Fuji Bank, which was invaluable in setting up our new subsidiary company just outside Tokyo. They worked closely with my American colleague Tom Bayha, who ran that operation, and gave him the same kind of support that I had received from Sumitomo. This is the kind of service support that the Western business person can expect from a Japanese bank in Japan, and it is worth remembering if one is interested in exploring marketing and financing opportunities there.

The banks function in Japan in a more segmented and specialized way than they do in the West. The large city banks, such as Sumitomo, Mitsubishi, Mitsui, and Fuji, act as important members of their respective industrial groups, operate extensive branch networks in Japan and all over the world, and are similar to the Bank of America or Citibank in the diversity of their operations. Some of these city banks have also expanded extensively overseas, and have acquired banks in the United States. Sumitomo has established its own branch network in California, for example, and the Bank of Tokyo, with its California First Bank, also has a strong presence in that state.

Japanese banks are also becoming active on the world's money markets and in underwriting huge share offerings by Japanese companies in London on the Eurodollar market. Their overseas expansion has been phenomenal, and traces back to the late seventies when the yen became such a strong currency that Japan became a net capital exporter for the first time.

The cross that Japanese banks have always had to bear is the "voluntary" purchase of huge amounts of Japanese government bonds each year. These pieces of paper are the means by which the Japanese government has financed its huge deficits over the past two decades. In return for all the support that the Japanese banks receive from the Ministry of Finance, they are expected to pick up the bonds that are given them at the start of each fiscal year. The total amount of bonds floated each year has been decreasing somewhat due to the efforts of the Ohira and later the Suzuki governments to cut government expenditure. Prime Minister Nakasone has followed the same lead. Nevertheless, over 30 percent of the government's budget is still financed through these low-interest-bearing compulsory bonds.

In addition to bankrolling the government, another important role for the Japanese banks is to bail out sick companies. The advantages of the *zaikai* groupings mentioned earlier are offset somewhat by the obligations imposed on group banks to take care of companies that have found themselves overextended for a variety of reasons. In Japan these affairs almost never come to public attention unless the situation is virtually hopeless. The reason is that no Japanese company president is willing to admit that his company is going broke. It inevitably means ritual resignation and sometimes disgrace for himself and his family, or even a suicide leap from a tall building.

The most famous bailout of recent years was the combined effort of Sumitomo Bank and the C. Itoh Trading Company to mitigate the Ataka Trading Company debacle. This large trading company was number nine or ten in the country, with an annual turnover in excess of $5 billion when it collapsed. The ostensible reason was overinvestment in a high-risk Canadian oil refinery, but there were other reasons related to management policies and world trading conditions. When Ataka collapsed the whole nation shuddered. It was similar to the Chrysler, Pan Am, and Lockheed crises, but the Japanese took the decision to strip the company and sell it off rather than resurrect it. The Sumitomo Bank put its considerable resources to work, and offered for sale all the units that C. Itoh did not want to absorb. I can recall the situation well because it was the first and perhaps the only time when a Japanese bank was knocking on the door offering companies for sale to foreigners. We had a close look at one of the Ataka companies that the bank was offering its "best customers," but decided not to proceed because the product lines were not particularly compatible with ours and too much new investment in plant and equipment would have been needed.

The many services that the large city banks perform for the *zaikai* groups and other customers, both domestic and foreign, are complemented by those provided by other parts of the Japanese banking structure. The Long Term Development Bank and the Industrial Bank of Japan are both extremely large institutions that have an important role to play in the financing of substantial projects both overseas and in Japan. These bankers' banks are further supported by the aggressive Ex-Im Bank of Japan, which offers concessionary finance for development projects and ties all the purchasing and services for the projects to the interests of Japanese business. In this role it is not unlike the American Ex-Im bank. However, the funding of the Japanese Ex-Im bank is almost double the American one, and it is able, because of the slightly different nature and charter of the organization, to offer rates of interest that are several points lower than those of the U.S. Ex-Im Bank.

The close marriage of banks and *zaikai*—and not just banks that are members of the *zaikai* are involved—has an important impact on how Japanese companies are financed as compared with most Western companies. The debt-to-equity ratio of Japanese companies tends to be amazingly high by Western standards, and that of the trading companies is higher than most others. In a work published in 1975 M. Y. Yoshino estimated that the (then ten) *sōgōshōsha* had an average debt-to-equity ratio of fifteen to one. Reflecting on the significance of this figure, one can gain a clearer idea of what the general trading companies are all about—they are, as I have said, the outward face of Japanese industry, the risk-taking cutting edge of the Japanese international economic effort. And despite the collapse of Ataka, the sheer staggering size of the *sōgōshōsha* ensures that they will remain better credit risks than the small to medium-sized Japanese companies, the mortality rate of which tends to be disproportionately high.

The relationship between *zaikai* member banks and *sōgōshōsha* is solidly based on mutuality of interest. Its present form dates back to the early days of regrouping, after the trust-busting, *zaibatsu*-breaking faction of the Occupation authorities was overruled by those who favored a rehabilitation of Japanese capitalism to stand as a bulwark against communism in East Asia. Even after the easing of restrictions on former *zaibatsu* member companies, the banks were allowed to hold no more than 10 percent of the stock of any one company. The *sōgōshōsha* were under no such restriction, and the traders thus took on the role of uniting the old *zaibatsu* into new-style *zaikai*, financed in these operations by the banks. Despite the issue of *zaibatsu* stock to the general public decreed by the Occupation authorities (SCAP), Japanese companies have never relied on issue of stock to raise the majority of their capital. Before the war the *zaibatsu* stock was in holding companies controlled by the *zaibatsu* families. The modern *zaikai* members prefer to hold one another's stock. Originally a device to get around the ban on holding companies, the system reinforces the solidarity of the group, and in addition obliges them to turn to the banks for financing, since they prefer not to issue stock to the general public.

The *zaikai* companies don't rely solely on member banks for needed capital. The competing *zaikai* have come to rely more and more on cooperating among themselves in order to finance overseas ventures. John Roberts cites a project in Australia for the mining of iron ore that went into partial operation in 1969. The Japanese share of the capital needed for the $300 million multinational venture—10 percent—was raised jointly by Mitsui and C. Itoh—rival *zaikai*. The *sōgōshōsha* have excellent worldwide credit, and for short-term loans overseas offices rely on foreign banks. But long-term money comes from Japan, and borrowing and lending of huge sums for high-risk overseas investment ensures that the *sōgōshōsha* and the banks both have a vested interest in maintaining the steady growth of the Japanese economy.

Incidentally, one of the secondary reasons why Japanese companies can afford to rely so heavily on borrowing is the saving habits of the Japanese people. As Albert Keidel has said:

> Corporate-retained earnings and government saving have made up the largest portion of Japanese gross savings, but private individual saving has also been traditionally high in Japan, accounting for a third of the total by the early 1970s. These figures represent a tremendous commitment to future growth at the expense of current consumption, especially when compared to much lower rates of gross savings in the United States (roughly 18 percent of gross national product in the early 1970s).[4]

Thus the Japanese people themselves have, in a manner of speaking, put up some of the capital needed for their economy's growth.

In recent years the world recession and the debt problem in the Third World have contracted the amount of money available for financing major overseas projects. A few large-scale projects involving Japanese companies have been financed by project financing, where banks lend money to the project directly, instead of to the corporations involved in the project. One such project in Western Australia, involving $10 billion in development of natural gas, is being financed by the Industrial Bank of Japan. Once the project begins making money, the bank will begin receiving repayment. If it is unsuccessful, however, there is no solid guarantee that the bank can recover its investment, despite the assurance the banks receive from participants of receiving some of the product in lieu of cash if worst comes to worst—in the above-mentioned case, the companies will undertake to provide natural gas to the bank. The bank must, however, rely largely on personal trust in such deals, because they cannot legally force the companies involved to cover the bank's liability. (This system would appear to be the bank's investment in the growth of Japan, a way of circumventing the inevitable limit to borrowing that even a Japanese corporation must eventually reach. It is a pure act of faith in future profitability and economic growth.)

Another way of circumventing stringent terms for industrial borrowers, which the Japanese are currently just beginning to exploit, is the option of leasing equipment and industrial plant rather than selling it. As one *sōgōshōsha* executive has said, "Leasing has much to recommend it. For instance, since there is no outright purchase, it is totally unrelated to the debt service ratio and doesn't appear on the balance sheet."[5] This strategy is particularly attractive to poor countries, which need industrial plant for development but can't afford to put up the necessary capital and absorb or write off the losses from depreciation. The general traders have been quick to become involved in leasing firms. The largest leasing deal so far signed was a $120 million contract to lease a large-scale fertilizer plant to a New Zealand consortium. Nevertheless, there will surely be a limit eventually to how far Japan can go in selling its goods and services to countries that don't have the cash to pay for them. If Japan is using its favorable balance of trade with the developed countries, and consequent inflow of hard cash, to finance its more risky Third World investments, the rise of protectionism could well call a quick halt to all such activities.

The Japanese banking and trading-company network, closely supported by the government itself, through the Bank of Japan and the Ministry of Finance (MOF), is a crucial element of Japanese business strategy overseas, and should not be overlooked in any assessment of why Japan is able to take business, such as large-scale development projects, away from the U.S.-European consortia that have traditionally handled such projects. In addition, the two entities (banks and trading companies) are the backbone of Japanese export and investment programs overseas. The newly developing East and Southeast Asian countries—South Korea, Singapore, Taiwan, and even those in the ASEAN block—are well aware of the success of the Japanese example, since it is so close at hand. European and American companies are finding that opportunities in Middle East construction and infrastructure projects have passed them by because Japan and the NIC's (newly industrialized countries) are pursuing these lucrative contracts more aggressively.

Some innovative ways to compete with the Japanese in these and other areas will be explored in the next chapter.

CHAPTER 13

HOW TO HOLD ON TO YOUR MARKET

Make no mistake about it. The Japanese are winning in the economic struggle that has seen the world's economic center of gravity shift from Europe to America and now, at an ever-increasing speed, across the Pacific to Asia and Japan. Japan has surpassed the West in annual improvements on everything from GNP growth to productivity and market-share increases. In 1969 Japan had just 4 percent of the world's GNP. It now has over 10 percent. Further, there is no slow-down in the rate of Japanese economic expansion either in the developed world or in the developing one.

In his recent book, *Japan as Number One,* Professor Ezra Vogel of Harvard predicted that Japan's GNP will pass that of the United States by 1990. Few Americans would believe that statement, but if Japan continues to grow at the rate achieved over the past twenty years, and Western Europe and the United States continue to show only marginal GNP gains, it is inevitable that Japan will surpass the United States at some point in the not too distant future—certainly before the turn of the century. Japan has seized the lead from the United States and West Germany in terms of market penetration in such areas as Southeast Asia and Africa, and they are whittling away at the traditionally U.S.-dominated markets of Latin America. The performance of Japanese companies in the Middle East grew from $627 million in 1969 to over $17 billion in 1981, and in 1983 were estimated to be over $22 billion.

These same percentage gains have been recorded in all areas of the world, including the developed countries. The Japanese trade surplus with the United States reached a record $14.5 billion in the first half of 1984, and this is a continuation of the trend that has prevailed since 1975, the last year when the United States had a trade surplus with Japan. The trade balance between Japan and the EEC has shown a similar trend, and the 1983 trade statistics show Japan with a surplus of over $15 billion with the Community. Gone are the days when large-scale international infrastructure construction and industrial-development projects (so-called megaprojects) automatically went to either Bechtel or one of its American competitors, or to an occasional European contractor. Nowadays it is usually the Japanese who take the lead in such projects. They may bring in specific foreign companies whose technology is useful to the project and relegate them to the role of junior partners.

Wherever you turn, from shipping to computers and fasteners to fashion, the Japanese are either in front or just behind the leader. No market where manufacturing, extraction, or construction is involved is safe from Japanese competition. They have seized the lead in consumer electronics around the world, and several large American and European companies have had to off-load their consumer electronics product lines or face the prospect of going broke.

The greatest strength of American industry has always been innovation. The British and other Europeans have also been outstanding innovators in high technology, with such successes as the Comet aircraft, the Concorde jet, and the CT scan to their credit. The European problem has always been marketing, which the Americans excelled at. Now both share the same weakness vis-à-vis the Japanese. The venture capitalists of Silicon Valley are unmatched anywhere else in the world, as are the entrepreneurial skills of individual American businessmen and innovative giants, such as IBM. In fields as diverse as the Josephson Junction in the computer world and biotechnology in the pharmaceutical world, the West is still in the lead. In military technology we have, by an accident of history, a quantum headstart on the Japanese. The first and possibly the most important way to stop losing market share to the Japanese is to continue to invest in R&D at an ever-accelerating rate and stay well in front in every possible field. Some Western business people delude themselves into thinking that product life cycles don't apply to them.

A glance at the electronics world of today makes nonsense of that claim.

Many large companies in both America and Europe have maintained their ratio of R&D to sales but have failed to exploit leading-edge technology quickly and *on a worldwide scale*. The financial men have taken over the boardroom, and profit growth through cost reduction and rationalization has superseded growth through investment in research and development and marketing. The reversal of this trend must be first priority if we can ever expect to hold our markets against the Japanese. For that very reason IBM, for example, continues to keep pace with the Japanese in getting new technology on the market. Finance men belong in the boardroom as advisers, but generalists, engineers, and marketing men should set the tone and direction.

A second critical factor in preserving Western leadership in the aircraft, electronic, computer software, and other high-technology industries (as well as regaining the initiative in areas, such as the semiconductor industry, where U.S. manufacturers have recently relinquished leadership), is to safeguard our technology through a willingness to invest in exploiting our inventions instead of selling or licensing them to Japanese companies without proper controls to ensure that the sale does not boomerang on the seller. Too many companies have gone for the quick and easy profit, selling their technology only to discover that the Japanese have turned around and wiped out the original company's market by selling their own improved version. As Boeing and other large aircraft manufacturers turn to Japan for component assembly and the manufacture of many critical sections of new aircraft, the eventual emergence of a strong Japanese aircraft industry cannot be discounted. The outright sale of Western technology to Japan in the fifties and sixties has been a major factor in Japan's ability to compete with the United States and Europe so effectively today. When a large company forms a joint venture in Japan with a giant like Mitsubishi or Komatsu, Toshiba or Hitachi, Nissan or Toyota, or any of the large and efficient Japanese manufacturers, they must be prepared for the eventual breakup of the joint venture that will occur when the Japanese are fully prepared to exploit, on a worldwide scale, that same technology (doubtless improved) against their erstwhile joint-venture partners. The Japanese recognize that the West still holds the keys to important technology, and, as mentioned in earlier chapters, they will stop at nothing to gain access to that technology.

The difficulties of exploiting our own technology include the high cost and low quality of labor in the West (as compared with Japan), the highly efficient and low-cost subcontractor consortia that are available in Japan to support worldwide marketing by major manufacturers, and the high cost of R&D in some industries, such as the aircraft industry, where a huge investment is needed to develop a new aircraft type.

Japanese industry has matured at different rates, depending on the industry. The pioneers in the recent expansion of Japanese industry overseas were the consumer electronics and automobile firms. They have now reached the stage where they command large market shares in the West, and can therefore reluctantly consider manufacturing overseas, since the gestation period for building demand for their products has been short-circuited through the development of a large market based on exports. This is why Honda and Nissan are building U.S. plants, and General Motors and Toyota are on the verge of entering into a joint venture to sell a jointly developed (but 50 percent Japanese-manufactured) model in an idle GM plant in California.

Other companies in high-technology industries that are less export-oriented, such as pharmaceuticals, are just now beginning to exploit the opportunities available to them overseas. The pharmaceutical giants of Japan have learned from other industries that have developed overseas before them, and they are insisting on joint ventures that will enable them to take full or at least maximum benefit from the fruits of joint-venture inventions. One company, Takeda (the largest Japanese pharmaceutical manufacturer), has gone into a joint-venture relationship in the United States with Abbott Laboratories in an agreement that will provide Takeda with a lever to open the door to setting up its own wholly owned subsidiaries in the future. The joint venture will exploit Takeda technology not only in the United States but also in Latin America and other American markets where it would not have been advisable for Takeda to make an investment on its own.

I cite this aspect of Japanese strategy overseas to show how Western companies should expand overseas. Western industry must learn never to sell or license leading-edge technology to the Japanese. At the very least, companies ought to look for a quid pro quo, where they are assured of getting some technology of equivalent commercial value through a cross-licensing agreement.

Another critical area where steps must be taken if Western firms are to succeed in maintaining their market shares in the face of Japanese competition is the need to balance our R&D investment between what has been called "seeds and needs," or original and applied research. The transformation of these concepts into R&D budgets and strategies is of critical importance, and the Japanese do this extremely well. They recognize their limitations insofar as "seeds" research is concerned. The Japanese corporate structure does not lend itself to discoveries of breakthrough technologies. For this reason the Japanese focus on finding out everything they can about the original research going on in the West, and then spend most of their R&D budget in improving the market acceptability of Western inventions, or in executing new twists on existing technology (for example, the Sony Walkman). The Japanese are no longer a nation of copiers—they have become a nation of improvers. The manufacturer studies and restudies what consumers want, and makes sure that they get it. A recent letter to the editor in the *Japan Times* (an English-language newspaper in Tokyo) compared the quality of American (Harley-Davidson) and Japanese (Kawasaki and Honda) motorcycles. Both have used the same basic technology, but the Japanese companies have excelled in giving consumers what they want through "needs" research:

> . . . in 80 years, Harley has just introduced minor improvements in their machines, which are completely obsolete. Their general performance isn't much better than a standard Japanese 400; vibration is painful, even dropping parts after a several hundred kilometers ride. Braking is below average; suspension induces a queasy stomach very easily; they are not provided with necessary tools; their 1,338 cc engine provides a modest 60 bhp, compared with Kawasaki's 120 bhp and 1,286 cc for instance. Acceleration (one important sales point) of Harleys is not better than most quick Japanese 250s.

And then the writer, who is obviously a motorbike buff, goes on to say:

> And they are more expensive than the most expensive Japanese motorcycles. The latter are faster, cheaper, better designed, better handling,

smooth, silent, offer you the choice between singles, vee-twins, two stroked water cooled twins, transverse and flat fours, transverse sixes, turbo charged models, DOHC, chain and shaft driven models, most with impeccable braking and suspension, fuel economy, overwhelming power and acceleration (what most fans look for in motorcycles) and few mechanical troubles.

Compared with my own transverse four, 16 valve, DOHC, 80 bhp Honda, any Harley Davidson is just an agricultural tractor on two wheels, far from the choice of most buyers. . . .[1]

This is just one man's opinion, obviously, and it is easy to discern that it is a subject dear to his heart, so that his thoughts may not be entirely objective. However, his letter was inspired by a call for protectionist legislation to allow Harley-Davidson a breather from Japanese competition, and this fact alone suggests that Harley-Davidson has suffered a body blow from Japanese competition. The Japanese emphasis is on achieving ever-increasing standards of excellence, whereas many Western firms seem content to rest on their laurels.

This focus on finding out what the consumer wants and proceeding to provide it is not magic, and it is not unique to Japanese business. American consumer product companies and service-sector firms are pioneers in market research and in tailoring the product to the market. These techniques can be used in all sectors; they need not be confined to the market for consumer perishables and services alone. If Western firms are to hold on to their markets, a continuing commitment to the highest standards possible in living up to consumer expectations is potentially the most important area on which to concentrate. The Japanese challenge in the area of consumer product and service is negligible because the Japanese know that they can, at best, find niches in the market for their specialty products, such as noodles and Benihana restaurants, soy sauce and sake. General Foods, Procter & Gamble, and Unilever would have no difficulty competing with Kao Soap, Lion, or Sunstar (three leading Japanese consumer-product companies) in Western markets. It is the manufacturers of machine tools, personal computers, automotive vehicles and machines, video discs, and refrigerators who have the most to fear. So far they have been content to provide the Western consumer with far less than the Japanese can deliver, and as a result, are the most vulnerable to attack. For example, in one case, an American appliance manufacturer decided to export refrigerators to Japan, but the project was a dismal failure because the refrigerators were too big and noisy for small, thin-walled Japanese homes. Such flagrant disregard for even the minimal requirements of the consumer is suicidal when competing with the Japanese, either in Japan or in one's own domestic market.

The question of export orientation is in fact related to that of product tailoring. Western companies must learn to compete with the Japanese in the overseas marketplace. Every Japanese company with a manufacturing capability is interested in export, and as explained in previous chapters, even the smallest manufacturing companies can become involved, either through the trading company or as part of a *zaikai,* whereby they provide parts and accessories for a finished product being exported by a large *zaikai* manufacturer.

One of the difficulties of export that is frequently cited by many medium and small-sized manufacturers in the West is that requirements for documentation are different in almost every country. Export also requires first-class market intelligence. It requires capable and dedicated sales engineers or sales representatives traveling the potential markets and backing up local agents with technical and after-sales support. Export business usually requires personnel with multilingual capability, and it takes patience and perseverance. Many American and some European companies simply can't be bothered. As a result they live in a cocoon of self-delusion, only to wake up one day to find that the Japanese are breathing heavily down their necks, poised and ready to enter their markets with a product that is both better and cheaper. If they had been active in the export market, they would have been forced to develop a competing product, and this in turn would have protected their market at home. The new export trading companies that are being formed in the United States by General Electric and others may give potential exporters an extra pair of eyes, ears, and hands that will enable smaller American firms to gain experience before venturing out on their own.

There is a tendency in the West to rely on time-tested methods of getting things done. This applies particularly in the manufacturing area. There are so many innovations in manufacturing these days that one could spend an entire working day just keeping track of innovation in a given manufacturing industry. The Japanese do exactly that. They regard having the latest manufacturing technology as a source of corporate pride. I can still remember the shock that registered on the faces of a visiting American congressional delegation when they were taken to Nissan's new automated manufacturing facility at Zama near Tokyo. The only jobs for people in this factory are checking dials and giving the computer occasional instructions. Similarly, in Yamanouchi Pharmaceutical's Yaezu plant near Shizuoka the computer controls everything from the "pick and pack" warehouse area to a totally automated pharmaceutical injectable filling area. Even the filled ampoules are light-inspected by an automatic inspection machine that is 100 percent accurate. Many American pharmaceutical firms still use female workers to physically inspect ampoules to check for foreign material. The Yamanouchi plant is now felt to be outdated (it is over ten years old) and a new modern facility is being built to take its place.

The following statistics are revealing of how far ahead the Japanese are in automation:

TABLE 4

Robot Population of Major Countries by Type of Robot (1981)[a]

| | PROGRAMMABLE | | | |
	SERVO-CONTROLLED	NON-SERVO	MECHANICAL TRANSFER DEVICES	TOTAL
Japan	6,899	7,347	53,189	67,435
U.S.A.	2,400	1,700	—	4,100
Germany, F.R.	1,120	300	10,000	11,420
U.K.	—	—	—	371

[a]Excluding manual manipulators.

SOURCE: *Japan 1982, An International Comparison* (Keizai Koho Center, Japan Institute for Social and Economic Affairs).

A typical Japanese tactic is to look for the soft underbelly of the competitors that they are targeting in a Western market. The weak point of most Western firms tends to be at the low end of the market where profits are not so exciting but where volume and turnover will justify a large-scale marketing commitment. Many American and European manufacturers surrender this end of the market to the Japanese almost without a struggle, since the accountants that seem to be in charge of most companies these days emphasize the negligible contribution that the low-end products have on the profit-and-loss statement. It happened in automobiles, it is happening in copiers, it happened in fasteners, it is happening in personal computers. From Silicon Valley to Boston, wherever American firms are developing new and exciting technology, there is a corps of Japanese liaison offices monitoring and evaluating the results to see if they can make something based on that technology which is cheaper, more efficient, and more in line with what the customer wants and can afford. My advice would be to concentrate on new low-end products and make it harder for the Japanese to get that first foothold.

Admittedly, defending the low end of the market can be expensive. Timing and a correct assessment of potential market share are crucial, as witness the fiasco at Texas Instruments when they decided to sell the 99/4A home computer for only $99. The computer retailed for $1,000 in 1979, when it was introduced. The ill-timed slash in the price, although it did succeed in putting the 99/4A near the top of the market, ultimately resulted in a loss—according to one estimate, perhaps as much as $50 per machine.[2] This mistake put Texas Instruments many millions of dollars in the red. The current price war at the low end of the home-computer market is a prime example of what happens when things get out of hand. The danger is that indiscriminate price cutting will make most of the U.S. firms abandon the low end. Then, of course, the Japanese will move in. If they arrive sooner, in the usual laser-beam fashion, using their customary impeccable marketing strategies, the already battle-weary American firms that might otherwise have stuck it out may well end up in full retreat. The decision to fight it out, especially at the low end of the market, is never an easy one. It must be taken only as the result of a carefully prepared strategy, and possible losses *must* be preplanned.

General Motors' move to recapture part of the low end of the small-car market by building an ultramodern plant in Spain is an example of the right way to go about building market share in this sector. The car being built in the new plant is the Corsa, designed by Opel, GM's German subsidiary. One of the factors that entered into the decision to locate in a small village in Spain was the lower cost of labor there, but cheap labor alone is not enough. In order to sell a car as well engineered and as cheap as Japanese autos, GM has enforced cost cutting in all possible areas, including maximum use of robots. They are also using another Japanese technique, the *kanban* system, where they order parts only just before assembly so that they can keep inventory costs down.

Although it is true that the present Japanese advantage stems not so much from low-cost labor (wages and benefits approach parity with those of other industrialized countries) as from automation, quality control, management, and other factors, nevertheless U.S. firms fighting for their lives will have to consider carefully the advantages of locating plants in low-wage countries. Automation, modernization, and improved use of human resources will be crucial in the long run, but for the present the multinationals may be forced to adopt this practice if they are to succeed in competing against the Japanese.

Although I have been emphasizing the importance of low-end market share, this does not mean that Japanese interest is limited to the low end. It would not be surprising to see the Japanese introducing large, luxuriously appointed rivals to the Cadillac and the Mercedes. Two likely candidates are the Nissan President and the Toyota Century. Now that they have the low end of the automobile market in full retreat, they can afford to set their sights on the high end as well. Ricoh and Canon have avoided taking on Xerox in the high-speed-copier market, but they have gained significant share at the low end—the slow, single-copy, small office copier. It is doubtful that the Japanese will be content to remain confined to this one market segment, and Western companies that make the mistake of complacently assuming that the Japanese aim for only one market segment may soon have a rude awakening.

Turning from marketing and manufacturing innovation, which is central to mounting any successful opposition to the Japanese, I should here reemphasize the need to alter our financial objectives to meet the Japanese challenge. I work for an American company that has over half its business overseas, and I recognize the difficulty of changing from a short- to a long-term view of the marketplace. Opportunities are missed daily at American companies because projects that have real market potential are shot down by the exigencies of the quarterly-earnings statement. The same must hold true for European firms as well. In contrast with this, the Japanese approach is to focus on growth and let the profits take care of themselves. This is part of the reason why Japanese companies are more prone to go into bankruptcy when the financial resources are strained by pursuing too many projects at once. Nevertheless, one seldom hears of a major Japanese firm heavily involved in exports getting itself into an unrecoverable situation. The one celebrated case, Ataka & Company, is highly unusual. (One reason for the fact that big Japanese companies seldom go under, despite heavy borrowing, is the special relationship they enjoy with their banks, which was discussed in Chapter 12.) When I say that the Japanese have a long-term point of view, I mean that once they have decided to enter a market they have the patience and tenacity to wait years for profits. It is rumored that it took Toyota eight years before it made its first profit in the United States. Investment spending, payout plans, and long-term strategies with worldwide marketing roll-out plans are highly expensive exercises, but they are part of the reality of a world where the Japanese are setting the pace.

Counterstrategies in the marketing, manufacturing, and finance areas are critical, but the main lesson of the Japanese experience in the past ten years is the emphasis on quality and after-sales service. Any manufacturing company in the West that has not heeded the lessons of William Ouchi's *Theory Z* and Pascale and Athos's *Art of Japanese Management,* both of which emphasized that quality control is directly linked to worker involvement, is going to have great difficulty with Japanese competition. In *Business and Society in Japan* is cited the tragic example of the price American semiconductor manufacturers paid as a direct result of insufficient attention to quality:

> For components such as semiconductor integrated circuits, reliability, that is, failure rates, is a very important consideration for potential buyers. By the 1980's, Japan had been provided with clear proof that their computer memory chips were more reliable than American ones. In a comparison that quickly gained attention in the industry, Hewlett Packard, one of the largest American makers of hand held calculators, small computers and other scientific instruments, tested over 300,000 memory chips from three American and three Japanese suppliers. *The failure rate of the worst Japanese supplier was six times better than the failure rate of the best American supplier.* [3] [My italics.]

In fact, the shoddiness of American goods has produced a feeling among ordinary Japanese that Japan can beat the Americans in any manufacturing industry in which they decide to compete seriously. This makes it difficult for American companies to sell their products in Japan, since the buyer/consumer who used to feel that foreign, and particularly American, products are usually superior to their own Japanese products, is now inclined to be dubious about the quality of most Western-manufactured goods. The Japanese import only a few thousand American cars each year, but none can be sold until the paintwork has been brought up to Japanese standards, and many parts of the interior finish have to be redone to satisfy the demanding Japanese consumer.

It is small wonder that Japanese manufacturers ran away with the small-car market in the United States. Fuel economy was admittedly the deciding factor. Nevertheless, Japanese quality control delighted consumers who had become accustomed to ripped upholstery and broken plastic door handles within a few months of purchasing one of the cheaper models turned out by Detroit. And women especially appreciated being able to buy cars with standard steering that didn't require bulging biceps to manipulate, as well as doors that can be closed easily even by those who are not weight lifters. Detroit has yet to learn some of these simple lessons. Indeed, the strenuous effort required to close the door of many U.S. models is possibly a "nontariff barrier" to the successful import of American cars to Japan, although the Japanese government can hardly be held responsible for the size of its people. It is by attention to such details of consumer preference, and a refusal to sacrifice quality in the name of cost cutting, that Japan has achieved success.

One vital area when competing with the Japanese is the commitment to the preparation of long-term counterstrategies. IBM is well versed in this. As early as 1977 it was employing several of its top sales engineers and research people in a counterstrategy team based in Tokyo and New York that monitored every activity of Fujitsu, Hitachi, NEC, and the other Japanese computer makers. IBM knew that the Japanese government was providing significant financial and coordinating assistance in the development of new techniques for the manufacture of VLSI (very large scale integration) chips. Over a five-year period the Japanese spent over $800 million in developing this breakthrough technology. IBM marketing teams prepared counterstrategies that have so far kept the Japanese at bay, although Fujitsu has recently managed to capture from IBM Japan the top position among computer makers in Japan. In the field of chip-making machines, the Japanese companies JEOL and Toshiba are now working on electron-beam equipment that should eventually allow them to write microcircuit diagrams directly onto silicon wafers by computer, thus ensuring absolute accuracy. According to an article in the *Economist* (January 15, 1983), just three years earlier almost three-fourths of the sophisticated equipment required in the Japanese semiconductor industry had been imported from the United States. But by 1982 domestic suppliers were providing 50 percent of the necessary equipment, and Japanese manufacturers of such equipment were expected to capture most of the rest of the domestic market by the end of 1983 and be ready to go into exporting to the United States. IBM has invested over $13 billion in the past ten years on new plant and equipment in order to counter the Japanese onslaught, and has now reorganized itself into independent business units to explore and exploit new markets and technologies. These units do not have to go through the entire corporate structure to get approval for new projects. IBM also has become more open toward cooperation and collaboration with other firms for the long-term good of IBM. If more American and European firms took the IBM approach, life would be more difficult for Japanese manufacturers. Significantly, IBM is one of the firms most often cited for the excellence of its management, and for its genuine commitment to including all employees as members of the team. It appears to be ready for the long haul—and none too soon, to judge by the speed with which the Japanese are determinedly overtaking America's headstart in the computer industry.

Another key to IBM's success in containing the Japanese is its strong position in the Japanese market itself. By being there and controlling a significant share of the Japanese market—it was a market leader until recently—it has been in a much better position to anticipate and counter the Japanese. A few American and European companies have followed the IBM example in this respect, and have significant benefits to show for their commitment. Texas Instruments, NCR, Control Data, Univac, Pfizer, and Bristol-Myers are but a few of the American firms that have gone into Japan in a big way. Although the primary motive in every case is to obtain a profitable market for their products in Japan, these companies have all benefited from the intelligence-gathering bonus that comes with full integration into the Japanese industrial scene. Large European companies, such as ICI, Philips, and Siemens, have also benefited from this strategy. The old saying "The best defense is a good offense" applies to the strategy of all companies that have been most successful in fending off a Japanese threat.

Even if the Japanese market does not give every company scope for investment, it is worth opening an office in Japan just to monitor developments, and to keep on the alert for potential opportunities in export and investment as well as joint ventures or reverse technology transfer. There are very few companies susceptible to Japanese competition that could not justify putting an office in Tokyo to keep an eye on their potential competitors at close quarters. Despite this fact, as of 1982 two hundred of the Fortune 500 companies still had no presence in Japan.

It is vital that a company have contingency plans worked out against the day when Japanese companies begin moving in on its markets. By examining vulnerable divisions or product lines before it is too late, and making it one's business to know what the Japanese are likely to do, the Western company will be able to launch much more effective countermoves. For example, it should be obvious to Boeing and Airbus that the Japanese are getting ready to make a major entrance into the aircraft industry. Pharmaceutical companies expecting to compete in the field of biotechnology should make it their business to know that Japanese companies are working furiously on developing this technology. The Japanese have targeted every high-technology industry as a focus for concerted attention to research and development and monitoring of worldwide trends. The Japanese are ready to move into machine tools and transportation machinery, agricultural equipment and earthmoving/construction equipment. If it weren't for the high cost of petrochemicals, it is likely that Sumitomo Chemicals, Mitsubishi Chemicals, and other large Japanese firms in the chemical field would be giving ICI, Dow, and Dupont a run for their money today.

Answering the Japanese challenge also means that some management methods sacrosant to Western managers are going to have to change. I do not advocate that Western executives immediately adopt Japanese management techniques, such as the *ringi* system, or spend every night drinking with their colleagues in order to promote *ningen kankei*. Such practices are too deeply rooted in particular Japanese traditions and circumstances to be transplanted successfully to the West. But there are some aspects of Japanese management worth adapting and emulating within our own cultural framework.

Topping the list of such management techniques is the breakdown of the artificial barriers between management and labor. It is simply counterproductive to have executive dining rooms serving dry martinis when the middle and lower ranks are confined to cafeterias serving soda pop. Japanese managers don't eat with factory workers, but neither are they segregated by rank into signposted enclaves of privilege. By eliminating ostentatious class barriers and taking such simple steps as encouraging a manager to have lunch with his staff, whether blue or white collar, a feeling of mutual participation in the activities of the enterprise can be fostered. Executives may bewail the lack of company spirit in their work force, but it is the attitude of management which molds that of all the other workers. The beauty of this simple policy change is that the place where the good ideas are—at the lower levels—can be reached and tapped. Many of the talented junior employees of large high-technology firms in the West have the ambition to go into business for themselves one day. One of the main reasons for this desire is to be free of the bureaucracy of large firms, but a more important factor is the feeling that no one above cares about the junior staffer's ideas for improving not only the operation of his department but that of the company itself. Suggestion boxes just don't do the trick (unless there is a very enthusiastic management push behind them), because there is nothing quite like having the chance to tell a sympathetic and interested superior what you would do if you were in his place. I remember trying this once in my junior trainee days and being told in no uncertain terms that as a trainee I wasn't expected to have ideas, that I should only learn from my seniors.

Peter Drucker was one of the first to point out the advantages of the Japanese de-emphasis of a demarcation between labor and management. In one of his books he says, "The purpose of an organization is to enable common men to do uncommon things."[4] The best Japanese firms (and the best Western ones, for that matter) never lose sight of this goal, and are well aware of the dearth of true genius, as well as of its erratic nature. Thus they are able to forge teams that work together for solid progress, have no patience with grandstanding, and do not suffer from the "superstar" mentality that operates as a demoralizing force among the managerial staff of so many

American companies. Introducing a shift away from the traditional management style will be hardest for British firms, where the gap between the ranks is highly formalized, but it shouldn't be as difficult for Americans, and the Germans are already doing it.

Another important but intangible way for a company to work at staying ahead of the Japanese is to have a long-range strategy—and actually stick to it. Many companies go through token "management by objective" (MBO) exercises that really do nothing but irritate the managers who have to submit to them, because they know that they will be judged on P-and-L performance and on today's performance, not tomorrow's. A good friend of mine, Jim Balloun, a director of McKenzie & Company and former head of their Tokyo office, has summed up this point beautifully in a recent magazine article:

> Simply put, the Japanese have developed a way to manage complex organizations with great simplicity. Interestingly, much of what they do is strikingly similar to practices we've identified in "excellent" American companies. . . .
>
> This similarity is seen in four pillars of Japanese organization—characteristics that I believe are the real sources of their success: (1) They treat people as members of the organization, not as employees. (2) They use shared values, not detailed procedures and controls to guide operations. (3) They take a "big think" approach to business strategy. (4) They are good listeners.[5]

One of the outgrowths of this management philosophy is the development of fierce loyalty and caring by members for the firm. My company, for example, has encouraged this kind of commitment by not hiring from outside and by not laying off. These are simple steps, but they can have a remarkable effect on the morale of the organization.

Another simple step is looking after retirees. This means nothing more than having the president of each operating division or group within the company write at least one letter a year to each retiree to see how he is getting on, and to try to help solve problems that are difficult for them to handle because of advancing age or lack of understanding of the latest company policy. Giving retirees a decent adjustment when inflation eats into their fixed incomes (something that British and Japanese companies always do, but few American firms feel is necessary) and publishing news of retirees in the company house organ are other positive measures which could be taken.

These small steps not only help retirees and their families but also affect the whole organization, since they are proof of Jim Balloun's first principle: "Treat people as members of the organization, not as employees." I was impressed when I was visited in Tokyo by a retired Procter & Gamble executive who wanted to ask me a number of questions about the problems of American businessmen in Japan. P&G had pulled him out of retirement to look into various aspects of company strategy in Japan, because they needed someone with both the time and the experience. His lifelong dedication to Procter and Gamble was self-evident, and was, moreover, being recognized and rewarded by the company.

Another key to Japanese success is the use of generalists rather than specialists in key management positions. Going back to Jim Balloun's point about making complex organizations simple, he criticizes the latest fad in American banks, the so-called matrix system:

> . . . we have an impossible paradox. On the one hand size and diversity lead to complexity. The ultimate rational response to complexity is the matrix, extensive planning and control systems, precise specialization reinforced by position descriptions, and accompanying massive staffs. This rational approach misses the need in modern business for innovation rather than efficiency, and skips over the fact that innovation comes from thinking generalists who cross organizational boundaries.[6]

As Peter Drucker has pointed out, the ultimate need in business is not efficiency but effectiveness. Inefficiently doing the right thing is a thousand times better than efficiently doing the wrong thing.[7]

The European response to the American attack on their markets in the fifties and sixties was to recognize the superiority of American management systems, and to reorient their thinking to accommodate such concepts as product management, marketing strategies, corporate planning, and vertical and horizontal integration. Management training is now flourishing in Europe, and Peter Drucker is as well known at Henley and Ashridge, Fontainebleau and Vevrey as he is at Harvard and Stanford. But how many American or European business schools are training tomorrow's corporate leaders to compete with the Japanese? According to the Japan-U.S. Friendship Commission, there are only a handful of schools that spend any time on Japanese management systems. The commission has developed a module on Japanese management systems that I was privileged to help evaluate when I was president of the American Chamber of

Commerce in Japan. This module, or something like it, should be integrated into the curricula of management schools throughout the West. There is no conceivable way for Western business to hold on to its markets if it fails to study and understand the factors that have made the Japanese challenge so formidable.

PART
FOUR

WORKING WITH
THE JAPANESE

CHAPTER
14

PLAYING THE HARP

An American businessman is quoted in Robert Christopher's book *The Japanese Mind* as saying, "In my industry the Japanese are coming on like gangbusters, and I either have to lick 'em or join 'em— or maybe a little bit of both." Those who intend to "join 'em"—or straddle the fence—will need to know not how to fight but how to get along.

This chapter is concerned with what foreigners have to do to gain entrance to the seemingly impenetrable workings of a Japanese organization and get the responses out of it that they are looking for. The chapter title is my metaphor for the necessary process of sounding all the levels of a Japanese company in order to produce a harmonious response. Before explaining how exactly to go about "playing the harp," I must expand on some of the points made earlier about the contrast between Western and Japanese-style management and organizational structure.

In the development of Western management thinking over the past half century, two conflicting schools of thought have emerged. On the one hand there is the "behavioral sciences" school exemplified by Douglas McGregor's Theory Y, which holds that an organization functions best when it allows employees to progress toward self-actualization and self-fulfillment through participation in decision making and establishing the objectives of the organization. In a sense this school puts people above products and profit, although the theory is that if people feel happy and are presented with adequate challenges, profits should follow. The McGregor school was a reaction to the older Theory X, which placed importance on the bottom line, contending that employees would function best if they were told what to do, how to do it, and then suitably rewarded financially when they did it.

The older mainstream trend of management thinking in the West has been the "management science" school. It is a descendant of the turn-of-the-century Theory X system in that it stresses achievement of corporate goals, but it has been updated and now emphasizes the use of mathematical models and computers to assist the manager in decision-making. Such scientifically managed companies are usually highly structured and hierarchical, with employees having well-defined roles and areas of responsibility. People are hired to fill these roles who are specialists in whatever area is required. Motivation of employees is important, but this school, led by Peter Drucker and others, puts a heavy emphasis on decision-making by scientific means, and on the importance of corporate profitability.

Elements from both these schools can be seen in the Japanese system, with superficially slightly more Theory Y than Theory X, but it also contains other aspects unique to it. The ideal Japanese organization maintains harmony and a unified sense of purpose among all its elements. One of the means of achieving this goal is to foster belief in and dedication to a fixed company culture and company philosophy. Employees (members of the organization) adhere to a code of behavior and generally have a deep faith that the company will always stand by them in the event of any personal crisis. One could call the dominant Japanese style of management Theory J, although management in Japan has not traditionally been approached in the scientific rationalistic manner common in the West. Some label the Japanese system as simply feudal, a grafting of the old *daimyo* system onto modern industries and corporations, but that is a gross oversimplification. The Japanese organization fosters a sense of personal responsibility in all of its members for what happens in the company, and backs this up by a concern for consulting and garnering the support of all the people involved. One writer puts it this way:

> Even when top-level managers formulate certain strategic projects, they do not finalize their plans until middle-to lower-echelon managers have had an opportunity to refine and often revise these strategies to

fit the means that middle- to lower-echelon managers have for implementing such plans. As extensive consultations take place among the individuals involved in implementing these plans who are scattered throughout the various subunits of the firm, a chosen course of action, once put into effect, is well understood by the corporate members.[1]

The key phrase here is "scattered throughout . . . the firm." There is no one right person to consult in order to proceed. There is a definite hierarchy, but things don't happen by executive fiat. This is quite different from the ancient feudal system. The only way in which modern Japanese corporations are more feudal than their Western counterparts is in their commitment to the welfare of their employees. Indeed, companies rigidly controlled by a chief executive who insists on having final approval over every decision are in one sense more feudal—and certainly more autocratic—than most Japanese companies. Getting a foot in the door of a Japanese company dedicated to a consensual, decentralized, sharing-of-responsibility approach is not a simple task.

When working with a Western company dedicated to Theory Y, one must investigate the organization carefully to see where the decisions are made that will affect the business proposal. Decisions may be made by group consensus, and in Theory Y organizations with matrix systems of management and committees for everything it isn't always obvious whom to cultivate. Also, to be easily accepted, the proposal should take into account the human element—i.e., it should not be a purely rational decision based on what is best for the quarterly-earnings statement, regardless of how it affects employees. Nevertheless, after a certain amount of exploratory groundwork, it is possible to discover where to go and whom to see for the specific project one has in mind.

In a scientifically managed company such explorations are usually not necessary. One merely looks up the relevant department in the organizational chart, and goes to see the person indicated. If the proposal makes sound business sense and fits into the strategy or marketing plans of the company, one can be assured of a fair hearing. The budget is a mighty instrument in such a company, and only if there is room in the budget, or if it is such a good idea that another budget item can be scrapped in its place, will the deal go through.

In the West both Theory X and Theory Y have the discipline of quarterly-earnings statements mandating an underlying similarity.

Because Theory J and Theory Y might seem to have a lot in common, I relate the following story to show where and how radically they differ. In 1981 I went on a tour of several American cities to speak on U.S.-Japanese economic relations. One of my stops was Chicago, where I spoke at a meeting of the America-Japan Society. The first day of the program consisted of visits to a number of Chicago-based companies that were assisting in the sponsorship of the conference. Most of those on the tour were Japanese businessmen, plus a few other interested members of the Tokyo delegation, including me. Our first stop was about a half hour out of Chicago at a company with a head office located in a garden adjacent to a large horticultural area. With paintings on the walls and atriums, the offices were truly gorgeous, and there was no easy way of telling which was the chairman's office and which the lowest analyst's. We were met by the company's dynamic CEO (who, incidentally, shook hands with the Japanese with all the grace and lightness of a water buffalo). He obviously had the company under his complete control, was very dedicated, and was trying to create as perfect a working environment as humanly possible in order to motivate his staff to meet the challenges of the 1980's. But his Japanese guests were not impressed. When we returned to the bus, the Japanese participants commented on the extravagance, the lack of differentiation between the various levels of the company, the incredible waste of space wherever the atriums and open areas were preserved, the general inefficiency—as it seemed from their point of view—of having most people in individual cubbyholes, cubicles, or offices.

Here was a clear physical example of the contrast between Theory Y and the Japanese system. To the Japanese an efficient office is a large open area filled with desks where everybody can hear what everybody else is doing. They consider the noise and constant ringing of telephones a healthy sign of activity. The boss sits at the end of the room and is available at all times to answer questions and monitor progress. There is a conference room for greeting visitors that can be used by almost anybody (in descending order of hierarchy and rank of the visitor) when it is free, and if it isn't, there are secondary conference rooms located throughout the building. There should not be an inch of space devoted to anything except the practical necessities, such as files and office equipment. After all, that is why one comes to work—not to look at pictures, gardens or interior decoration. Anything that is distracting in the workplace other than slogans exhorting the employee to work diligently would take his mind off the seriousness of the job at hand. It is true that the cost of office space in downtown Tokyo and other urban centers in Japan prevents most Japanese companies from finding space for anything except essentials, but the Japanese seem to regard such amenities not as an impossible ideal but rather as a waste.

The Theory Y behavioral approach to management—giving the workers a sense of fulfilling their individual desires for "self-actualization" and offering them outstanding facilities to work in—is completely alien to the Japanese. Therefore, when working with the Japanese, it is important to remember that they regard these kinds of luxuries—in fact, anything that is not strictly functional but merely aesthetically pleasing—as inappropriate for a workplace. By contrast, conference rooms are usually decorated in accordance with the rank of the average users. *Kachō*-level conference rooms are stark and practical, whereas the conference rooms on the executive floor are beautifully decorated because they are not considered "work areas." As explained in previous chapters, the higher you go in a Japanese company, the more ceremonial the executive's function becomes.

Because the Japanese orientation is different, inexperienced Westerners with a business proposal to put before a Japanese company will have a tough time figuring out where to start. If they are in Japan the task will be easier. Trying to get the Japanese company interested in any major proposal without coming to Japan is perhaps possible but highly unlikely. Routine transactions of buying and selling, exporting/importing of commodities, and so forth, can be and are done by and through the overseas branches of Japanese companies, but anything of major financial or strategic significance can be decided only at the head office in Japan.

Often the Western company wants to deal with the manufacturer of a product but is prevented from doing so by the trading-company margins and financial activities surrounding the sale or purchase (as discussed in Chapter 12). In such a case it again means that the Western businessman must come to Japan to try to resolve the issue. But once he arrives in Japan after such fruitless preliminaries, he will find that the real mystery awaits him. If he walks into the reception area of a large Japanese company without an appointment and asks to see "the man who deals with widgets," he will be confronted by a very confused receptionist. In the end she will probably ask the visitor to either give her a name and make an appointment, or, at

best, fetch some English-speaking employee to serve as an interpreter. But this is unlikely to help much, because the interpreter
won't have the power to do anything but make polite sounds of
disappointment and suggest that the visitor contact the Japanese
company's U.S. or European branch, "which deals with this sort of
thing."

Obviously, no Western business person will try such a crude approach for a matter of any importance—it rarely works anywhere.
However, even assuming that one has the name of the right person
to see, one is still light years away from getting an answer. There is
no one entry point or window where a proposal is first mooted. Even
after the Japanese company nominates a liaison person with whom
one is to deal officially, one is still expected to work a proposal
through every level of management and every concerned department. By doing this the *ringi* system (described in Chapter 7) will be
put in motion. Everyone involved must put their seal of concurrence
on the proposal before it becomes a reality. Only when the outsider
has obtained a favorable response from all those concerned will he
have sounded the chord he needs to hear from the corporate harp.

Speaking from years of experience in this area, I would strongly
recommend that Western executives have realistic objectives before
they begin the flight to Tokyo. If this is the first time a subject or
proposal is being broached, one shouldn't expect anything except a
hearing. Before leaving home, they should send out feelers to discover if they can contact anyone who knows anything about the
company they are interested in. If they turn up someone who will
provide a letter of introduction, so much the better, since the Japanese like to operate on a person-to-person basis. If no such contact
is possible, the next best procedure is to write to the commercial
section of one's country's embassy in Tokyo requesting information.
Alternatively, it is possible to get such information from JETRO (the
Japan External Trade Organization). JETRO will certainly be able to
provide the necessary information, but there is a drawback: since
JETRO's purpose is to assist Japanese business, it will inform any
Japanese who cares to inquire of the interest you have shown in
Company X.

Once one has found out the name of the person to be contacted,
one should write to him, clearly explaining everything about one's
company, its background, its financial situation, its bank references,

its links with larger companies, and its present situation in Japan, and enclose annual reports for the past five years. In the next letter, to follow the acknowledgment of the first letter by the correct *kachō,* the proposal should be outlined in general terms, stressing the mutual advantages but without giving details. Only after a reply has been received to this second letter, with a positive expression of interest or at least a commitment to study the matter closely, should a trip be proposed.

Before advising the Japanese company directly of an intention to visit Japan, it is beneficial to examine the entire project as carefully as possible, trying to anticipate every technical question or other problem that the Japanese might raise. Next, Japanese translations of key technical summaries should be prepared to make it easier for their technical people (who are less comfortable in English than their marketing and sales counterparts) to understand the gist of the proposal. I would recommend that if one is from a European Economic Community country that he contact the commercial sections of the EEC legation and his embassy again, and ask them to do a profile of the Japanese company concerned. The American business person will find that the foreign commercial service officer at the embassy is the best person to contact. These reports will almost always be inadequate, because this function isn't given the priority it deserves at the embassies in Tokyo. Instead of maintaining reference books and files about their own industry for the Japanese, the Western embassies should be maintaining information on Japanese companies for their own business people. In this area they could follow the example of the defense attachés, whose sole job is to know what is going on in the host country.

There is one final step that must be taken before the Western executives book their tickets. A vital element is missing, one that almost every Western business person completely forgets. Who will do the follow-up? Once a Japanese company is interested in something, matters cannot be expected to go smoothly unless there is someone on the spot in Japan to follow up after the initial advances have been made.

This follow-up person will play the harp before, after, and in between visits from people in the home office. He will keep them advised on how the proposal is faring within the Japanese company. If technical questions seem to be holding up progress, he will pass along this information to the Western company's head office before the Japanese do, because until they know an organization well, they will be reluctant to do anything that might embarrass it. Having a person based in Japan avoids the classic situation that arises when Western management is looking for a quick response from its "Japanese project," and all the concerned executive can say is that everything was fine when he was there two months ago, and that he hasn't heard anything to the contrary since then. To work with the Japanese, one must play the harp all the time, not just when one happens to be on the scene.

It is quite easy to find people in Tokyo, Osaka, and Nagoya to do this follow-up at a reasonable price. There are a number of well-placed American and European businessmen running their own consultancy business who specialize in this type of activity. However, if the project is big enough, an arrangement with a consultant should last only as long as there is any doubt about the viability of the project. With a suitable incentive to ensure that such doubts are quickly dispelled, the consultant will be ready to take a backseat when the time comes and assist the persons whom the company eventually stations in Japan.

When Western business people approach Japanese companies in order to get something done or to work with them on a project, it is important to make certain that every level of management in the Japanese company, from bottom to top, has had ample opportunity to look at the proposed activity and give it some thought. They should be prepared, when the official proposal is put forward and when the *ringi* system goes into effect, to make their mark on the piece of paper approving the action. In Tokyo I used to spend hours and hours playing the harp in the Japanese companies that I worked with. I had some five companies that I had direct daily interaction with because we had actively marketed products with them and, in addition, some eight product development relationships that required at least monthly if not more frequent meetings.

To give an example, when it came time for the annual marketing plans to be prepared and approved, I had to ensure their acceptance in the five companies with which we had marketing relationships. I would usually spend a lot of time within my own company making sure that we had considered all the aspects relevant to the marketing problems of the product on which we were trying to work with the Japanese. At the same time I would begin the task of letting the Japanese company's marketing group become aware of some of the key elements of our marketing plan so that they would already be familiar with them when we officially presented our plan. I would send my marketing manager or his deputy to the marketing manager of the Japanese company to explain informally how we regarded the following year's advertising and promotional activities, and to make sure that he was in general agreement with us. Once the plans were more or less final, and again before presenting them formally to the Japanese company, a second stroking of the harp would take place, once again at the marketing level. I would meet with the marketing manager or deputy manager of each company to discuss informally the general outline of the proposed plan. Then would come the final day when the presentation would take place. Here the selection of venue was important, and we made sure at least a week beforehand that the Japanese company had copies of everything we were recommending and that there were no surprises. As mentioned in previous chapters, there's nothing the Japanese hate worse than a surprise. In fact, a formal meeting is usually nothing but a confirmation of what has already been decided on an informal basis. Each side tends to read out their proposals and decisions in a ceremonial fashion. Very little is decided at such formal meetings; what happens is that decisions are "confirmed."

Once the plan was presented at the formal meeting, we would ask our Japanese opposite numbers to tell us when they thought they could inform us if the plan was approved, or if not, what changes they would require. Because we had taken care to give plenty of time for the proposal to percolate through the Japanese company prior to our presentation, they could usually give us a rough timetable. But the job was not finished here, because it was necessary to take the plan that had been approved in principle by their marketing department on up the ladder to the managing director or executive managing director, and sometimes even to the chairman in person, so that they were aware of the key elements. If there was anything controversial, we would give a rationale for it. This prevented the plan from being shot down behind our backs, as it were, and ensured that our point of view was presented to all levels.

Playing the harp is important not just for major decisions, such as the one for the annual marketing plan, but also in any contact with the Japanese where the Western business person feels that what is being proposed has more than routine significance. For example, if Westerners working with a Japanese company wish to propose any kind of idea, whether business-related or not, they should always present it to several levels within the company, always exploring from the bottom up rather than the top down. The only time an exception to this rule might be valid would be at an informal after-drinks exchange with the top executives of the Japanese company, when one senses that the atmosphere is sufficiently relaxed to allow the proposal of an idea, while realizing that one will still have to go back through formal channels. This informal probing may occasionally be possible in order to get a reaction before beginning the process of harp stroking, but much depends on the relationship that the Westerner enjoys with the senior Japanese.

Getting a prior reaction is possible only in such informal circumstances as those I have just described. When I was still fairly new on the job I discovered this fact the hard way. One of our U.S. subsidiary presidents called me at two in the morning with what he felt was a revolutionary new idea on how my company might work together with our Japanese joint-venture partner. He described the concept in some detail, and despite my drowsiness, I, too, was enthusiastic about the idea, but was sufficiently new to Japan not to recognize the danger signals when he told me to take the idea to the president of the Japanese company in order to explore it with him confidentially and get his reaction before proposing it to the lower levels. This was a classic American approach, and one that could work very well in the United States, but it was completely opposite to the Japanese way, particularly in companies where the president or chief executive is not very strong or does not wish to operate without a complete consensus behind him. Nevertheless, I followed instructions and presented the idea to the Japanese president the next day. His reaction after listening to me was to say he had no comment until he had a chance to discuss it with his subordinates. This was another of my rude awakenings, underscoring the realization that it is almost impossible to take a new concept and expect a quick, off-the-cuff answer from a Japanese executive.

Most Japanese companies have a culture or philosophy, and it is important to adapt to a firm's particular style in order to work with it successfully. As mentioned previously, one should never make the mistake of treating all Japanese companies as if they were more or less the same, for in reality they often differ radically. In the pharmaceutical business, for example, Sankyo and Yamanouchi are almost complete opposites in style, yet they are both major factors in the pharmaceutical market in Japan today. Learning and sensing and becoming identified with the company culture and what it means are very important. Occasionally a company culture, especially one that has international operations and dealings, will be heavily centered on the personality of the chief executive. For example, when Dr. Naito of Green Cross died in 1982, there was a definite change in the atmosphere and philosophy of that corporation, both at its headquarters and in its various operations around the world. One might say that Akio Morita of Sony holds the same kind of influence over his corporation, and that when he eventually retires, there will be a significant change at Sony. In most Japanese companies, however, the culture continues almost unchanged as chairmen and presidents come and go, since their basic function is to embody the historic goals and purpose of the corporation, to make sure that their firm adapts slowly to the external environment, and to bring the company as close as possible to the number one position in its industry. Downplaying their own personal contributions and any individual quirks they may have is part of the job description. One might even say that the offices of the chairman are practically never used, except on ceremonial occasions, where the emphasis is on style rather than substance.

With the exception of Western companies that have important, long-standing relations with Japanese companies, foreign business people seldom see the chairman or president of a Japanese company. After several meetings, if it looks as if the proposal might be of interest to the hosts, the Westerners may find that during a meeting with a number of Japanese colleagues there will be a knock on the door and a smiling young woman will enter with a note announcing that the chairman is now free to receive the visitors. This entails a five-minute social call and exchange of gifts, after which the meeting will be resumed. Seeing the chairman of a Japanese company may turn out to be a rare event. According to some, it is also an irrelevant exercise, although this depends on the Japanese company in question. The main point of such a brief meeting is a confirmation of the importance and seriousness of the business proposal under discussion.

I have chosen the metaphor of playing a harp to describe the constant contact necessary for a successful relationship with a Japanese company because it graphically suggests the necessity of proceeding up and down the company, touching down at points all along the way. But I don't mean to suggest that the procedure is merely a matter of manipulation. The skill, artistry, and feeling with which a harp is played determine the quality of the music, as well as that of the player. Thus it is not sufficient to perform the exercise only when an important matter is at stake. A musician who never practices is bound to be a flop when he tries to perform on the concert stage. To be a success with the Japanese, a foreigner must gain their confidence and make them feel that frequent visits by him can be routinely anticipated. They don't like to think that you will be around only when there is something urgent and important to be dealt with. Regular calls on the different sections of the Japanese companies the foreigner deals with, and the close contacts in the organization that he makes through such visits, should keep him abreast of what is happening and what the company's thinking is on most of the major issues affecting it, including their attitude toward the foreigner's company and his position or his problems. This aspect of playing the harp relates very closely to *ningen kankei*, or human relations. I employ a different phrase to describe the procedure of systematically going up and down the organization, getting reactions and garnering support, because it is a skill more strictly related to business than *ningen kankei*, which can be used in a more general sense.

I return for a moment to the example of the marketing plan. Beyond the formal decisions regarding implementation, I used to make trips throughout the country to all the branches of each of the Japanese companies to explain to the branch managers what was involved, and what they could specifically do to assist. I would always try to have a representative of the marketing department of the Japanese company with me so that the branch manager could be reassured that what I was saying was not just what I would like to see happen, but company policy. This was also playing the harp; even though a decision had been made and would be passed on down the line, so that the branch managers would in any case be obliged to comply with it, by making these trips and personal visits I was able to ensure an understanding and willing cooperation, rather than a grudging or routine treatment of our products or plans. The main benefit the Westerner will obtain from playing the harp when dealing with a Japanese company will be a sense of full participation with them in the evolution of a mutually desirable business outcome.

When I was leaving Japan, I was overwhelmed by the expressions of regret and warm good wishes I received from employees in the companies I had dealt with during my years in Japan. One comment in particular stands out in my memory. At a farewell geisha party one company president said to me, "You have established strong relationships at every level of my company. Please don't allow them to wither away." This remark underlines the importance of continually cultivating relationships with Japanese people. A neglected harp quickly goes out of tune, and a neglected friend quickly forgets what it was he liked about you. Since leaving, I have tried to maintain my contacts, paying courtesy calls whenever I am in Japan to indicate how deeply I appreciate the warm relationships I continue to have there.

CHAPTER 15

JOINT VENTURING

If a Western company is really interested in penetrating the Japanese market (instead of licensing technology or exporting a finished product to agents), joint venturing is often the best way to go about it, despite the fact that the Japanese generally prefer to deal with Western companies at arm's length, by licensing. They tend to regard a joint venture with the same dread that a Westerner would feel on stepping into a cage of vipers. A joint venture obliges both sides to adjust to nearly unfathomable differences in culture, language, and general business approach, but since most of the adjusting has to be done by the Japanese company, it usually means that they have to sacrifice some of the intracompany harmony that is so highly valued in Japan. The Japanese prefer licensing because they can thereby avoid the painful adjustments that joint venturing entails. Usually, once the hard job of negotiating a contract or licensing agreement has been completed, the commercialization of the technology is left to the Japanese licensee in accordance with the terms of the agreement.

The main reason that joint venturing was so popular among foreign companies in the past was the foreign-investment laws, which, up until 1976, made government approval for any other type of direct investment very difficult. The amount of royalty payable on licensing agreements was also kept deliberately low, and the licensing of Western technology to the Japanese, while common in the postwar period up until the early 1970's, was recognized as unprofitable when compared with direct investment. In the foreign-investment liberalization phase that began in 1972 and culminated in the 1980 Foreign Capital Control Law, the legal barriers to 100 percent foreign equity investment were largely dismantled, but even today joint ventures are still the most commonly used method of market entry, since they significantly reduce both the risk and the cost of entry. A Japanese partner can be of significant assistance in providing access to the complex distribution system, local-marketing knowledge, and superior production facilities and techniques. Nevertheless, the joint venture is no panacea, and in this chapter the experiences of several successful and unsuccessful joint ventures will be examined, and advice offered on how to avoid certain common pitfalls.

There are many types of joint ventures, and many reasons for forming them. Once a Japanese company has overcome its initial reluctance by realizing that there is no other way to obtain the desired Western technology, established brand name, or marketing expertise, it will typically regard the joint venture as a more or less permanent alliance, a relationship like an old-fashioned marriage, which both partners enter into with the clear understanding that they will stick together through good times and bad. A joint venture with a Japanese company means that even if changes in technology and business conditions make the original commercial objectives of the joint venture obsolete, the formal relationship is likely to remain. A good example of the indissoluble nature of such joint ventures is one that my company formed in the 1960's with a medium-sized Japanese pharmaceutical company. The purpose of the relationship was to export bulk pharmaceutical chemical products to my company's overseas affiliates. After a five-year period of intense business activity, the ability of the Japanese partner to supply the products at competitive world prices began to erode because of process improvements by local and European competitors which lowered their costs. In order to stay competitive it became necessary for us to buy from other suppliers. The original business purpose of the joint venture gradually disappeared, and we were left with a shell. Nevertheless the relationship is still in existence after twenty years, though it is at least fifteen years since any significant business activity took place. Every year we convene the annual board meeting with a dinner at a posh Tokyo restaurant, with either the Japanese partner or my company acting as host on an alternating basis. The conversation each year is the same, centering on a discussion of how to find a suitable business that can breathe new life into the joint venture. At least four or five new ideas are brought up each year and discussed, and sometimes are looked into in some detail. Nothing ever comes of them, since neither partner can offer the other anything that would justify new investment. To the Japanese firm the idea of simply giving up the relationship is unthinkable, and out of respect for their sensitivities—they are also our distributors—I have never brought it up. And so year after year we go on compiling this obsolete joint venture's financial reports, which are needed by my head office for any entity in which we have an investment.

Although perhaps an extreme case, this example illustrates the enduring nature of business relationships with the Japanese, demonstrating why it is vital for the two partners to explore fully the short-, medium-, and long-term objectives, and to consider carefully the possible impact of changing circumstances before entering into the negotiating stage.

One of the main reasons why Western companies enter into joint ventures with the Japanese is to establish a foothold in the highly profitable Japanese market. The return on investment (ROI) figures for American companies in Japan is estimated by the Department of Commerce (and verified by an extensive survey done in 1978 by the American Chamber of Commerce in Japan) to have averaged 18 percent over the ten-year period 1969–1978. British companies report even higher figures for the same period. Thus the problem with investment in Japan is not lack of profitability; rather, it is having the capital not only to establish operations, but also to sustain them for as much as five to ten years before payback starts. Many Western companies are prepared for this and have gone after the market with a wholly owned subsidiary. It is widely rumored that Procter and Gamble, which took this route, spent over $70 million in getting their detergent and toiletries business off the ground. Most companies don't have that kind of long-range thinking, nor can they afford the financial sacrifices in the short term that the 100 percent equity investment route requires. This is the main attraction of the joint venture.

Probably the second most important reason for joint venturing is that the Japanese partner can usually promise and deliver access to his own dedicated distribution channels and retail shelf space. For a new company to gain access to either is an awesome job because of the exclusive nature of the distribution system (no wholesaler will push competitive products unless consumer demand forces him to, and even then he will give them second priority). Another benefit of the joint venture is that the Japanese partner will take over the problem of finding qualified people to staff the venture and provide a ready-made management team by using recently retired executives. (This system can backfire if the Japanese company is not wholly committed, because it will sometimes use the venture as a place to shelve its own deadwood.) Additional factors that attract Western companies to the joint venture as a method of entry include the Japanese partner's knowledge of how to get product and project manufacturing and research facilities, and to create a company culture based on its management philosophy.

On the Japanese side the joint venture, while second to licensing in preference, is nonetheless an attractive prospect when it brings otherwise unobtainable technology, fits into the long-range plans of either the government of Japan or the family group of companies to which the Japanese partner belongs, offers access to a marketing system or internationally famous trademarks and brands, or helps them neutralize competition. Ideally, from the Japanese viewpoint, the joint venture in Japan will be mirrored by a joint venture in America or Europe that will enable them to establish operations overseas with market-entry objectives similar to those of their Western partners in Japan.

Whatever the reasons that each partner has for entering into a joint venture, and whether it is intended to operate in Japan or in any other market, it is vital that both partners understand the objectives and motives of the other in order to avoid future misunderstanding and frustration. One of the main points of disagreement that is often responsible for causing most problems has been the financial expectations of each partner. The Japanese are usually not as concerned with profitability; they will be delighted to plow money back into the operation and hire more and more people (or, even better, transfer excess staff from the parent company to the joint venture) in order to capture market share. The Western partner wants a return on its investment, and is usually opposed to the "growth for growth's sake" philosophy of the Japanese partner. When Dow Chemical tried to reduce its work force at its joint venture, Asahi-Dow, in order to bolster profitability, it could do so only by gradual attrition and retirements. The Japanese regard Western-style "rationalization" (cost-saving programs) with suspicion when it comes to redundancies or other types of layoffs. It is an un-Japanese approach, and affects their reputation in the business community. It should also be mentioned here that accounting systems in Japan are very different from those normally practiced in the West. Balance-sheet items such as land, buildings, and machinery tend to be undervalued, while such items as reserves for retirement, contingency reserves, and any other place where taxes can be avoided by declaring a lower profit are usually fully funded. The Western partner must obtain clear-cut assurances on how these financial questions are to be treated.

As mentioned above, one of the main reasons foreign firms have for setting up joint ventures in Japan is that it seems the best way to establish a base in Japan. Many firms hope that the experience of operating a joint venture will pave the way eventually for a wholly owned subsidiary. This is not always easy to do, but some foreign firms do manage it.

Pfizer-Taito is an excellent example of a firm that managed to achieve this objective. Pfizer was lucky enough after many years of joint operation to use the venture as a springboard to a majority-controlled entity in Japan. One of America's pharmaceutical and chemical giants, Pfizer wanted to establish operations in Japan back in the early 1950's. They contacted Taito Sugar, which had a medium-sized but well-established pharmaceutical division making penicillin-based antibiotics. K. Masuda, the American-educated head of the Taito pharmaceutical division, recognized that if the division was to survive it would need new antibiotic technology, and a joint venture was formed in 1956. By 1968 Pfizer had increased its share of the equity to 80 percent, by 1976 to 95 percent, and by 1983 to 100 percent. Taito gradually withdrew because it needed the funds for its expanding sugar business. The result was to make Pfizer the largest foreign pharmaceutical company in Japan, with net sales of $300 million in 1983. Perhaps one of the reasons for this happy outcome was that Taito's main business was in a field far removed from pharmaceuticals, and thus the balance naturally gravitated toward the company whose core business it was.

A more recent and more dramatic example of a joint venture becoming a pathway to majority control is the takeover of Banyu Pharmaceuticals by Merck Sharp and Dohme. Several years ago Merck formed a joint venture with Banyu, although Merck already had a Japan branch. In 1981 they acquired a 30 percent share of a smaller Japanese company, Torii Yakuhin. Then, in a dramatic move in July 1983, they acquired not only the joint venture with Banyu but also a majority position in Banyu itself. One week later it was announced that they had increased their stake in Torii from 30 percent to a position of majority control. Merck now has direct control of a sales force of fifteen hundred men, giving it the largest pharmaceutical company sales force in Japan. The takeovers came as a shock to the Japanese pharmaceutical industry. Nothing like it had ever happened before. During my visit to Tokyo in August of 1983, every Japanese pharmaceutical executive I met was bemoaning the loss to the *gaijin* of these two large and well-established companies. Under the old foreign-investment regulations it is unlikely that Merck could have pulled off such a remarkable coup, and it is a sign of the times that the boards of both Japanese companies agreed to the takeover, probably because they felt that the company's survival depended on it.

An example of a creeping takeover similar to the Pfizer case occurred when the S. C. Johnson Company of Racine, Wisconsin gradually acquired a controlling interest in its joint venture with a large Japanese consumer-products company, and today Johnson Company Ltd., under the able leadership of Hachiro Koyama, is the number one marketer of industrial maintenance products in Japan, with a large share of the consumer wax, polish, cleaner, and air-freshener markets. Another example, in a different industry, is the joint venture between Hewlett-Packard and Yodagama Electric. This joint venture was founded in 1963, employs two thousand people, and has sales of over $250 million. Yodagama–Hewlett-Packard (YHP) sells not only Hewlett-Packard products in Japan but also manufactures electronic instruments for sale worldwide. In 1983 Hewlett-Packard increased its equity from 49 percent to 75 percent by purchasing new shares, and now has control.

As stated earlier, one of the main reasons for Western companies to form joint ventures is to gain access to a distribution system. In the consumer-products field there are two or three good examples. The Ajinomoto–General Foods joint venture was formed because after General Foods had tried to make a go of it on its own, despite initial success it realized that it needed the marketing muscle of a well-established Japanese consumer-products company in order to compete successfully with Nestlé and a host of Japanese coffee companies. In 1973 the joint venture was formed on a fifty-fifty basis, but day-to-day management remained in the hands of Ajinomoto. General Foods brought its technical expertise in coffee and other food products to the joint venture, and Ajinomoto its Ajinomoto-*kai*, or network of wholesalers, which gave shelf space to Maxwell House coffee and Maxim instant coffee in thousands of mom-and-pop grocery stores—the backbone of the Japanese food trade. General Foods hasn't looked back since, and its market share in Japan has risen steadily on the crest of this quantum leap in distribution capability, coupled with outstanding television-advertising campaigns.

Borden of the United States and Meiji Milk initially worked together under a licensing arrangement to allow Meiji to sell Borden's ice cream in Japan under the brand name Lady Borden. They chose licensing for the initial project of entering the untapped household-consumption market for ice cream. (Previously ice cream had been a novelty item, eaten primarily on summer outings.) Borden retained the right to take an interest in the production and marketing of Lady Borden, a product that ended up revolutionizing consumer attitudes toward ice cream. After the success of this first venture, Borden decided to enter the domestic cheese market, which was of quite a different character. Because several companies (including Borden's rival, Kraft) were already competing in this market, it was felt that a joint venture would be the best way to proceed, and it has been very successful in the consumer cheese market. By late 1983 they had captured 18 percent of a greatly expanded cheese market by a process of consumer-education similar to that used in the ice cream campaign, originally on the simple theme of how to use cheese, and then shifting to a focus on cheese as a healthful food, capitalizing on the growing health awareness in Japan. Sales of domestic cheese by the joint venture have now reached $18 million. Perhaps some of the success of this joint venture can be attributed to that of the previous licensing arrangement, which allowed the two companies to become acquainted, and gave Borden time to learn about the Japanese system before entering it fully.

Another type of joint venture is one that is created to exploit a foreign marketing concept. Perhaps the most successful of these has been McDonald's-Fujita's in the fast-food business. This venture's prosperity can be attributed at least in part to the skill and enthusiasm of Den Fujita, who is one of the most dynamic entrepreneurial marketing men in Japan. In less than ten years he has built McDonald's Japan into a network of almost three hundred fast-food outlets, and Ronald McDonald is as familiar to the urban Japanese schoolchild as he is to his American or British counterparts. The success of McDonald's has been phenomenal, and the Ginza branch has sold more hamburgers than any other McDonald's outlet in the world. Fujita has gone beyond the original American fare, and although the ubiquitous hamburger remains the backbone of the business, McDonald's in Japan offers a wide variety of fast-food products that have been developed especially to appeal to the Japanese palate. The Kentucky Fried Chicken–Mitsubishi joint venture has also enjoyed a tremendous success, and similar joint ventures by Denny's, Arthur Treacher's, the Wendy's hamburger chain, and several others have all found niches in the market. European companies have been slow to exploit this opportunity, and although Wimpy's of England (Trust House–Forte) have opened a few stores, Trevor Abbott, who runs their operation, has confessed that their financial commitment just isn't sufficient.

In a parallel development, the "7-11" convenience store chain (Southland) has also done extremely well in Japan, again in joint venture with Mitsubishi. Not only does the Japanese partner bring to such ventures the benefits already mentioned, such as offering access to distribution channels and political connections, but it can also greatly assist in site selection, which can be a problem in crowded Japan. An influential Japanese partner, such as Mitsubishi, can use its real estate and banking arms to locate and finance site location and acquisition.

Many medium-sized firms establish joint ventures solely to gain experience in Japan, with the ultimate objective of either acquiring or dissolving the venture and setting up a wholly owned operation. Such moves are not viewed kindly by the Japanese, but they have learned to expect this approach. The important thing to remember is that a firm risks creating enemies for itself if it is not frank with its proposed Japanese partner on this point at the outset. It is easier to set up this type of joint venture if there is a reciprocal venture in the territory of the foreign firm, so that the Japanese partner has the same option eventually to either take over or break away. Sankyo Pharmaceuticals was not happy about having to alter or dissolve two joint-venture relationships in the space of a year because their foreign partners wanted to start up their own operations. Parke-Davis–Sankyo was a highly successful joint venture that lasted for many years, but after Parke-Davis was acquired by Warner-Lambert, the latter adopted a strategy of consolidating all its operations. Similarly, Sandoz of Switzerland had a long-standing joint venture with San-kyo, which was replaced by a marketing agreement after Sandoz set up its own manufacturing facilities in Japan. However, apparently Sankyo is still on good terms with both companies, and the foreign firms certainly benefited from their long association with one of Japan's top marketers in the pharmaceutical business. The close con-tact with top foreign pharmaceutical companies also helped Sankyo in gaining the necessary technical knowledge to become productive developers of new drugs in its own right, and now Sankyo is expand-ing aggressively overseas through both licensing and joint ventures. Thus it can be inferred that despite Sankyo's reluctance to "divorce," both the Japanese and the foreign partners had outgrown their need for such close association. ICI of Britain went through a similar expe-rience with Sumitomo, and has recently established its own indepen-dent marketing operation while maintaining close contacts with Sumitomo. Recently these contacts have resulted in ICI being given the right to sell one of Sumitomo's outstanding new antibiotics in most of the world's leading pharmaceutical markets.

For larger companies, such as Dow Chemical and Dupont, the joint-venture route is usually part of a diversified strategy of market penetration, which may include wholly owned subsidiaries selling specialty products as well as joint ventures manufacturing bulk chemicals, where the cost of importing the finished product to Japan would be uneconomical.

In general, the only way to be successful in Japan is to have a presence there, and this entails direct investment. Whether a foreign company should choose the joint-venture route or decide to set up its own operation depends on many factors. If the option chosen is to go it alone, at the head of the list of requirements for success is a willingness to commit millions of dollars with an extremely long payout period. IBM, NCR, Texas Instruments, Procter & Gamble, BASF, Ciba-Geigy, Shell Chemicals, and many other companies have been successful in building up their own operations from scratch. Central to each of these firms' success has been its ability to invest vast amounts of time (from seven to ten years) and money in order to capture a profitable market share.

Some large companies have at least initially preferred joint ventur-ing to the long uphill fight to establish a wholly owned subsidiary.

Fuji-Xerox is one example of such a venture. Acquisition is another option that many companies find attractive, but usually the only situation where acquisition is a viable alternative is one in which the Japanese target company is in bàd shape financially and agrees to allow foreign equity as a means of staying alive and keeping faith with its employees. Even then the likelihood of acquiring majority control at the outset is slim, unless the Japanese company is in such dire straits that it is about to go under.

According to a recent *Business Asia* article on foreign acquisition of Japanese companies, most companies acquired in the period between 1955 and 1981 were in some financial trouble, and tended to be small firms that generally were in a weak position within their industries. Sometimes such firms preferred takeover by foreigners, who would usually prefer to keep local employees in place, rather than by a Japanese firm, which would be inclined to insert its own people. Thus an important factor in a successful acquisition is a commitment to the existing personnel.

One final element in a successful partnership is to make sure of government (FTC) approval. Although it is not required, the FTC has the right to review international contracts at any time, and generally will look at a contract after it has been approved by the Foreign Investment Council and the concerned ministry, so it is best to make sure everything is acceptable before going through this process. (The FTC is concerned only with international contracts, so to avoid difficulties it may be useful to conclude the agreement by means of a local branch office or subsidiary.)

The Merck acquisition mentioned earlier would appear to herald a thawing of the frosty attitude toward foreign acquisitions that has prevailed in Japan up till now. From now on we may see more Western firms acquire a controlling interest in their joint-venture partners. In this connection it is worth remembering that this race is not to the swift; careful long-range planning and a genuine commitment to and understanding of Japan will be the keys to success. Many a hare has appeared confidently at the starting line in Japan, but somehow only the patient tortoises appear at the finish line happily counting their yen.

For Western companies that are interested in exploring this subject in more detail and evaluating which entry strategy appears to offer the best alternative for them, some of the publications of the American Chamber of Commerce in Japan are invaluable. One of them, *High Adventure in Joint Ventures,* published in 1972, is a case study of a hypothetical joint venture, Edo Widgets, and is still good reading today. A more objective and quantifiable report is a study of U.S. manufacturing investment in Japan done by A. T. Kearny & Company for the Chamber in 1978. It is an exhaustive report on the performance of different American companies in Japan since the war, and includes a section on entry strategies and opportunities. A more recent publication (1980) in booklet form is entitled *Successful Entry into the Japanese Market,* and includes helpful advice on every aspect of entering the Japanese market, from how to open an office in Tokyo to site selection and factory construction. Case studies of two joint ventures, Asahi-Dow (Asahi Chemicals and Dow Chemicals) and Ajinomoto–General Foods, are included in this publication. In 1983 the Trade Study Group, a joint U.S.-Japanese group that looks at trade and investment problems and is closely affiliated with the American Chamber, published a worthwhile study by McKinsey & Company entitled *Japan Business: Obstacles and Opportunities.* As the title suggests, it is a broad-ranging look at the Japanese market and offers advice on how to approach it in the 1980's and 1990's. Similar studies were also carried out by the EEC chambers of commerce in Japan (EEC Steering Committee), in cooperation with the EEC legation. The British Chamber of Commerce in Japan also did an investment study, but I think my European business friends in Japan will agree that the American studies are the more exhaustive. In fact, several European companies, among them such companies as Bayer, British Oxygen, Beecham's, and Boehringer-Mannheim, took part in the 1978 investment study of the American Chamber.

I turn now to the examination of a few unsuccessful joint ventures, with some comments on why they failed.

The failure of the Bucyrus-Erie/Komatsu joint venture has been mentioned in previous chapters, but it merits a closer look. Bucyrus-Erie is an American equipment manufacturer, which teamed up with Komatsu in a joint venture that seemed for several years to be satisfactory. But ultimately the failure to anticipate long-range strategy and changing circumstances led to a breakup of the venture. The overt cause was the Japanese government's intervention, in the form of a Fair Trade Commission (FTC) ruling. The FTC is a watchdog agency that is supposed to concentrate on administering the antimonopoly laws in Japan, but in practice it also tends to view itself as the protector of Japanese interests in business dealings with foreign companies. It accused Bucyrus-Erie of having imposed unfair clauses in its joint-venture agreement with Komatsu. The clause in question prevented Komatsu from exporting products of the joint venture to markets where Bucyrus-Erie already had sales activities. The real reason for the joint-venture break up was Komatsu's desire to exploit the attractive China market with joint-venture (i.e., Bucyrus-Erie) technology when business relations with China resumed in the mid-seventies. (It is worth noting in this connection that Japanese business has had a tendency to overestimate the importance of the Chinese market because of Japan's ancient history of association with China.) Komatsu wanted to use Bucyrus-Erie joint-venture products as part of the export program it was mounting in China, but the American partner pointed out that it was already active in China and the planned activity by Komatsu would therefore violate their agreement. At this point the Fair Trade Commission stepped in, undaunted by the fact that the contract had been in force for years, and ruled the clause unfair. Shortly thereafter the joint venture was dissolved.

Generally speaking, Japanese companies feel as honor-bound in their relationships with foreign firms as they do with domestic ones, but there are exceptions. That is why the selection of a joint-venture partner is critical, and the maintenance of good relations even more important. A Japanese company would also never dare to damage its relationships with domestic firms by using questionable means to gain an advantage if there was any possibility of the company losing face thereby. Similarly, despite the cultural gap, a Japanese firm will generally apply the same standards to its dealings with foreign companies, particularly if the foreigners make an effort to work closely with them and try to understand their customs. Foreign firms that make a point of doing business Japanese style will discover that their Japanese associates will not find it easy to write them off as outsiders, thereby justifying acts they would never commit in dealing with fellow Japanese.

A foreign company entering on a joint venture should never forget that there is at best only a limited convergence of interests between them and their partner. A joint venture is always a compromise of sorts, and a long, hard look at the reasons for forming it can save a lot of trouble. Wishful thinking must not be allowed to play a part in the decision. Obviously, if the Japanese company originally wanted a licensing arrangement, it is the technology of the Western firm that it is really interested in. Although, as noted, the majority of Japanese companies are scrupulous, in letter and in spirit, about their agreements, nevertheless it doesn't hurt to safeguard against any undesirable leakage of technology to the joint venture's Japanese parent firm by establishing and maintaining excellent and open relationships with people at all levels in the Japanese company.

Dispute over financial objectives is a common cause of insoluble differences in a joint venture. Such a situation occurred when my company and a large Japanese engineering firm entered into a partnership to exploit our pollution-control technology. After a spectacular start, in which some forty-eight plants were built all over Japan for the secondary treatment of municipal sludge, we found that although the sales were impressive, there were no profits. Despite continuous prodding we couldn't convince the Japanese firm that it should allocate its profits to the joint venture rather than to the parent company that was doing the actual construction of the plants. The net result was that in 1976 the joint venture was dissolved and reverted to a straight licensing-royalty arrangement, and my company is now beginning to see a return on its investment.

Occasionally the Japanese enter into a joint venture in order to neutralize a potential competitor; this was the case with Colgate and Kao Soap, a giant Japanese company manufacturing detergents and toiletries. Colgate had been trying to build a business on its own in Japan and had gradually expanded the franchise of Colgate toothpaste and other products. Suddenly a rumor started that Colgate toothpaste had a harmful ingredient, and the business started to disintegrate. Colgate turned to its archrival, Kao, and offered to form a joint venture that later became known as CKR. The result has been that Colgate sales in Japan have stayed at minuscule levels. The only place where Colgate has anything like the franchise and market share that it normally achieves is in Okinawa, where it retained control of the business.

The case of Dow Chemical and Otsuka Pharmaceuticals is yet another example of an unsuccessful joint venture. Here the reason for the failure was entirely different, and it bears a detailed explanation, since it represents another common type of misunderstanding. Dow Chemical acquired Merrell, the ethical pharmaceutical arm of Richardson-Merrell, in 1979. This acquisition gave Dow a $900 million worldwide pharmaceutical business (the figure includes the business of other Dow pharmaceutical subsidiaries). But despite its prominence in the field, Dow had almost no business in Japan, the world's second largest pharmaceutical market. The company decided that the joint-venture route was the best way to enter this market, and settled on Otsuka, an aggressive and capable drug manufacturer from Osaka. Eventually the partnership formed, and was front-page news in the trade press. Two years later the joint venture was dissolved. Otsuka had expected that Dow would immediately license the venture to exploit Dow-Merrell technology by way of new pharmaceutical products, but at that particular time Dow had nothing suitable on hand. What Dow really wanted was a structure that would market its existing products (most of which were already licensed to other Japanese companies and therefore not immediately available) and be ready to take on new products as they became available. This example again shows the importance of realizing that the Japanese view a joint venture as a second choice to licensing. If the foreign partner expects a Japanese company to join hands in the expectation that new technology will become available sometime in the indefinite future, the life expectancy of the relationship will be short indeed.

The highly successful joint venture between Smith Kline & French and Fujisawa Pharmaceuticals sprang from a situation nearly opposite to that of Dow-Otsuka. Here the American partner had a blockbuster of a new drug, and Japanese companies were standing in line. The drug, a new antiulcer product called Tagamet, has worldwide sales of close to a billion dollars, and SKF had ironclad patents in Japan. The result was a happy marriage, which was further sweetened, from the Japanese point of view, by the agreement to open a reciprocal joint venture in the United States.

In joint venturing, it is worthwhile to remember that the Japanese style of negotiating—a low-key, nonconfrontational process of building trust between two parties—may well leave foreigners with the wrong idea about what has been decided. This cuts both ways, of course; the Western way of doing things can be just as confusing to the Japanese as their style is to us. When a joint venture comes apart at the seams, it is a bit late to realize that studying and being sensitive to *haragei* and other forms of indirect communication used in Japan is not just a pleasant extra bit of expertise. Such knowledge may represent the difference between a prospering enterprise and a dismal failure. Smith Kline & French was lucky enough to have a sure winner, but when the situation is more equivocal—as it usually is—

a foreign company would do well to proceed cautiously.

There is another factor that can jeopardize a joint venture. When a Western company forms a partnership in Japan, it must be prepared to see its other relationships in the same field gradually wither, since it will be understood and expected that priority will be given to the joint venture. The Western company which finds it more profitable to play the field and avoid entanglements with any single Japanese company should bear this in mind before it seriously considers a joint venture, unless it is so narrowly focused (i.e., one product, technology, or submarket) that relationships with other companies are not threatened.

These various examples show that it is an easy task to isolate the factors crucial to a successful joint venture. First, there must be a definite product, technology, marketing system, or brand that the partnership can immediately and profitably develop and exploit. Second, the Western firm must have a clear understanding with the Japanese partner regarding short-, medium-, and long-range objectives and profit expectations. Third, the foreign partner has to be prepared for a relatively long payout period, and to accommodate this fact in its calculations when establishing financial objectives. Fourth, the foreign partner must remember that the Japanese look upon a joint venture as more than a simple business arrangement. They will view it just as they do their relationships with suppliers, distributors, agents or trading companies—as a relationship of trust that is expected to endure the test of time. One sure way to poison a joint venture is to flirt with the Japanese partner's direct competitors without first explaining why and how it will affect the relationship.

Beyond these generalizations, the Western company contemplating a joint venture on a basis of less than majority control should think hard and long about whom it sends to Japan to represent it, and how to position this person in the joint-venture structure. It is not wise to send anyone who has not had extensive experience either in Japan itself or at least in other foreign cultures. The ideal candidate would have demonstrated in the course of his career flexibility and adaptability—essential attributes when dealing with the Japanese. As mentioned in Part I, it is also desirable for the Western company representative to have a flair for languages and be ready to make the necessary sacrifices to learn the language reasonably fluently within two years of his arrival.

Another important asset that the person selected should have is to be a seasoned veteran in the parent Western company, and have access to, and the confidence of, top management at the head office. This latter point is all-important, since the Japanese firm will soon bypass any representative of the foreign firm and go straight to the head office if it feels that it can get faster action. Also, when the senior executives of the Japanese partner travel abroad, they expect to see the chairman and president of the Western partner and not be fobbed off on underlings. Only a well-respected and senior company representative will have the clout at home to ensure that no such gaffes are committed.

Then there is the ageism of Japanese society to contend with. A young man will not command the respect that he needs in order to be effective. Finally, the Western company should avoid at all costs sending someone to Japan who is likely to be caught in the double bind of having neither the full confidence of his local staff nor the wholehearted support of his head office. Such situations occur when the foreign firm does not assign enough importance to its Japan operations or fails to take into account the unique nature of business there.

Because the role of the Western partner's executive representative is crucial, it must be clearly defined. Ideally, he should function as the executive vice president (*fukushachō*) of the joint venture, with veto power over financial, marketing, and technology-related policy matters. The day-to-day running of the partnership should be Japanese style, and matters such as personnel administration, industrial relations, production, and local purchasing left to the Japanese partner. Since the representative of the Western company will be its eyes and ears inside the venture, it should be made clear to the Japanese partner that the representative must be kept informed about all developments that affect the attainment of the agreed objectives, and that he should be regarded as an important member of the strategic planning process. There is a great temptation on the part of the Japanese staff to bypass the Western company representative on the grounds that "he will never understand." The staff may also feel that briefing him is an unrewarding chore. This tendency must be fought at every stage, and therefore much depends on the executive selected and whether or not the Japanese partner feels, or can be made to feel, that the Westerner can make a contribution.

One final word about the selection of staff for the joint venture.

Earlier I mentioned that the partnership is usually staffed by the Japanese company, but the Western partner should screen the selection process carefully in order to be sure that deadwood isn't being hired. In the beginning it is fine to have a few recently retired professionals to assist, but as soon as possible the joint venture should begin recruiting its own freshman staff from the good universities and training these recruits in the company culture, which may be a fusion of the Japanese partner's traditional policies and the more dynamic approach of the Western firm. Older executives retired from the Japanese parent company will often find it difficult to adjust to this new atmosphere after decades of service in a firm whose structure and culture are likely to have been quite different. The joint venture should not end up as a retirement home for Japanese executives judged not fit to be promoted to true "lifetime employment" as a director of the parent company.

Key joint-venture staff should be given the opportunity not only to visit and observe the workings of the Western parent company but to receive a working assignment that will help them understand how the Western firm operates, and to make friendships that will greatly assist in overcoming the communication problems that are bound to arise from time to time no matter how hard both parties strive to avoid them.

It should also be remembered that adjustment is a two-way street. The Western partner can learn a lot from the Japanese one, and this knowledge can become a tremendous asset in the marketing and manufacturing as well as product technology base of the Western company in its operations both inside and outside Japan. Among the most frequently mentioned benefits of close contact with a Japanese company are superior production techniques and efficiencies, product improvements, packaging innovations, development of related products using the same technology, cost reductions, process improvements, and opportunities to exploit the technology of the Japanese partner in the Western company's home and other markets. Joint financing and shared resources in the development of new products and technology are other significant side benefits of joint ventures with the Japanese, who will usually offer their partner the right of first refusal on any related new technology.

The joint venture is an attractive alternative to going it alone in the Japanese market, where, aside from the numerous cultural and bureaucratic difficulties, everything from land and wages to the cost of television advertising is astronomically expensive. The factor of paramount importance in selecting the right partner is to make certain that both parties share the same aspirations for the performance of the partnership, and that each understands the objectives and expectations the other has in both the short and the long term. A true understanding of any relationship entails a realistic appraisal of all possible weak points, from the main fact that it nearly always represents a compromise for both parties, right down to the personality of the Western executive chosen to be the representative in Japan. But in the long run the good faith of both parties in the constant struggle to communicate and achieve their mutual goals will be the deciding factor.

CHAPTER
16

EXPORTING TO JAPAN

Despite significant progress in recent years, the problems that face American or Western European companies wishing to export to Japan range from rigid customs regulations to a plethora of nontariff barriers designed to keep (or at least have the effect of keeping) foreign goods out of Japan. In deference to the disproportionate influence wielded by Japanese farmers on the ruling Liberal Democratic party because of outmoded election boundaries, the Japanese government still clings to established quotas for some products, most of them agricultural, setting maximum limits on the amount and value of imports in a given period. Exports of chemicals, automobiles, machinery, cosmetics, any many other items are also subjected to varying degrees of harassment and interference by the Japanese.

Over the last two decades or so there has been a decided shift in the way that Japanese consumers view foreign goods. In the past they traditionally believed foreign merchandise to be superior to their own, but that is no longer true. In light of this, and of the unique nature of the Japanese market, when considering exporting to Japan it is important to adapt one's product to the market. In the past a number of American and Western European goods have sold in Japan even though they were unsuitable, because equivalent products did not exist. But such success is always shortlived, since Japanese companies will swiftly move to fill in the gap. For example, when Sears decided to export large refrigerators to Japan, they were bought by consumers who really did not have adequate space for them but couldn't find a large enough Japanese model. In the intervening years since Sears had its big sales surge there, each manufacturer of refrigerators has expanded its line to include all possible sizes. These manufacturers are careful, of course, to tailor their products to specific Japanese requirements, and so are quickly able to recapture market share lost to Western companies, which are usually ill prepared to meet the challenge.

When exporting foreign consumer goods to Japan, it is necessary to keep in mind that the Japanese have preferences in colors, flavors, and fragrances that are decidedly different from those of Westerners. As just one example, the Japanese regard the color yellow and the smell of lemons to be unacceptable for toiletries. They tend to associate lemons largely with dishwashing or clothes washing rather than with perfumes or fragrances. Product tailoring is the key to exporting to Japan, and serious prior market research on the suitability of foreign products for their market is essential.

Japanese consumers also have idiosyncratic ideas about what constitutes value for money. They are prepared to pay up to $7 or $8 for a bottle of ordinary aftershave lotion but find the idea of paying $2 for a package of disposable moist towelettes to be too expensive and wasteful. They will pay $20 to $30 for a melon (considering it a luxury item suitable for gift giving), and yet will quarrel with storekeepers about the price of tangerines and vegetables. In general, the price of consumer products in Japan is at least double that in the United States or Europe. In the case of manufactured goods this is due largely to the highly expensive distribution network, for the manufacturer's price of many goods is almost the same as in the United States or Europe.

Another peculiarity is that the Japanese consumer likes to see beautiful packaging. If a high-quality product is packaged in economical containers, the consumer will not recognize that the ugly duckling is actually a swan. Trying to sell toiletry products in Japan in Western packaging is a surefire way to failure. Bonus or special economy packs are generally restricted to such mundane household items as detergent and soap, while toiletries or cosmetics must be packaged in the most elegant and expensive-looking packaging available. This emphasis on style and manner of presentation is very Japanese, and its roots lie deep in the culture. Advertising agencies that come to Japan soon find out that when Japanese consumers shell out their hard-earned yen for those expensive products, they want to feel that they are purchasing something special, with stylistic overtones suggesting hidden emotional benefits. They are not like hardheaded American consumers, many of whom take their pocket calculators to stores to help them figure the price per ounce, and are often willing to sacrifice quality for quantity and a cut in price. Japanese consumers have a gut belief in the practical importance of style.

The characteristics that attract Japanese to foreign products usually include a certain aura of exoticism and fantasy. An elegant and carefully fashioned advertising campaign, calculated to stimulate their interest in a product as being mysterious or special, is one of the best routes to success. A foreign product promising subtle emotional advantages not available from routine Japanese products is far more likely to be a hit than one that emphasizes rational, practical features. Outstanding success in this kind of product-image creation has been achieved by the Estée Lauder and Clinique cosmetic lines in Japan, as well as by Revlon in its packaging of Aramis men's toiletries. An attempt to use the same package or advertising campaign in Japan as in the West is usually a dismal failure. Many of the giant American advertising agencies have offices in Japan, and most of them know this.

After a company gathers the information it needs to enter the market, it must find a well-established agent or trading partner to promote its product. It is essential to have a local agent or trading partner to handle sales, after-sales service, and representation. As mentioned in the previous chapter, companies that have potentially high volume products should consider joint venturing or direct investment. Even in such cases export experience can be a good way to learn about market potential. One major drawback is that any form of market testing tips off Japanese competitors and gives them enough time to copy the product. They can thereby forestall a full-fledged entry, since by the time the Western company completes successful testing, numerous local competitors will have already prepared excellent imitations and introduced them in forms that are particularly suitable for their market. There are no easy answers to this problem. It may seem suicidal to launch a full-scale marketing effort without any testing, but if the testing takes longer than three months, it may turn out to be an equally bad move.

Imported industrial goods are often presented initially to the Japanese customer or buyer through trade shows or special promotions put on by the trade-promotion section of the relevant embassy. For example, such organizations as the U.S. Department of Agriculture, through their foreign agricultural service, and a number of Japanese government-sponsored import agencies, such as JETRO and MIPRO (the Manufacturers Import Promotion Council), frequently sponsor trade fairs for imported industrial goods. There are also showrooms and display facilities maintained by most major European countries that are managed by either the embassy or the Chamber of Commerce of the country in question.

Once the Western company has established that the product it wishes to sell in Japan is likely to be well received, has arranged for a trading partner, and is satisfied that it can establish a good working relationship with this partner, it will be in a much better position to consider direct marketing in Japan. Some possible partners would be a Japanese trading company, a Japanese importer, a Japanese retail outlet, or a Japanese industrial agent. Other possibilities include U.S. trading firms, such as Wilbur Ellis & Company, William Kyle & Associates, and a number of other Western firms that operate both in the United States and Japan. There are also many British trading companies that maintain offices in Tokyo, such as Dodwell's, Jardine's, the Swire group, Hutchison's, and other Hong Kong–based companies. It is vital for an exporter to select the right trading partner, one who is likely to give a product the priority it deserves and promote it actively.

Finding a partner in Japan is not always easy. Many Western firms have looked to the *sōgōshōsha* for help, but this often does not work out. The unique nature of Japanese general trading companies has already been discussed in Chapter 12, and while they are superb in their efforts to establish Japanese business overseas, usually they are not the best choice when it comes to promoting a foreign product in Japan. The history of the *sōgōshōsha* militates against it, for the trading companies were formed to bring raw materials in, and ship manufactured goods out. When a *sōgōshōsha* imports a foreign manufactured product, it is seldom given the access to the distribution system that it needs or the level of priority it deserves. All too often the trading company will import limited quantities, distribute them imperfectly, and then have one of the manufacturers in its *zaikai* make an excellent imitation that will undermine whatever limited market share the imported product has managed, against all odds, to achieve. Thus, while the *shōsha* are always scouting around for new products, it is probably unwise to rely on them.

Generally speaking, American companies have never been much concerned about exporting. In Europe, on the other hand, many countries, have been export-oriented for years, but their zeal simply doesn't compare with that of Japan. Aside from the historical fact that, rightly or wrongly exports have never been perceived as vital to the U.S. economy, one of the factors in the United States that have discouraged exports has been the laws preventing the formation of Japanese-style general trading companies. With the passage of the Export Trading Company Act in 1982, which allows U.S. banks to be the principal investors in U.S. trading companies, perhaps alternatives to the *sōgōshōsha* may come on the scene. Although it is too early to tell whether anything approaching the Japanese traders in skill and scope will ever develop in America, it does appear that at least a few U.S. companies are considering taking advantage of the new law. General Electric, for example, has announced its intention of forming a general trading company. Perhaps sometime in the future, then, the task of finding a good partner who knows the Japanese market will be considerably easier.

It is not enough just to have a trading partner. An exporter also needs a local lawyer who will be responsible not only for legal matters but also for interpreting Japanese commercial law, and to help the exporter anticipate some of the inevitable legal and bureaucratic problems that a Western exporter to Japan faces, no matter what its product or service. One also needs the services of a well-established accounting firm with offices in Japan. (Most of the Big Eight Western accounting firms maintain offices in Tokyo.) The accountants can assist the exporter on tax aspects as well as anticipate some of the problems arising from the difference between Japanese and Western accounting practices. In addition, a freight forwarder or broker is an important member of the export team, although this can usually be arranged by the trading partner, and thus the exporter may have limited contact with this facet.

One of the worst stumbling blocks encountered by any foreign business with interests in Japan is the communication gap. In addition to all the problems already described, exporters face special difficulties because they usually do not have a physical presence in Japan. Forgive me for calling attention to the obvious, but first of all, the letters, telexes, and telegrams sent to Japanese trading partners must be simple and clear-cut. Although many Japanese—and probably most of those connected with a foreign exporter—can read English, that does not mean that they will be able to comprehend long, involved sentences or jargon and idioms. They are likely to be incapable of reading between the lines, so anyone who wants to be understood had better be specific. Moreover, the trouble the Japanese have with letters is nothing compared with the confusion that a telephone call will engender. It is usually useless to telephone a Japanese partner; he may well panic and fail to understand a word. Anyone who has passed the written portion of a foreign-language exam and miserably failed the oral will be able to understand this problem.

One useful communication device to keep in mind is the telefax, or facsimile service, which can be very effective. (Japan has the most widespread and broadly organized telefax system in the world.) Finally, before trying to get in touch with anyone in Japan or bemoaning seemingly inexplicable delays, one should be sure to consult the Japanese firm about its schedule of holidays, as well as times when it may be inconvenienced because of work slowdowns—that is, the Spring Struggle, or *shuntō,* the annual nationwide campaign in the last week of March and the first week of April when labor organizations demand wage increases.

One significant problem faced by Western exporters to Japan is the difficulty of achieving acceptability under Japanese standards. This is not the same as tailoring the product to the local market, which is necessary to be sure that people will buy it. The Japanese government has a plethora of special regulations designed to protect the consumer from inferior merchandise; these have the additional effect of keeping numerous foreign products out of the market. Examples of highly regulated categories, where meeting product standards is virtually impossible the first time around, are automobiles, agricultural products, toiletries and cosmetics, pharmaceuticals, sports equipment, and transportation equipment of any type.

In the field of cosmetics and toiletries the government maintains a list of approved chemicals only, and ignores a huge number of chemicals and chemical ingredients that are neither approved nor disapproved. There has been some progress toward improving this situation, but it has not yet been streamlined. Either through his trading partner or directly, the exporter to Japan must find out what the government position will be with regard to the import of non-specified commodities. In many Western countries there is a negative list of banned ingredients and chemicals, but not in Japan, although there is some thought of preparing such a list. Frequently Japanese standards are much stricter than those in the West, and the ingredients that can be used as additives, colors, and stabilizers are far more limited. They are often permitted only in quantities that would make them ineffective. In order to obtain approval for additives, it is necessary for the exporter or his agent to have lengthy discussions with the ministry concerned (usually Health and Welfare or Agriculture) in order to determine what kind of testing will be required before the ingredient can be considered acceptable. Often the testing is so expensive and time-consuming that it is easier to reformulate the product rather than try to import it using the same ingredients as in the West.

In the case of automobiles, foreign pollution-control equipment, such as exhaust pipes, catalytic converters, and catalytic converter trays, are often not up to Japanese standards, and they are usually ripped out and replaced when the automobiles arrive in Japan. (The fact that Japan had one of the worst air-pollution problems in the world—a situation that is now largely under control—explains the strictness of these requirements.) The small number of cars imported into Japan from the West (approximately sixty thousand) is a clear indication of the great difficulty that foreign companies have experienced in attempting to get their products certified by the Ministry of Transportation (MOT). (Of course, the lack of product tailoring has also been a problem.)

In recent years there have been some attempts to improve matters by stationing MOT inspectors at the manufacturing plants of exporting companies so that they can give "type approval" to the products before they leave Western factories, and thus expedite the clearance process of the cars on their arrival in Japan. To date, however, this system of prior certification has not worked very efficiently. Local inspectors will frequently take it upon themselves to disapprove many of the devices installed in the cars, and insist on their replacement or installation of additional devices, often thus greatly inflating the cost of the final product. The most successful Western automobile manufacturers have been those that have especially tailored their products to the Japanese market and made all the necessary adjustments in accord with both consumer and government requirements before shipping to Japan. German manufacturers, such as Mercedes Benz and BMW, tend to dominate the imported-car market, while such American automobile companies as General Motors and Ford have found their sales declining over recent years largely because of their unwillingness to make the highly arbitrary and expensive modifications demanded.

In addition to product standards, which form a very significant barrier to the entry of foreign goods, the Japanese also maintain a quota system for a number of products, particularly agricultural ones. U.S. orange growers are allowed to export to Japan only between the months of March and October because the Japanese *mikan* (tangerine) season begins in November and lasts until the spring, and *mikan* growers are an important political constituency. Aside from the time limits imposed, obtaining quotas of any significance for oranges and some other citrus fruits is difficult. (In fairness, it should be said that the *mikan* growers have a far larger capacity to supply the market than is realized by those who feel that such barriers are unjustified. Moreover, labor and land-intensive Japanese fruit farming could not hope to compete in terms of price with American-style mechanized farming.) Selected importers have been allowed to bring citrus fruit into Japan, but it is a highly risky business. Often the inspector from the Ministry of Agriculture, finding one imperfection or seeing one fungal growth or any kind of insect infestation, will reject an entire shipment rather than segregate bad fruit from good. The same is true of lettuce. During January and February the cost of one head of lettuce in Japan can run from $3 to $5, but despite the fact that California growers can import it for $0.18, the California Lettuce Growers Association has had bitter experiences trying to get lettuce into Japan because many shipments have been found to be less than perfect by local standards. In such cases the risk has to be borne by the exporter. No insurance company will provide coverage, since the idiosyncratic and unpredictable nature of the views of Japanese Ministry of Agriculture inspection agents is well known. On many occasions hundreds of thousands of heads of American lettuce have been judged unacceptable and dumped into Tokyo Bay.

The question of importing beef into Japan is another sore subject in international trade. Severe quota restrictions exist on beef imports, and both Australia and the United States are interested in seeing that these quotas and restrictions are lifted. These laws are designed, of course, to protect the Japanese cattle growers. Not only do they constitute a powerful political block in the electing and maintaining of the Liberal Democratic Party in power, but they could not hope to compete with foreign beef producers. The whole beef controversy is something of a tempest in a teacup, at least as far as U.S. beef production is concerned. A 1983 study by McKinsey & Company for the U.S.-Japan Trade Study Group revealed that Australian beef would almost certainly be considerably cheaper than American beef in a quota-free Japan. And to put the whole quota and tariff question into perspective, an examination of the practices of EEC countries—in more than one of which there exists blatant discrimination against Japan—reveals that Japan is no worse than most, and often better than many, when it comes to the amount of duty charged and the length of the lists of items that come under quota restrictions.

When considering Japan's agricultural quotas, one should realize that Japan must import the majority of its foodstuffs and is the largest single customer for American agricultural products. Japan has no hope of ever becoming self-sufficient. This situation has given rise to two basic schools of thought. One might be called the realists, who feel that clinging to outmoded protectionism will not save Japan in the event of a catastrophe that cuts off supply lines, and that such barriers therefore do more harm than good because they antagonize Japan's trading partners (in addition to driving up consumer food bills). But probably the majority of Japanese still feel that Japan should strive to remain as self-sufficient as possible and not allow the domestic food production industry to collapse. So it is not likely that there will be dramatic progress in this area in the near future.

When exporting to Japan, or even sending samples, it is necessary to provide the trading partner with complete details of the ingredients, formula, or other breakdown of the constituents of the product. Japanese customs duties are based on the *exact* contents, and failure to state them can hopelessly delay clearance of a shipment from customs. It is critically important to obtain prior clearance and customs determination of all products intended for export to Japan, since without this prior clearance the Western exporter will have no way of knowing how the product will be treated when it lands at customs. Therefore, don't delay or become paranoid if your trading partner telexes a request for information on a product's exact constituents, stated in percentages. Without such information it may be impossible to obtain customs clearance. This is another reason why exporters had better team up with a partner whom they trust.

Customs inspectors vary from port to port, and from airport to airport. An assessment of a product by the customs office in Kobe, for example, may differ from that in Tokyo or Narita. This is another problem that has been brought to the attention of the Japanese government, and steps are being taken to eliminate these inequities. Incorrect or incomplete documents, or the discovery of banned ingredients or any kind of imperfection in the product, can result in costly demurrage charges while the product is held in customs. The exporter should solve all of these matters well ahead of time. Studying the trading partner's customs-clearance problems in detail will help ensure that costly and embarrassing delays do not occur. Even a firm that has extensive experience in exporting should adapt its normal exporting procedures to the unique requirements of Japan.*

The bureaucratic maze that exporters to Japan face is vexing, and I have no desire to add to the confusion and emotional obfuscation surrounding it. Faced with the prospect of quotas and tariffs on their own goods, Japanese authorities have come to realize the necessity of simplifying procedures to bring them in line with international practices and to make them fair. The problem lies in pinpointing the areas where change can be most effective, and in persuading the slow bureaucratic machinery to agree. The way to ensure that neither side gives up in the negotiation process is to constantly review the actual state of affairs and not allow a few emotionally inflated issues, such as oranges and beef, to obscure the facts.

Until very recently, people in the Japanese government have by and large been operating under the traditional "Japan is vulnerable, so we must protect her" ideology, which causes many or most Japanese to see their country as a special case in the community of nations. This point of view has produced the tendency to stonewall and throw up barriers to foreign goods when tariffs have been forced to fall because of pressure by the international community. The Japanese government has begun to acknowledge that these old attitudes are no longer viable. Thus the government has conceded the need to dismantle these nontariff barriers, but there is not always agreement as to what constitutes a nontariff barrier. In addition, the government is not a monolithic entity, and there is by no means a

*There is an excellent and practical booklet on exporting to Japan, written by Richard Bush (a long-term American resident in Tokyo who specializes in importing from the West), published by the American Chamber of Commerce in Japan (1982). Any exporter who is serious about investigating the Japanese market should read this booklet.

consensus among all concerned ministries that foreign goods are not a threat to Japan.

Still, after years of frustration, Westerners are finally getting action on their complaints about the difficulties of exporting to Japan. However, there is a tendency on the part of some to label situational difficulties as nontariff barriers (NTB's)—for example, when Detroit finds that despite no duty on imported automobiles it still can't sell cars there, it blames its problems on NTB's. The argument is that if our cars can't meet Japanese standards, it's the standards that are wrong and not our cars. In such cases it is crucial to separate the many genuine complaints from the cases of scapegoating.

In short, constantly crying about the same few highly inflated trade issues places Japanese-Western economic relations in jeopardy, and retards progress on the real problems because it provides Japan with an excuse for believing that foreigners' complaints are just sour grapes.

A genuine case of a nontariff barrier that is, as of this writing, still being negotiated is that of metal baseball bats. This case received wide coverage in the press and came to serve as a symbol of the problems faced by foreign manufacturers wishing to export to Japan. Before telling this tale, however, it is important to emphasize that while metal bats may seem trivial, the case represents only the tip of the iceberg. Few outside of the business realize that most cases of harassment and discriminatory practices during customs clearance of foreign goods do not come to light. Often the circumstances are nebulous because the word of the importer is set against that of the customs official. In addition, during my term as president of the American Chamber in Japan, I found out that most small Japanese agents and importers acting as liaison for U.S. exporters were unwilling to approach the U.S. embassy with their complaints because they would have had to give names and full details. The embassy can do nothing about allegations couched in general terms. If a Japanese whose business was importing foreign goods made public allegations against a particular customs official, his business could be jeopardized. Many such small importers came to me when I was president to tell me of their troubles, and why they couldn't state them publicly. The inability to cite specific cases is a great handicap when trying to negotiate an end to NTB's. Thus such public cases as that of the metal bats assume an importance somewhat out of proportion to their purely commercial significance.

The metal-bat incident is a classic example of what can happen to a promising import into Japan. In 1973 metal baseball bats were first introduced into Japan, where they quickly became popular. In the beginning virtually all of them were imported from the United States, but domestic manufacturers quickly came up with their own versions, and locally made bats began displacing the imported ones from the market. However, some of the local bats were defective and broke apart at the grip. Many accidents occurred, but a real hue and cry was not raised until a broken bat hit a spectator on the head, causing injuries that left him unconscious for several months. Under the Japanese Consumer Product Safety Law, metal bats were then placed on a list of "specified products" that needed a special "S-mark" of approval affixed on them before they could be sold. The Japan Rubberized Baseball League (JSBB League) made its own standards for bats used in their games, and six Japanese manufacturers received approval.

This was the situation that American manufacturers faced when they again became interested in exporting metal bats to Japan. First they tried to get JSBB League approval but were unsuccessful, and the manufacturers realized that they would have to get S-mark approval from the government anyway. After the U.S. and Japanese governments became involved in negotiating the problem, the JSBB League agreed to modify its standards so that if a bat met the S-mark requirements, League approval would follow automatically. But again there was a snag. There are two ways of getting the S-mark in Japan: lot inspection or factory registration and model approval. Japanese manufacturers followed the latter procedure, which is cheaper and faster, and carries criminal penalties for violations to guarantee its effectiveness. Foreign suppliers were required to apply for the S-mark under the lot-inspection system, which involves costly delays in customs that would make the price of imported bats prohibitively high. A further irony in this requirement is that it forced stricter inspection on American-made bats, while it was the defects of the early Japanese-made bats that had given rise to the stringent safety laws. On top of all this, after the S-mark approval system was instituted, there were virtually no incidents of metal bats breaking because of manufacturing flaws.

The first U.S. firm that applied for S-mark approval did so under the system of factory registration and model approval but was turned down. So again the American government became involved in negotiations about metal baseball bats. Eventually the problem was resolved by removing bats from the list of "specified products" and instituting a different procedure of affixing an "SG-mark," which was further modified to accord the same treatment to foreign and domestic suppliers.

But this solution has not addressed the heart of the matter, which is still under discussion—that is, the fundamental nature of Japan's certification system. This involves a difference of opinion between the Japanese and American governments about the interpretation of the Preamble to the General Agreement of Tariffs and Trade (GATT), of which both the United States and Japan are signatories. The Japanese maintain that the Preamble allows any country to exclude a product if the reason given for doing so is that the government judges that it poses a possible threat to human life or the environment. The United States government has taken the position that this is an incorrect interpretation (possibly based on problems with the Japanese translation of the Preamble), and that in fact it states that no country may establish discriminatory certification procedures that have the effect of excluding foreign suppliers from the market. The United States used to discriminate in this way, subjecting foreign suppliers to lot inspection and reserving factory registration for domestic firms, but in the interest of promoting free trade this system was abolished in the 1950's. The Japanese were major beneficiaries of this revision. In light of this, it seems evident that the metal-bat problem has uncovered a clear-cut case where the Japanese government still maintains an archaic discriminatory attitude, which is directly contrary to the principles of free trade.

Although the list of products that require the S-mark is not long, it is the principle involved that makes these special cases so important. The length of time it has taken the Japanese to move on this issue is indicative of the long way left to go before an atmosphere of genuine free trade can flourish in Japan. And I fear that the ominous rise of protectionist sentiment in the West may end up forestalling this much needed development—with an impact on world trade that may well prove disastrous.

To give some added perspective on the dimensions of this problem, I cite a few examples from my own industry. Whenever a foreign pharmaceutical company wishes to change its manufacturing site, a laborious and painstaking procedure is invoked by the Japanese government, even though no inspection system is provided. In other words, if the Western pharmaceutical company registers a plant in the United States as a supplier of a certain pharmaceutical material, and then later on decides to switch the location to Puerto Rico or Europe, the company is required to undertake a series of bio-availability and stability studies to show that the product characteristics remain the same in the new plant. This procedure can take as long as two years. An additional barrier to drug imports is that all studies to prove the safety and efficacy of a drug must be repeated in Japan, despite the fact that these tests were probably performed under higher-quality laboratory conditions in the country where the product originated. The cost of repeating these studies can run into millions of dollars—and frequently does. Despite the fact that foreign-origin pharmaceutical products accounted for over 40 percent ($6 billion) of the Japanese pharmaceutical market at the retail level, out of a total market of approximately $15 billion in 1981, the Japanese government has promulgated the idea that only products that are manufactured completely in Japan are acceptable. Activities by Western exporters of drugs to Japan have focused on getting the Ministry of Health and Welfare to accept both laboratory and clinical research done abroad in order to ease the rules for transferring manufacturing and import licenses to new manufacturing sites, and to reduce the requirements necessary for changing the source of bulk chemicals or finished products. Easing the requirements of repeating stability studies and having the Japanese government give up its attempt to force foreign companies to manufacture everything from the chemical to the finished product in Japan are other issues being focused on by exporters to Japan through their various chambers of commerce. The Health Care Study Group of the American Chamber is particularly active in this area.

One disputed area that was finally resolved in 1979 opened bidding on Japanese government procurement contracts to foreign companies, which had previously been effectively prevented from doing so by bureaucratic barriers. This is a potentially lucrative ($8 billion per year) market. A barrier that foreign firms are learning how to evade is the far too short lead time that the Japanese government allows, usually either thirty or sixty days to make a bid after the public announcement. This is ludicrously inadequate for preparing a major bid, and the only way to deal with it is to hire a consultant (usually a man recently retired from the ministry concerned) to keep his ear to the ground and give prior warning about upcoming announcements. Firms interested in submitting bids for Japanese government contracts should obtain *Procedure Manual for Tenders to the Government of Japan,* an excellent pamphlet by Robert F Connely.*

In an additional move to forestall criticism, the government of Japan announced in June 1983 several proposals designed to relieve trade friction. Of these the most important, if put into effect, is to lower the commodity tax on autos with 2,000 cc or more engine displacement from 22.5 percent to 17.5 percent. Most imported automobiles fall into this category, so cars exported to Japan will be slightly more cost-competitive. These measures are unlikely to make a significant dent in the trade imbalance, but they at least display a certain willingness on the part of the Japanese to make concessions.

One of the major factors in making it difficult for Japanese companies to import products that might otherwise have found a good market is the high dollar-yen exchange rate, which makes dollar-denominated imports into Japan far more expensive than they were just a few years ago, when the exchange rate was about 30 percent more favorable for the importer than it is today. (In October 1978 the exchange rate was ¥178 to the U.S. dollar, and in 1984 it remained steady at approximately ¥246 to U.S. $1.) This has also had the effect of greatly increasing the attractiveness of Japanese exports.

Another major barrier is the so-called commodity tax, which varies by category but can add as much as 30 percent to the value of an imported product, for it is an additional tax beyond any customs duties. (Products manufactured in Japan are also subject to this tax.)

There are few cases of successful long-term importation of finished products into Japan by Western companies. Although there have been significant success stories, such as those involving Scotch and imported cosmetics, as well as other beverage products and specialities, particularly from Europe, even these profitable markets have been eroded by Japanese imitators and competition. The example of Scotch whisky is a good one. Traditionally the Japanese have considered Scotch an ideal gift. During gift-giving seasons imported Scotch, particularly Johnnie Walker Black Label, has been preferred for both business and personal gift giving. Formerly gifts of Scotch were sure

*This invaluable publication is available through the American Chamber of Commerce in Japan or in the United States can be ordered from Procurement Services International, P.O. Box 17960, Irvine, CA 92713. It has also been translated into seven European languages with the cooperation of the Commission of the European Communities.

to be appreciated, but the situation has now changed. Due to the differences in exchange rate and a number of changes in the customs regulations, Scotch prices have fluctuated wildly over the past few years, and as a result the Japanese buyer is no longer sure of the real value of the present he is giving. In America such valuation is not important, but in Japanese etiquette the exact value of a gift can mean the difference between correctness and insult. Suntory, a Japanese whisky maker, conscious of this problem, has developed a line of highly expensive and well-packaged local whiskies that have gradually eroded the franchise of the Soctch makers, since the recipient of the gift knows exactly how much the donor paid for the item received, whereas in the case of a bottle of Johnnie Walker Black Label it's possible to pay as low as ¥3,000, or as high as ¥8,000, depending on the outlet and the exchange rate.

Exporting to Japan is a thankless business, often resulting in disappointingly limited market shares and sales, imitation, or both. There are many drawbacks aside from the uncertainty and competitiveness of the Japanese marketplace, among them the unpredictable exchange rates and the havoc that product tailoring can cause in European or American manufacturing plants. Special product tailoring often requires increased overhead in the shape of retooling and other changes needed to meet the more exacting specifications of the Japanese market. Considering all these problems, I'm almost inclined to advise that (except in the case of high-commodity agricultural products, raw materials, and unique products that are impossible for the Japanese to imitate) exporting to Japan is only a realistic option when undertaken as a market-testing device prior to local manufacturing in a joint venture or other direct investment in manufacturing. But in good conscience I cannot really be this drastic. The pragmatic, results-oriented businessman in me tells me that this is the only realistic attitude toward exporting to Japan, but there is another side to the question. From one point of view, an operation in Japan that makes no money or perhaps even loses it may yet end up tremendously benefiting the firm undertaking it. The company will gain experience in the toughest market in the world, will have to upgrade its products to meet the most demanding standards, and, perhaps most important of all, will learn how to compete with the Japanese —knowledge that may prove invaluable in combating a Japanese challenge in its home market.

Before the reader becomes exasperated at being advised to lose money in Japan out of some quixotic notion of challenging the challengers even if the cause is hopeless, let me add that I don't believe that it is impossible to succeed in exporting to Japan. I *do* believe it is frustrating, time-consuming, and very difficult. But establishing a base in Japan will certainly give a company an advantage. Relying permanently on agents can be self-limiting. Also, exporting parts for assembly in Japan is far easier than exporting finished products, and the customs clearance process is much faster. Thus I would recommend trying to export components to one's own company for assembly in Japan rather than finished products to a third party.

Even if a firm has an excellent relationship with its partner in Japan, it may still end up outgrowing the partnership. This has probably happened with Kodak. Their original partnership with Nagase Trading worked wonderfully when there was no competition, but now that Fuji is battling with them for market share it would appear time for Kodak to commit itself more directly to the Japanese market. (It has been my experience that there are beginning to be problems in the distribution of Kodak film in Japan. On a trip to Amanohashidate, one of the most beautiful tourist spots in Japan, a place that simply cries out to be photographed and where film is second only to sushi as a popular tourist purchase, I could not find Kodak film anywhere, despite a diligent search. Amanohashidate is 45 miles from the nearest city of any size, so local distribution is critical.) But since Kodak and Nagase Trading have been happily wed for years, untying the partnership in the interests of growth may be difficult.

Exporting to Japan *is* tough, and one can easily be defeatist about it. But then the positive examples of two quite different men come to mind. The first I have already mentioned more than once—Akio Morita, and the story of his fight to establish the Sony brand name in America. That is a story of dogged determination to beat the odds that Westerners concerned about the trade imbalance would do well to recall. The other concerns a more obscure figure, who has determination equal to that of Morita. Donald ("Skip") Conover is a former U.S. marine who is the representative director of Schlegel Engineering (K.K.), a small upstate New York manufacturer of specially weatherproofed glass, with applications in the automotive and building industries. The company started out by joint venturing, but when Conover found it wasn't making money, he boldly dissolved it, decided to go it alone, and started knocking on doors. By absolutely refusing to give up, he has managed to make a success of it against all expectations (despite the fact that the name of his company is virtually impossible for a Japanese to pronounce).

The example of Schlegel Engineering proves that to succeed in Japan a company must come in with an absolute commitment to making it, no matter what the obstacles. Small to medium-sized manufacturers in particular will have a terrible time. They must come prepared to take on the market on its own terms, but also to vigorously pursue and publicize instances of harassment and discrimination via any avenue open to them—the embassy, the Chamber of Commerce, the U.S.-Japan Trade Study Group, the press, and any other available means. In short, foreign companies face an uphill battle, but the only long-term solution to the current precarious world-trade situation is for American and European companies to struggle to achieve in Japan what the Japanese have achieved in the United States and Europe.

CHAPTER
17

WORKING IN A JAPANESE COMPANY

Foreigners who work for the Japanese, particularly at the management level, must struggle to overcome the Japanese tendency to
exclude foreigners from the innermost councils of the company, to
distrust their loyalty, to feel that a foreign worker can never give as
much to the company as a Japanese would. The Japanese have considerable justification for this attitude: the Western habit of changing
jobs frequently, the headhunting, the attachment to self rather than
to the company, and the Western individualism, in general, disturb
the Japanese profoundly. Not only does this negative attitude lead
them to distrust foreign employees even more than they would normally, given their natural xenophobia, but it also sometimes hampers
the efficiency of their overseas plants. In *The Japanese Mind*, Robert
Christopher says that he was surprised at how many Japanese industrialists had reservations, unexpressed publicly, about the way their
American plants were run. Nonetheless, many overseas Japanese
manufacturing facilities have productivity rates virtually equal to
that of their domestic counterparts.

Still, it has been adequately demonstrated that many of the techniques commonly used in Japan can be effective anywhere, although
local culture must be taken into account before they can be implemented. Specifically, a company's commitment to motivating ordinary workers and integrating them as important members of the
enterprise is probably the most important thing we can learn from

Japan. Nevertheless, most Westerners are not willing to make the kinds of sacrifices typically demanded of Japanese workers. This may be why productivity in Japan is sometimes higher than that in Japanese-managed enterprises largely staffed by foreigners. While in itself admirable, the recent trend in the West of employees taking a much publicized cut in pay to save their company is only one aspect of what the Japanese mean by sacrificing for the company. It is not at all uncommon for Japanese employees to forgo their six-month bonuses for the company in a bad year. Most Japanese are emotionally committed to their companies in a way incomprehensible to Westerners, except possibly those labeled fanatics or workaholics. The cultural gap is enormous, and anyone who wants to get ahead in a Japanese firm must be willing not only to study his co-workers and learn to understand them, but also to respect them and participate wholeheartedly in their way of doing things.

One of the first things an ambitious person wishing to make a career for himself in a Japanese firm must decide to do is to learn Japanese. The importance of learning Japanese for anyone stationed in Japan has already been emphasized, but a knowledge of the language is equally essential for anyone embarked on a career in management at a Japanese firm. Without fluent Japanese, it will be difficult for a foreigner to have fruitful contact with the head office. Even just making an attempt to learn the language will at least demonstrate sincerity and commitment. Executives will open up to a Japanese-speaking employee as they never would—or could—with an employee who doesn't know the language.

Learning Japanese may not be practical for everyone, but even those working at a level where it is not needed will find that studying about the country and its people will be of great help in understanding the motivations of the boss, as well as those of the company. For one thing, even if the president speaks one's native tongue, he is not going to communicate with the same detail, clarity, or style with which a European or American would express himself. As explained earlier, blunt, forceful communication is taboo in Japan. Although Japanese accustomed to dealing with foreigners realize that their own way of expressing themselves is not always understood by foreigners, any Japanese who has left the country as an adult will find enormous difficulty, for example, in being strongly negative. Sometimes a Japanese, realizing that foreigners don't talk as diplomatically and circuitously as Japanese do, will go too far in the other direction and adopt a tone that may appear rude or even insulting. Understanding a Japanese superior's difficulties in communicating will help reduce friction and lessen the employee's own frustrations.

Although working in Japan may be far harder in the long run on an individual than simply working for a Japanese-run company overseas, the Western resident in Japan has the advantage of a personal experience of its society. Those living there see around them every day the social milieu that produced their colleagues and bosses. An American or European who works for the local-branch office of a Japanese multinational may well find the thought processes of his boss opaque, and start believing the myths of Oriental inscrutability. To cope with this situation, one must master the Japanese style of indirect communication, or remain in danger of never understanding what is really going on. The nuances of such speech cannot be absorbed right away. First, one has to learn how Japanese values differ from Western ones. Anyone committed to working in a Japanese organization should read *Japanese Society,* by socioanthropologist Chie Nakane. Other books discuss history, literature, and the arts in greater detail, and while those aspects of the country are also important, Nakane's book goes straight to the heart of what you will need to know—i.e., the principles of Japanese organization, social and otherwise. Nakane discusses extensively how business, bureaucratic, and political groups and organizations function. (It is dangerous, however, to take one work, no matter how authoritative, as gospel, particularly when it concerns a subject as complex and controversial as the structure of an entire society. One should make it a point to read anything and everything on Japan until one acquires a feel for the subject. The bibliography at the end of this book would be one place to look for sources of information.)

Those who are not resident in Japan should consider joining a local cultural organization that promotes understanding of Japan and its culture. The Japan-America Society, for example, has sixteen member societies located throughout the United States. Its purpose is "bringing the people of Japan and the United States closer together in understanding, appreciation, and cooperation."* Attending the meetings and cultural affairs of such a society not only would help broaden one's understanding of Japan, but also could serve as a useful

*The address of its headquarters in New York is Japan Society, 333 East 47th Street, New York, NY 10017.

source for personal contacts. One might also consider subscribing to *Japan Echo*, a quarterly magazine that publishes translations of abridged versions of selected articles that have appeared in important Japanese magazines and journals.* Unfortunately, there is no organization equivalent to the Japan Society in the United Kingdom, although there are a few organizations that engage in more limited activities.

Doing one's homework is important, but, obviously, it is not by itself going to guarantee success and happiness in a Japanese company. Keen observation of how the company works is essential. What is the company's reputation in Japan—is it number one or an also-ran? The answer to this will affect the caliber of executive sent abroad. Is the management centralized or decentralized? Do employees wait in fear and trembling for directives from Japan, or are they working on their own initiative? Generally speaking, managers in a Japanese company should not look for overt direction. The typical Japanese executive expects subordinates to come to him with their group's ideas charted out—and this becomes more true the higher one rises in the company. After a certain period the new Western middle manager in a Japanese company will typically start tearing his hair out, and exclaim that if they would only tell him exactly what to do and what they expect, he'd be delighted to buckle down and do it. But they usually will not tell the manager what to do—exactly, that is. Instead, the Japanese prefer to set general goals and targets, and try to inculcate in everyone in the organization an instinctive feel for the firm's needs, norms, and general direction, so that specific orders are not needed. To be successful, one must develop a kind of sixth sense, a hypersensitivity to subtle hints, that is an essential skill for working in a Japanese environment.

In an ordinary Western firm, management not only will set general goals and targets but will order specific assignments to be achieved by certain approved methods. In a highly bureaucratic company these may be fairly rigid and strictly enforced. Even in a less structured firm there will still be much more overt direction than in a typical Japanese company. If employees do not perform up to standard, they will usually be informed of this quite directly. In Japan, direct criticism is taboo, but the employee "senses" if his perform-

*TBR Building, 10-2, Nagata-cho 2-chome, Chiyoda-ku, Tokyo 100 Japan. Airmail is extra.

ance is satisfactory. A Japanese manager is more likely to be open about his own faults than a Western manager, because the Japanese have not only more job security but also more group support and tolerance of individual shortcomings. Once a Japanese is accepted into a group and abides by its norms, he has the right to expect his colleagues' nearly unconditional loyalty and support. In such an atmosphere, criticism takes on the connotation of a direct personal attack; therefore people avoid criticizing one another, but indirectly and subtly let it be known where improvement may be needed.

There are many differences between Japanese and Western organizations, but in the area of understanding people's motivations and coordinating a group effort, the Japanese are in fact more realistic than most Americans. Americans like to think of themselves as straight-talking and hardheaded, but experienced managers soon learn almost reflexively to pussyfoot around their employees' shortcomings unless they have made up their minds to fire an incompetent. It is a simple fact of human nature that criticism is usually perceived as an attack, and leads to defensiveness or demoralization. Neither reaction is conducive to a resolution of the problem, and for this reason alone no-holds-barred criticism is often counterproductive. The Japanese know this instinctively, and employ subtle signals to convey to an employee where he stands in terms of performance. There is likely to be a tacit acknowledgment among the members of a work group that one person is a whiz, another a duffer, and a third average but reliable. Integrating all these personalities and abilities so that they form an effective team is what management is all about in Japan.

This system works in Japan because the Japanese are accustomed to interpreting nuances of behavior and are trained to work in groups. But all this subtlety may be lost on the Westerner, who often is not skilled in reading even the heavy-handed hints of a typical Western boss. Pascale and Athos comment in *The Art of Japanese Management* that many Americans are caught by surprise when they are fired, although hindsight reveals that the boss dropped plenty of hints, if only the employee had been paying attention.

It has already been emphasized that Japanese management style typically gives more latitude to lower-level managers than is common in Western firms. One area where the difference is particularly noticeable is in sales. The head office in a Japanese firm will set overall strategy and targets for the year, but specific implementation is left to the regional branch managers. The branch manager occupies an important post because he is the regional representative of the company, and he must be a walking advertisement for his firm. There will usually be more emphasis on performance at this level than at some others; branch managers who don't perform will be demoted to a lesser branch or to a staff job at the head office. To a Japanese such a demotion would be a terrible blow because it would cause him to lose face. Thus, even though the so-called lifetime employment system ensures that a manager will almost never be fired, the system does hold out the threat of punishment in other ways.

A Westerner who is demoted in a Japanese company may not have face in the Japanese sense, but he does have pride. However, protesting that the demotion was unjust—a typical response of hurt pride —is not the way to get back into favor. The only approach is to maintain a low profile, perhaps apologize for any mistake (apologies are important in Japanese society), and then work as hard as possible in order to show that one desires to regain face.

An excellent way to gain acceptance in a Japanese company—after studying Japanese and obtaining a thorough knowledge of the overseas subsidiary of the company—is to request an orientation trip to the head office in Japan for several weeks or months. This contact will prove an invaluable experience, which will help to improve a Westerner's standing in, and familiarity with, the company's operations.

The nine-to-five attitude so prevalent among Westerners is difficult for most Japanese to understand because of the intense personal identification with the workplace that is endemic to Japan. The Japanese invest much of their emotional life in their work, not so much for its own sake, necessarily, as from a concern for not letting their fellow workers down. For example, when journalist Satoshi Kamata worked in a Toyota factory for six months to find out what it was like, despite the hellish conditions he faced there he felt guilty when taking days off, and even slightly sheepish about quitting at the end of his six-month contract. The reason was that he knew his absence would place a terrible burden on his co-workers.

Perhaps it should be clarified that what has been said so far about working for a Japanese company applies mostly to office workers. Few foreigners have ever worked at blue-collar jobs in Japan. Manufacturing investment by Japanese companies in America and Europe has been increasing in recent years, resulting in some remarkable success stories, but it is impossible to tell how Japanese management really feels about their foreign blue-collar workers. In Japan, despite quality circles and a commitment to worker involvement, it is nonetheless true that in one sense there is a sharp division between management and labor. Japan is often called a meritocracy, meaning that anyone who passes the exams to go to a university can leave his humble origins behind. But the other side of the coin is that anyone who fails is relegated to lower-status jobs for life. There are no second chances, and this "narrow gate" creates a sharp class division in Japan, although it is after the fact and not based on birth (though it has been established that families who can afford expensive private schools and tutoring have a better chance of getting their children into a university). Japanese are naturally not eager to publicize this aspect of their society, and it is difficult to determine the sincerity of a company's pronouncements about its attitude toward its blue-collar workers.

Kamata's book, *Japan in the Passing Lane,* which describes his experience at Toyota, is a chilling indictment of life on the Toyota assembly line as it was in 1972–73. Kamata claims that the situation has actually worsened since then, and that Toyota achieves cost reductions by speeding up the work and hiring fewer workers. He goes so far as to allege that the way Toyota has implemented automation has actually made it more difficult for workers. Quality circles, at least when Kamata was there, were perceived as a burden, and like the suggestion boxes fashionable at one time in U.S. factories, the ideas adopted often did as much harm as good, since it was not a genuinely integrated process, as quality control must be if it is to be truly effective. (This is not to say that quality circles cannot be extraordinarily effective if undertaken in the right spirit.)

If there is truth in Kamata's allegations, one wonders what GM will "learn" from Toyota as a result of their U.S. joint venture. It is clear that American workers will never acquiesce to such draconian methods. If Toyota treats its workers as if they were soldiers in a commercial war, and this is the "secret" to their success, it won't be of much help to Western auto industries. Neither patriotism, fanatic company loyalty, nor intense devotion to one's fellow workers can be relied on to motivate workers in a Japanese company in either Europe or America.

Toyota is rumored to be a worst-case example, but even more humane working conditions will not elicit the same dedication from *gaijin* as from Japanese. One young American who works in Sony's

California plant commented in a *Time* magazine interview that he was personally satisfied with his job, but implied that it was not exactly the anchor of his spiritual existence. He said that Japanese management had yet to comprehend fully that most of their blue-collar employees live for the weekend. Even in Japan this may be more true than management would like to think, but peer pressure, combined with subsidized evening meals and company entertainment, will usually succeed in maintaining a high level of dedication even among those who do not wholeheartedly believe that the company is the fount of all goodness.

Foreign blue-collar workers in a Japanese company will be happier if they can feel a true dedication to the company and trust its management. In Japan such trust is mutual, and even at Toyota, where worker grumbling was apparently quite common at the time Kamata was there, most workers felt respect for the lower to middle managers with whom they came in contact and sympathy for the problems of the foremen. If the old adversarial relationship of management and labor can be dismantled in the West, the Japanese example will have precipitated an important chapter in modern history.

Still, it is obvious that Japanese methods cannot be imported wholesale. In Sony's California plant, for example, management made the wearing of company smocks optional, and few workers chose to wear them. More ominously, workers in the Centerville, Ohio, Honda plant refused to wear Honda hats and wanted to wear union ones instead. This incident had all the makings of a head-on collision between Japanese management and American workers. To Japanese management the insistence on wearing union emblems rather than company ones suggested that their workers did not believe that they were full members of the company they worked for, that they did not trust management, and had no particular attachment to Honda. In short, these workers were fulfilling the worst fears of the Japanese about American and European labor. On the other hand, the workers felt that they were union men, and since the union was, at least in theory, a workers' organization, they probably felt at some level that to wear company hats would be conformist, whereas union hats expressed individuality and pride in self.

In *The Japanese*, Edwin O. Reischauer points out that much of the individualism in Western cultures is illusory, and that while the Japanese build impossible myths of perfect harmony, we indulge in impossible images of ourselves as perfectly free and unfettered individuals. A *true* nonconformist would refuse to wear either a company hat or a union one, and would be incapable of functioning in an organization. Thus the wearing of uniforms per se was not an issue here—the workers had declared their willingness to wear a uniform by wanting to wear union hats. By doing so, they sent a clear message to management that they regarded managers as guilty until proven innocent. American and European managers usually return the compliment and regard workers with equal suspicion.

What is at issue here is not just how to get along in a Japanese company, but whether or not Western workers and managers can evolve fast enough, learning to disregard the old adversarial relationship and try something new, in order to save traditional industries and prevent new ones from succumbing to the same disease. Japanese direct manufacturing investment is touted as a solution to the trade imbalance, but it can be successful in the long run only if it helps precipitate a revolution in management-worker relationships and working attitudes among blue-collar Americans and Europeans. In fact, the Japanese companies with the best records in foreign manufacturing are often those that have avoided industry-wide unions and instituted a company-wide union instead.

Anyone who is considering working for a Japanese company should know that "the British disease" is a common phrase in Japan. It refers to a widespread belief that the basic problem of British (and other Western) industry is laziness, apathy, and lack of devotion to the company on the part of workers. This is obviously a view that is simplistic to the point of absurdity. British class hatred is a festering sore that has far more to do with "the British disease" than supposed worker laziness. Nevertheless many Japanese firmly believe that *gaijin* are lazy. Sophisticated Japanese executives with international experience have a more complete view, but the American or British worker must prove that laziness has nothing to do with it, and that they can respond to the needs of an organization that includes them as genuine members with full rights. In turn, it is up to the Japanese company to prove that it does in fact manage its organization on this basis. Many Japanese companies with successful foreign operations have succeeded primarily because management has been able to motivate the enthusiasm, trust, and loyalty of workers.

What has been said about blue-collar workers applies equally well to clerical workers. Japanese clerical workers don't get a much better deal than American ones. There is less scope for promotion, in part because many companies have a policy of gently discouraging female employees from staying on after they are married. But the main reason is that executive secretaries don't exist in Japan in the form that they do in the West. Managers draw on secretarial and clerical services as they are required, but even the top executives are not usually assigned a personal secretary who looks after all aspects of their business and social lives. This is another example of the lack of special perquisites and privileges of rank in a Japanese office that contributes to a feeling that all employees are working together. The rewards of performance, rank, and seniority in Japan are less tangible than in the West. This is one reason why Japanese companies can command such worker devotion, because their system provides visible evidence that executives are working hard for the good of the company and not merely to achieve wealth and power. The efforts to include everyone in the company culture extend down to the clerical pool. Even the lowliest stenographer is expected to be able to recite the official company philosophy, to be familiar with its industry ranking, and to be knowledgeable about other details. Western clerical workers who feel genuinely enthusiastic about their jobs will be far better suited to a Japanese company than those who don't understand the importance of such things as company songs or who feel cynical about them.

Frequently I have asked Western executives (particularly in middle-level management) about the group turnover or sales of their corporation, and have been surprised when they don't seem to know, and can only quote the figures of their own subsidiary or division. This would be inconceivable in Japan, where any executive can tell you about group turnover, division turnover, branch turnover, the relative change from the prior year, and his company's standing in the industry—all of which he knows by heart. Japanese companies take themselves seriously, and believe that only through the unified and enthusiastic efforts of all their employees can the organization prosper. If you look at it in this way, it appears to be mere common sense. Such a strong and vital organization will have a tremendous advantage over an old-fashioned company riddled with conflicts and contradictions.

The reason why I keep making generalizations about Japanese companies is that no two are exactly alike. Taken as a group, they share many characteristics that distinguish them from Western organizations, but individually they differ considerably. When joining a Japanese company, it is essential to orient oneself to the company culture as soon as possible. It would be even better, of course, to find out before being hired what its atmosphere is like, what its principles of organization are, and what role its management foresees for its foreign employees. If it is possible to get this information, a prospective employee will have a better idea of whether he or she can fit in. Once hired, the foreigner had better be prepared to quickly get a feel for both the official and unofficial philosophies of the company by observing how the staff interact and what elements are given priority.

One chronic problem of foreigners who work for or with Japanese is that many of them will start to feel a sneaking sense of superiority to the Japanese. This is a totally irrational feeling, which one may not even be aware of. There are several reasons for it, chief of which are: Westerners tend to be taller than Japanese; feeling superior is one way of guarding against the effects of culture shock; racism, conscious or unconscious; self-defensiveness, most commonly a result of the attitude that it doesn't matter that the Japanese are beating us hollow on the trade front because we are somehow morally superior; xenophobia and ethnocentricity, often lurking in the shape of beliefs so central that one doesn't realize one holds them.

The tendency to feel superior is insidious, and it must be fought against. It is a stubborn weed, and its root is always a bit deeper and harder to get at than you thought when you started digging. Espousing a traditionally liberal, egalitarian ideology will not be enough to keep one from making this mistake. It is essential to begin with a set of *examined* assumptions. This is particularly important for those who are going to Japan for training or on business, or to settle there. Steven D. Myers, an American businessman with extensive experience in Japan and an old friend, recommends that those going to Japan should draw up a list of their values, make a point of noting in their reading about Japan where their values differ, and also be aware of the cultural clashes they experience when they arrive in Japan. Myers emphasizes that one should develop a strategy for dealing with these clashes that is neither self-defensive nor patronizing.[1] By being aware, curious (though not pointedly so), open, and nonjudgmental, one can learn a lot and avoid the dangers of a superiority complex. The Japanese are extremely sensitive, and may be able to detect a negative attitude even if the foreigner doesn't himself realize that he has one.

Japanese are also better than Americans are at detecting phonies. If an employee enthusiastically participates in company activities designed to increase personal contact and esprit de corps but fails to maintain a rapport with his co-workers when in the office, they will not be fooled. Indeed, they are likely to resent it if a foreign boss, for example, is willing to go out with them for a drink after work but is unwilling to become truly interested in their personal affairs. Most Japanese prefer a boss who demands a lot but is understanding, and supportive of their personal problems, to one who is not so tough but is aloof. Japanese are usually far more sensitive to slights than Westerners are, and indeed may find certain behavior on the part of a Westerner insulting when no such implication is intended. The opposite also holds true, and both sides must keep the cultural gap in mind at all times.

One Western pastime that is unlikely to be tolerated in a Japanese office is toadying to the boss in the hope of wheedling a promotion from him. This aversion to sycophants stems from the emphasis on teamwork and group achievement in a Japanese company. Human nature being what it is, it is not that a Japanese boss would be unsusceptible to flattery or the temptation to indulge in favoritism; rather, it is the system that militates against it. However, Japanese companies do have factions, and the leaders of a given group tend to become "godfathers" to its junior members, giving and expecting a high degree of loyalty in return for preferential consideration for promotion to jobs controlled by the godfathers. This is in contrast to the practice fashionable in America of promoting superstars and whiz kids over the heads of older members of the company, which seems absurd to the Japanese. Their philosophy tends to the belief that merit will out, and contributions to the company will be rewarded in due course—that is, when the junior employee has collected enough seniority to be in a position to be in line for such a job. The Japanese believe in the long-term benefits of promoting harmony among the staff, since by the very nature of the system over- and under-achievers will always have to work side by side. Japanese companies have made a few tentative moves toward awarding merit raises and promotions, but it goes against the grain of the culture, and employees often oppose the idea. To what extent a Japanese firm will modify this system in their Western affiliates will depend on the company. Few Westerners have the patience to wait for their reward to come in the fullness of time, if at all, so it seems likely that the

Japanese will find it difficult to retain this policy when hiring foreigners.

Even in Japan itself employment patterns and practices are changing. More women are being hired for real jobs, beyond the occupations of tea lady and escalator girl that were the main options before. It is still extraordinarily difficult for a woman graduate to find a job with a large established Japanese firm, but the new small high-tech entrepreneurial firms, which have trouble attracting high-caliber employees because most highly qualified Japanese prefer to work for large established companies, have started hiring women. There is also some limited scope for qualified foreigners interested in working in Japan to find jobs with such firms. In the February 1982 edition of *Business View* (an English-language cassette-tape magazine directed at Japanese businessmen) there was an interview with Ben Hollin, a young American electrical engineer who was working in Japan on a two-year contract with a small Japanese semiconductor firm. On receiving his degree from a California university, Hollin turned down offers from several large American firms and accepted an offer to go to Japan because he felt that it was "where the action is" in the field of semiconductor technology. He found the Japanese staff to be shy at first, but once his language improved to the point where he could begin communicating, relations improved and co-workers opened up to him. One difficulty he did come across was due to the different curricula followed in Japanese and U.S. engineering courses. The Japanese he worked with expected him to know certain details he hadn't been taught in American schools. On the other hand, he had learned some things that the Japanese didn't know.

Hollin's experience suggests that the exchange of technical knowledge and viewpoint between Japan and the West could be greatly facilitated if more American and European engineers could go to work there. Unfortunately, given the nature of Japanese business and society, it is rather pointless to expect many Japanese to come to work in Western firms, and there are problems for Westerners working in Japan. One point Hollin emphasized was the difficulty a foreigner will experience in securing a work permit. The attitude of the government is basically protectionist, and visas are hard to come by for any kind of work that can be performed equally well by a citizen. Of course, the same is true of Western governments' policies on issuing work visas for Japanese going to the United States or Europe.

No one who works for a Japanese company should ignore the fact that most Japanese dread overseas postings and, even if they like living abroad, will usually be apprehensive (with good reason) about how they will fit in on returning to Japan. The move is especially difficult for those who have families. The Japanese educational system is rigid, and even a few years spent abroad may place in jeopardy a child's chances of getting into a good university. Thus the expatriate Japanese executive faces the prospect of either leaving his wife and children behind in Japan or bringing them along at substantial risk to the children's educational careers. Also, a Japanese posted abroad may be apprehensive that he will fall out of touch with his home, office, friends, and business contacts in Japan. Perhaps the career escalator will leave him behind, since he is so far from the center of things. Chie Nakane comments that Japanese abroad, even more than most other nationalities, often tend to form little closed societies of expatriates who don't mingle with local people at all. These problems and insecurities may diminish an expatriate Japanese's effectiveness and, moreover, make him even less inclined than he would normally be to explore and adapt to the new culture in which he finds himself. I recall an interview with a Japanese executive who said that the first time he was posted abroad he made no contacts in American society. On his second tour he was determined not to repeat this experience. He joined some business organizations, and in one of them was amazed that he was elected to chair a committee over the heads of Americans both older than he and with longer standing in the organization. Such a thing could never happen in Japan, a society where hierarchy plays such an important role, and which, moreover, is closed to those it perceives as outsiders. Japanese managers whose task is to motivate foreign employees will have to break out of their shell, but it should be recognized that this involves considerable effort for them.

As the Japanese internationalize their business operations, the task of influencing Japanese business toward a truly global perspective will fall to a certain extent on the shoulders of foreigners who work for Japanese subsidiaries. Japanese companies are beginning to invest in foreign manufacturing facilities not because they want to but because they have to. It is in the interests of the global economy that Japanese business lose its parochial orientation, and a significant step toward this goal will be the success of Japanese companies in establishing strong foreign operations. A necessary condition for that success will be harmonious relations with their Western employees and the promotion of foreigners to senior management positions over Japanese support and technical staff. This will happen only if the local employee makes the effort to meet his Japanese superiors halfway.

CHAPTER 18

WE NEED EACH OTHER

The West has underestimated Japan's importance in the world for far too long. Europeans are perhaps more guilty of this practice than Americans, but Washington cannot be entirely exonerated of the charge. Now that the developed nations of the West have begun to wake up to the fact of Japan's strength, their reactions have tended to be hostile and accusatory. Japan, meanwhile, has allowed itself to remain in a cocoon of unjustified belief in its specialness and unique vulnerability, and under continued attack seems to favor the posture of the injured innocent. Both these reactions are dangerous, for Japan and the West cannot afford to drift apart. We need each other. The present divisiveness and "Jap-bashing" is useful only to the enemies of a free-world economy. We must decide to hang together, or, as Benjamin Franklin said in another context, we shall, most assuredly, all hang separately.

The United States and Japan have had a special relationship ever since World War II, and one could even make a case that the specialness of this bilateral relation stretches back to Admiral Perry's adventure more than a hundred years ago. Most nations regard the Japanese negatively; only in the United States have the circumstances created a cadre of influential men who are favorably disposed to Japan. (The Chinese understand their neighbors better, perhaps, but the painful memories of Japanese militarism linger.) When history forced Europeans out of their Madame Butterfly daydreams of a toy country full of docile maidens and obliging gentlemen, the perception swung to an opposite extreme: of demoniac conquering hordes, or, in the latest manifestation, dehumanized fanatic workers—economic predators who can hardly be distinguished from the robots they are so fond of installing.

The relationship of Europe with Japan is not and cannot be as close or as vital to the interests of either as that between Japan and the United States. Indeed, due to the inability of the Japanese to explain themselves, the task of explaining this country to the world has fallen largely to Americans. It may well be that only a strengthening of the U.S.-Japan bond can avert the present threat of a global trade war as country after country begins to close its borders to Japan, and then to other countries, with disastrous consequences. Asia needs Japan, the United States needs Japan, and even Europe needs Japan, if Europeans will only admit the fact.

The U.S.-Japan relationship, which has been deteriorating in recent years, must be repaired. The prescription necessary to achieve this end has two components. One is that Japan must develop a more truly international outlook and leave behind its outmoded insistence on Japan as a special case, somehow exempt from the obligations of other major nations. The other necessary ingredient in any lasting solution to current trade frictions is a commitment on the part of other developed nations to restructure their economies. Using Japan as a scapegoat for all the economic ills of the West may be a useful ploy serving the interests of politicians by providing them with a handy excuse for their domestic economic problems, but in the long run such an approach will only destroy Japan's respect for and reliance on the West. Moreover, it will also ultimately enfeeble Western nations because scapegoating foreigners distracts attention from the vital necessity for changes at home.

Because I am a businessman, I am not susceptible to the *tatemae* blandishments of Japanese bureaucrats who have convinced some Westerners that the Japanese are only guilty of the crime of winning the game. When foreigners assert that Japan is in many important ways still a closed market, it is not just a matter of the defeated party self-defensively accusing the victors of cheating (though it certainly serves the interests of the Japanese to make it appear that this is so). No—Japan has far to go in establishing itself as a free and open market, such as Europe and the United States are. It is time for a bold new Japanese initiative aimed at encouraging imports from all developed nations and reversing the policy the country has followed ever since World War II of political isolationism coupled with economic expansionism.

As many commentators have pointed out, it is only in the United States that the Japanese have found fast friends. Our economic and political strength, together with our relative lack of insecurity in an increasingly dangerous world, have enabled us to view the defeated Japanese magnanimously, and to help place Japan in the position it holds today of a stable, developed democracy. Having a strong, solid ally in such a strategic region of the world is critical to our national interest. Despite the Japanese preference for seeing themselves as neutral and peace-loving, the U.S.-Japan bilateral relation is an alliance that is vital to our mutual and individual interests.

The essential source of current problems in Japanese-American relations is the bilateral trade deficit. One of the most profound bonds linking Japan and the United States is our common economic system. Therefore to a certain extent it is ironic that economic issues are driving the two nations apart. The clash was inevitable, given that U.S. industry in the fifties and sixties was not foresighted enough to recognize that economic dominance cannot be maintained without constantly monitoring trends and adjusting to them as circumstances change. The West is currently suffering the effects of the failure of business to take the long view twenty years ago. But it is still not too late to respond, and indeed the high-tech growth industries have already acknowledged that Japan cannot be ignored. Perhaps it is too late for other, older industries, such as steel, but even the Japanese face an uphill fight in their traditional heavy industries against the newly industrialized countries (NIC's).

In this sense, Japan and the other developed nations of the world are basically in the same situation, all needing to readjust their economies away from traditional mainstays. Japanese-style business is geared to the long term, and if Western business is prepared to begin focusing its sights past the next quarter, it will come to realize that Japan and the West are economically interdependent. The United States and Japan have a $75 billion bilateral annual trading relationship. If this came to a halt, virtually the whole world economy would be affected. Japan is the largest single customer for U.S. farm products, and we are Japan's best customer for its manufactured goods. Our two economies are deeply interdependent, and we cannot afford to let simplistic protectionist reactions to bilateral trade imbalances damage this vital relationship.

If the economic relationship between Japan and the United States is important, our military relationship may be even more so. Japan is the headquarters of the U.S. Pacific fleet and one of the most important bases for U.S. forces in the Pacific. In exchange for this, the United States offers Japan a place under its nuclear umbrella, and guarantees Japan's territorial integrity against foreign aggression. With the increase in Soviet military activity in the Western Pacific, the Japanese have more need than ever of American protection, and the United States of a strong ally in the region. It is America's nuclear shield that has given Japan the security it needs for its successful economic progress. Whether or not Japan has been getting a "free ride" at the expense of U.S. taxpayers, as some have charged, there is no denying that the U.S.-Japan alliance is vital to both.

Another reason why the United States needs Japan is that Japan serves as an example to other East Asian countries that free enterprise flourishes best in a democracy. Dictatorships in newly industrialized countries continue to be an embarrassment to U.S. foreign policy, and a force for instability in their regions. The significance of the Japanese example is that it has achieved its successes by invoking a national consensus that has consistently elected a party dedicated to free enterprise. Japan has never needed to resort to the strongman tactics favored by many of its neighbors, where a dictator is supported, or at least tolerated, by business interests. In this sense, Japan is a role model for Asia; since South Korea and other neighboring countries seem inclined to take a leaf from its economic textbook, perhaps they will also learn some political lessons from Japan. One argument against imposing protectionist measures on Japan—isolating it is a sort of pariah for supposed economic crimes of opportunism —is that, as Robert Christopher has pointed out in *The Japanese Mind*, the Liberal Democratic Party would probably not be able to survive a severe depression. If such a depression was brought on, or perceived to have been brought on, by economic sanctions imposed by the West, it is unlikely that the LDP's replacement would win the election based on a forgive-and-forget platform. U.S.-Japan relations could then be irretrievably damaged and Japanese democracy itself imperiled.

Even though Japan and the United States are far apart in many respects, it should not be forgotten that the two societies share many common goals and values. It would indeed be a pity if we sacrificed the considerable goodwill Japan has toward the United States on the altar of a futile protectionism. Already Japanese confidence in the United States is much eroded because of the defeat in Vietnam and the economic slump of recent years. But improving relations cannot be solely up to us. Japan must pull out of its "Japan first" isolationism and wake up to the realities of its responsibilities as the second major industrial power in the world. As Mike Mansfield, the U.S. ambassador to Japan, has often commented, the U.S.-Japan bond is unquestionably the most important bilateral economic relationship in the world.

As emphasized throughout this book, the main issue dividing the United States and Europe, on the one hand, and Japan, on the other, is trade. The chief target of attack is Japan, though bilateral disputes between the Common Market and the United States are not rare. There are many who are ready, willing, and indeed eager to point a finger at Japan. There are others who, perhaps out of some sort of exaggerated anti-xenophobia, are given to overdefending Japan, minimizing Japanese faults, and magnifying American and European ones. A prominent journalist and an academic have each written a book propounding Western guilt and incompetence and lauding Japanese virtues. Such views are as distorted as those of any simpleminded denigrator of the Japanese. Liberal breast-beating and an "Ain't we awful" attitude will do nothing to save our dying industries. Excessive negativism is a shortcut to an unjustified despair.

However, the advocates of a "Learn from Japan" ideology perform a certain service by contrasting our weaknesses with their strengths, thus preventing any honest person from seriously maintaining that the Japanese have merely exploited our generosity. The fact is that we are not comfortable with an economically strong Japan. The United States and Japan had such a cozy big-brother–little-brother relationship for so many years that we conveniently forgot that even if junior still owes us respect, he can grow up to overtake us. And an adult sibling has the right to decide whether or not his elder brother behaves in a way deserving of deference and admiration.

Perhaps the biggest problem preventing both Americans and Europeans from really understanding Japan is our ignorance of Japan's history of economic modernization. It is a common misconception that Japan somehow catapulted its way to industrialization in a few years following World War II. It is true that Japan compressed its industrial revolution into half the time it took in the West; it managed to do so in one century, while Europe and America underwent a more gradual evolution over the course of two centuries. But although a century represents a rapid pace in this time frame, it is a far cry from a few decades.

It should be recalled that the Japanese copied Bell's telephone just two years after it was invented, and duplicated the light bulb within eleven years of its invention by Edison. It was no mean achievement, but while foreigners misconceive of the Japanese as a recently backward people who sneakily caught up with the West using dubious means, Japanese go to the other extreme. They tend to misinterpret the cause of their rise as the only fully developed nation in Asia by ascribing it to some unique Japanese tribal characteristic that sets them apart from other peoples. The truth is that there is a more pragmatic explanation. From ancient times Japan has been an isolated island culture, far more unified in religion and culture than most Asian nations, and with a long tradition of a strong central government. There should be no mystique about Japan's hitherto unique position as an Asian developed nation; the examples of Taiwan, Singapore, and Korea are enough to prove that Japan's success is no freak. As Edwin Reischauer points out in *The Japanese,* in the distant future the West's headstart of one or two centuries in the Industrial Revolution will be perceived as a mere detail. Taking the long view, it is evident that China, now that it has left the madness of the Cultural Revolution behind it, is likely to pose the same "threat" eventually to the older developed nations that Japan and the NIC's pose today—that is, if we choose to perceive as a threat the advance of a nation from weakness and poverty to strength and wealth.

Japan was in a desperately weak position after World War II. Some, who dislike ascribing Japanese success to American weakness, have even gone so far as to suggest that one of the key advantages that the country had was that it had to rebuild most of its industrial plant after World War II, because the U.S. armed forces had done its industry the favor of flattening most of it to the ground. This "advantage," if it can be called such, forced the Japanese to modernize in the fifties. But they have also continued modernizing, continually straining to keep pace with changes and improvements in production techniques. U.S. industry should have been doing the same, even though it was not lucky enough to attract uninvited aerial demolition crews happy to pulverize its outmoded equipment at no charge.

Less tangible factors have also entered into the "miracle": Japanese national pride, its burning desire to catch up and blot out the humiliation of its defeat in the Pacific war; the fear of vulnerability —the export-or-die mentality of a resource-poor nation. This last factor has hardly been intangible in practice, and while Japan may be justly proud of its achievements, the fact is that it sheltered its vulnerable, infant industries until they were large and strong and could take care of themselves. As pointed out at length in Chapter 17, the residue of this old protectionist attitude lingers, not just on the government level, but also in the minds of its people, and is substantially damaging to Japan's relations with Europe and America.

The basic foreign policy of Japan ever since the war has been to export manufactured goods to pay for the raw materials it must import. It is the driving need for foreign exchange to enable the country to fulfill its energy and food requirements that has stimulated its rise to the top. Whether Japan was right or wrong in practicing protectionism in the past, this policy is clearly an anachronism in the 1980's.

The Japanese have not faced up to the new reality, and the older generation still nourishes a "To hell with foreigners" attitude that works against the country's national interest. This old ideology must be rooted out. In coming years it will not be enough to have mastered the technique of cracking foreign markets. The Japanese will have to learn about foreign peoples as well. To break out of its centuries-old isolationism will be a revolution more profound than any Japan has yet undergone, but it is a revolution that must take place if Japan truly wishes to be number one. A leader among nations has responsibilities as well as privileges—and the former tend to outweigh the latter, especially since one of those responsibilities is defense.

In *Misunderstanding*, Endymion Wilkinson cites the following figures: "Per capita, in 1981, the United States spent $760 on defense; Britain $572; France $483; Germany $405; Italy $155, and neutral Sweden and Switzerland $455 and $154, respectively. Japan spent $98."[1] Defense is a thorny issue in Japan. Technically speaking, it is questionable that the self-defense forces are in fact legal. The country's constitution has a no-war clause that Japanese often point to when foreigners press for a more equitable contribution to defense expenditures. But the self-defense forces do exist, and despite much initial opposition from the Japanese Left, it has been many years since there have been serious protests. The legal limit on defense spending of 1 percent of GNP is in fact violated by means of excluding certain expenditures, such as military pensions, that are included in most other countries' defense-budget figures. By international reckoning, Japan actually spends 1.6 percent of its GNP on defense. Since its GNP is huge, this is not an insignificant amount; nonetheless, when the United States, with an even larger GNP, spends 6.5 percent (1983 figures), there is considerable scope for Japan to increase its contribution.

Japan's pacifist foreign policy has been remarkably effective up to now, and any dramatic increase in its military strength would no doubt alarm its neighbors. Bitter memories die hard. Given the current world situation, it is politically impossible for Japan to go nuclear at any time in the near future. Only if there were to be some calamitous threat to its internal security would Japanese public opinion swing to support a domestic nuclear capability. The possibility of such a change occurring is not remote, but at present it is not necessary, and in any case it is doubtful that a Japanese bomb would be in the interests of the United States. It could well drive us apart, since it would be likely to occur only if Japan perceived us as too weak to offer a credible defense.

There is plenty of room for improvement in Japan's conventional forces. The present Prime Minister, Yasuhiro Nakasone, has on several occasions demonstrated that he believes in a more effectively armed Japan, so there is reason to hope that the country will gradually move in this direction. It is not simply more and better armaments that are required. The Japanese defense forces do not coordinate the operations of the different branches. Because of Japan's experience when the military got out of control in the 1930's, it has built civilian control into the present defense structure. However, this retards progress toward better organization. There should be one senior military man responsible for overseeing all the forces, in a position similar to that of the chairman of the Joint Chiefs of Staff in the United States. In addition, the country must learn to cooperate more effectively with its allies; Japanese, American, and Korean forces should be working together to promote the security interests of all three. The old enmity between Japanese and Koreans makes progress in this area difficult, but closer cooperation must be achieved eventually if the region is to be defended adequately.

As I repeatedly emphasized, one factor that consistently inflicts great damage on Japan's relations with the West is the unfortunate tendency of Europeans never to take Japan seriously (except in the cartoon form of a Yellow Peril), and for Americans to take them seriously only sometimes. The Japanese still referred to the "Nixon shocks," often and indignantly, eleven years after they occurred. These were a series of moves directly affecting Japan that Washington took without consulting Tokyo. The deepest insult was President Nixon's visit to China, which was not announced previously to the Japanese government. Tokyo had always understood that its loyalty to Washington's Chinese policy, despite its desire to reestablish relations with China, gave it certain rights and privileges. When Nixon utterly ignored them, the Japanese took it as a direct insult—a matter of face. Intentionally or not, Nixon's action showed his—and Kissinger's—low estimation of Japan's importance. When, in the early 1970's, Nixon moved unilaterally to cut off exports of soybeans to Japan because of a temporary shortage in the United States, the abrupt suspension was greeted with dismay and panic in Japan, ever sensitive about its dependence on imported food supplies. This ill-considered action fueled Japanese determination to remain as self-sufficient as possible in food producing.

When President Carter appointed former Senate Majority Leader Mike Mansfield ambassador to Japan, the country was delighted with what appeared to be, at long last, a recognition on Washington's part of Japan's importance. Ambassador Mansfield has been very effective in Tokyo; his age (culturally an important factor in Japan), his distinguished political background, his emphasis on the importance of the Japan-U.S. bilateral relation, and his scholarly background in Asian history have all contributed to his success. The Carter administration occasionally undermined his effectiveness, however, by such actions as its attempt to impose a worldwide ban on fast breeder reactors. Whether or not one supports nuclear energy, any reasonable person must acknowledge that the time is past when the United States can impose its values on the world—if it ever could.

The Japanese believe in the importance of gestures. When Washington, either in blissful ignorance or with malice aforethought, attempts to impose a policy on Tokyo without even a show of consultation, it reaps a harvest of bitter ill will in Japan. As Robert Christopher pointedly remarks, it is nearly unbelievable that the Carter administration had the gall to demand that Japan achieve a fixed rate of economic growth, determined by Washington to suit its own purposes. Imagine the U.S. government delivering such a demand to France, Germany, or even India—the idea is laughable. The United States government must break the irrational habit of assuming that little brother Japan can be told what to do. One day Japan will get fed up, and the fund of goodwill is sure to become exhausted. The Reagan administration has also been guilty of myopia toward Japan in more than one instance. Washington's consistent failure to understand Tokyo and give the Japanese their due is one of the most dangerous factors among all those that have driven—and are driving —a wedge between Japan and the West.

Another bone of contention between East and West is Japan's contribution to Official Development Assistance (ODA), which aids developing nations. Japan's ODA fell from 0.32 percent of GNP in 1980 to 0.29 percent in 1982. Moreover, up until quite recently, nearly all development assistance offered had to be used to buy Japanese goods, and even now a great deal of it is offered only with strings attached. Japan can ignore its responsibilities only at the cost of ill will on the part of both the developing and the developed nations.

Strong forces link Japan and the United States, and strong forces drive them apart. The threat of a world trade war looms, as even the United States and the EEC take to squabbling over such things as stainless steel and butter. It should be the top priority of all free nations to do everything possible to avert this threat and mitigate the effects of the bad blood that has already come between us. In the fight to keep mercantilist, protectionist sentiment at bay, business has a vital role to play. Those who manage noncompetitive industries must cease making excuses and lobbying for the privilege of being coddled with tariffs and quotas. If an industry has been sabotaged by unfair competitors, let it demonstrate its grievances and its willingness to fight and change before it can qualify to receive help from the federal government. There is no reason why American consumers should foot the bill for a generation of mismanagement that tries to place the blame for its failures on everyone except itself.

Western management systems are archaic. Labor and management must develop a new relationship with each other, and obliterate the old atmosphere of fighting each other tooth and nail. The present system is not merely inefficient but destructive of industry, leaving each side self-righteously isolated. Class divisions and mutual suspicion cannot be done away with overnight, but the attempt must be made in this generation, in the hope that by laying down the cudgels now we will bequeath a more efficient, satisfying work environment to our grandchildren. Giving all workers a chance to show their loyalty and initiative has reaped tremendous rewards in the many Japanese and few Western companies where the system has been instituted. In 1983, during its annual meeting of top management, General Motors took a step in the right direction by announcing a new company creed that emphasized quality products and services, long-term management thinking, and putting the stockholders a bit further down on the list of beneficiaries of the company's success by placing employees and business partners first.

I can't deny that as an executive I enjoy the fringe benefits of the job, but I believe the present system of maintaining such hierarchical symbols as executive dining rooms is outmoded and productive of divisiveness within a company. An essay by Andrew S. Grove, president of Intel Corporation, published in *Newsweek*, [2] makes the point that the lack of executive perks at his company is not just a laid-back West Coast affectation; it is a matter of necessity. Intel, one of the industry pioneers in integrated circuitry, works with leading-edge high technology. Although senior managers in the organization have technical backgrounds, the field moves too fast for anyone not actively involved on a day-to-day basis. If the main decision-makers were all senior people, the company would quickly cease to be competitive. By eliminating most of the privileges of rank, the firm ensures that its junior people, the ones who are really up on the latest developments, are integrated in decision-making as equals. Fewer and fewer industries these days are unaffected by rapid changes in technology; Intel and firms like it may soon come to be the rule rather than the exception.

Another archaic practice that must be dispensed with is the debilitating tendency of firms to worry about the price of their stock. No company should ever go to Wall Street defensively. Whatever a bold move may cost a company in the short term, an excess of caution with an eye on the next quarter is almost certain suicide in a world where Japanese competitors are striding ahead toward goals five and ten years down the road. Further, stock exchanges throughout the world tend to react favorably to top-quality long-range planning, such as IBM's move into personal computers. Western business must get out from under the tyranny of the next quarter. One of the best ways to do so is to take a leaf from the Japanese book, and start rewarding managers for successful long-term plans rather than for short-term achievements. Of course, to make this feasible, the system will also have to change to make sure that managers stick around long enough to see the fruits of their long-range thinking.

Yet another area in which the Western business record is dismally bad is in the area of exports. Up till now, American companies have generally favored going multinational and opening overseas manufacturing facilities rather than exporting. This policy has been successful to a certain extent in increasing American exports, because overseas manufacturing tends to pull exports after it in the form of domestic ingredients and components around which the foreign-manufactured product has been designed. Up to 40 percent of a U.S. foreign-manufactured product may consist of elements imported from the United States. The Japanese, on the other hand, dislike direct manufacturing investment, mainly because they feel they can't rely on foreign labor. Thus the two economies are structured differently. But the United States and Europe are going to have to shift more toward an emphasis on exports of manufactured goods if they are to regain world competitiveness. Because of this isolationist attitude, too many companies have virtually ignored the world market for their products, while Japanese competitors were moving in and thereby forestalling the possibility of Western entry.

If the West's focus has been too internal, Japan's has been too external. The quality of life in Japan could be vastly improved by increased domestic spending. Housing is one critical area. If the Japanese emphasis were to shift a bit from its panicky export-or-die orientation to a greater commitment to improving the quality of life in Japan itself, it could ease bilateral-trade frictions. In order to achieve this shift in emphasis, however, the Japanese will have to learn to tolerate increased inflation.

To return to the tasks facing Western business, the trend of recent years toward "rationalizing" divisions in trouble is suicidal. This kind of paperwork wizardry, dedicated to improving the cosmetic appeal of the balance sheet, is sheer folly. Companies are beginning to realize that when the going gets tough, the tough do *not* have a chat with their accountants. They decide what their core business really is, and they refuse to budge unless and until they lose the war. Huge old American companies scrambled over one another to divest themselves of money-losing businesses when the Japanese decided to muscle in. Perhaps some of these industries were already doomed, but one can't help imagining what the scene in consumer electronics, for example, would be like today if Western business's idea of pragmatism were not to simply cut and run. One of the Western industries that have suffered most under the impact of Japanese exports and cost advantage has been the automobile industry. Only when the Japanese began to encroach in this core sector did the United States wake up. Imagine GM deciding to rationalize its automobile division. It seems a ludicrous notion. Fortunately, there seems to be a limit to Western industry's inclination to surrender without a fight.

In those industries that have not thrown in the towel, it is becoming fashionable to try Japanese methods in an attempt to fight fire with fire. Perhaps nothing has been more talked of than "the quality circle," which can indeed be a powerful factor in improving quality control and reducing costs—but only when it is not used as a Band-Aid. The sinner who goes to church on Sundays but has no true repentance will not be saved. In other words, a weekly quality-circle meeting must be part of an integrated process that operates continuously, and is a genuine top priority of management, with clout and substance.

Because the natural bias of Westerners is to blame the Japanese for all ills, the emphasis in this book has been on the weak points of Western business. On home ground there can be no excuse for ignominious defeat, but when doing business in Japan is a different story. It is a widely held view in the Japanese government that the efforts of American and European business to crack its market have been puny. There is a modicum of truth to this charge, but it is in most respects grossly unfair. Until the late 1970's, the bureaucratic roadblocks placed in the way of foreign business alone would have been enough to daunt potential exporters and investors, quite aside from the language, cultural, and distribution problems. When the most obvious legal restrictions were finally removed, there still remained plenty of nontariff barriers dreamed up by various ministries to protect Japan from what it perceived as the threat of foreign economic domination. There are many good reasons to invest in Japan, and by now few if any major companies can afford *not* to be there. Nevertheless, it remains true that the Japanese market is one of the most difficult of the free markets to enter. Moreover, the government continues to harbor plenty of bureaucrats who believe the old rhetoric about Japan being a special case and needing to be nurtured. Although it is difficult to define exactly what constitutes openness in a market, the very fact that Japan continues to niggle and haggle before ever admitting the existence of a nontariff barrier demonstrates that it stands self-accused in the matter. He who has nothing to shelter or hide does not act defensively.

Some of the most difficult barriers are structural rather than legalistic, and the distribution system is undoubtedly the greatest. Its roots (described in Chapter 10) lie deep in the culture, and there is no way that complaining foreigners can force Japanese wholesalers and retailers to change their ways. However, history has shown that once Japanese are convinced that a new approach is needed they can move swiftly. Perhaps the government could mount a campaign to show the public that it is an embarrassment that foreign companies must struggle for years in order to break into the Japanese distribution system. Ways could be found to ease these difficulties. If Tokyo seriously wants to promote foreign investment, such a campaign, coupled perhaps with some kind of incentives, could begin to change the atmosphere. At the present time it takes years for any newcomer —Japanese or foreign, but especially foreign—to build up the contacts necessary to put together a viable distribution network. It would be a major step forward if this lead time could be shortened.

The distribution system is far from being the only barrier to foreign investment in Japan. All the nontariff barriers to imports discussed in Chapter 16 must be eliminated—the unreasonable certifications and standards, the quotas, the unpredictability of customs officers. Most fundamentally, the attitude of both bureaucrats and ordinary citizens must change. It is my hope that someday people in Japan will wake up to the fact that blandly denying foreign complaints about disguised protectionism is an unpatriotic act. The situation has become critical, and the old excuses are no longer acceptable. Whether it is official development assistance, defense expenditure, or its attitude to foreign investment, Japan has shown that while there may be talk about internationalism, there is not much substance behind the talk. The Japanese remain insular in the most profound sense of the word. It may not be entirely their fault that most other peoples perceive them in terms of negative stereotypes, but it is surely in their most vital interests to work to combat these images. There is no other nation more dependent on free trade and an uninterrupted flow of goods and services. (Ironically the Japanese claim that their very dependence on the free market exempts them from the obligations of other nations. This is the tired old "special case" remark that one hears so often. It is simply not so; many other nations depend on foreign raw materials, and Japan is far from being unique in this sense.)

The vulnerability complex that hampers Japan, preventing it from taking its proper place in the world, has its roots in its citizens' most basic attitudes toward their country. The Japanese educational system passes down the "special case" theory to generations of schoolchildren. This practice of emphasizing the uniqueness and specialness of Japan is dangerous. Granted, it is a source of cohesion and strength within the society, but in the long run it works against the country's true interests. Although the ultranationalist militarism of the thirties and forties is unlikely to be repeated soon, it remains an object lesson demonstrating the dangers of inculcating excessive patriotism. The recent controversy over the revision of World War II history textbooks shows that certain Japanese would like to have the past recalled in a more favorable light than the facts warrant. The government agreed to withdraw the new textbooks, which offered a softened version of various Japanese acts of aggression in the Pacific war, only under strong pressure from the governments of some countries formerly colonized by the Japanese. This is a dangerous trend. If the country is to lose its insularity, its children should be taught to disavow xenophobic nationalism rather than to make excuses for it.

Nowhere in Japan is there a single top foreign executive of a domestic company. Many people of Japanese origin are in positions of power in the United States, and increasingly in Europe. There has never been a delegation from Japan to foreign countries for the purpose of promoting foreign investment. It would never even occur to a Japanese prefectural governor to try to lure foreign business to his prefecture, whereas the governors of American states often visit Japan to try to convince its industry of their state's suitability for its manufacturing investment.

The lack of a true international spirit in Japan is nowhere more evident than in its abysmally poor record of foreign-language teaching. The United States is often criticized for a lack of commitment to foreign languages in school curricula, but the American record pales beside that of Japan, where every student studies at least some English, often for several years, but almost none end up being able to speak it. The system emphasizes rote memorization of esoteric grammatical points. Actual fluency counts for nothing in the university entrance exams, and may even be a handicap. Even the English teachers are not usually fluent in spoken English. Obviously, they have a vested interest in maintaining the status quo, and the non-English-speaking English teachers find allies among their peers who fear that widespread fluency in foreign languages will somehow undermine Japanese society, leaving it vulnerable to Westernization. Even so distinguished a Japanophile as Edwin Reischauer allows an exasperated tone to creep into his writing on the subject of English teaching in Japan. As he points out in *The Japanese,* there is no way that the country will be able to live up to its international responsibilities if foreign-language learning is not encouraged and rewarded. It may seem arrogant to insist on their learning English rather than our learning Japanese, but the reality is that English is an international language, and Japanese is not and never has been.

Certainly, anyone closely involved with Japan and its citizens should learn their language. But in the present scheme of things it is far easier to implement good teaching of English (and other foreign languages) in Japanese schools, where English of a kind is already being taught, than to expect many ordinary Americans and Europeans to learn Japanese, where the historical precedent is simply lacking. A side benefit to an emphasis on language learning in Japan would be that study-abroad programs would become more common as a result. The more Japanese go abroad to study, especially if the atmosphere in Japan shifts to favor such exchanges, the more truly internationalized the country will become.

I could cite many other areas in which the Japanese display an introverted nationalism that prevents them from effectively making their case before an accusing world, but will confine myself to giving one more example: the practice of assigning to top-level negotiations silver-tongued *tatemae* experts, whose mission is to be glib and verbally accommodating while at all costs preventing substantive concessions. This tactic has obstructed progress time and again. I suppose the purpose of the assignment is to buy time while various concerned ministries pore over the evidence to find out what the most minimal action possible is. Among themselves, Japanese may well understand the difference between *tatemae* and real intentions, but foreigners may not, and lack of clear understanding leads to confusion and resentment.

American negotiating teams, on the other hand, go to the other extreme, and tend to arrive in Japan armed with the conviction that it is time to lay down the law. They lecture and condescend to those they have come to meet as if they were converting savages to the one true faith. Washington exacerbates this situation by carrying affirmative action a step too far in assigning youthful nonconformists and women to Japan. No matter how brilliant and dedicated a female or younger official is, such people simply have no credibility in Japan. I realize that the opposite could be argued—that assigning important posts to such people is part of a national commitment to equality, and that it should take precedence over the preferences of foreigners. Nonetheless, it would not deal equal opportunity a death blow, and would be far more effective, given the cultural context, to assign older men who have experience in Japan to work there.

Although some commentators have gone overboard in praising the Japanese, thus producing a backlash of criticism, an evenhanded study of what the Japanese have done right can prove fruitful. One should not examine them with a view to slavish imitation, but with balanced admiration, weighing good and bad, and noting the most ingenious and imitable aspects of the system. If the United States adopted as much from Japan as Japan has from the United States, the link between the two countries would be strengthened to the point of being indissoluble. The lessons of Japanese employment practices have already been discussed at length, but some other Japanese practices, such as government tax breaks to encourage private savings, are also worth emulating.

The savings rate has been an important factor in providing capital for the investment that has fueled the country's steady economic growth. Of course, the Japanese tendency to save and the Western tendency to spend cannot be viewed simplistically, as if they were merely national character traits. Given a limited amount of cash to distribute, as long as Western industry depends so heavily on domestic consumption it is obvious that if consumers put money in the bank they would otherwise have spent on consumer goods, the slack demand will result in an industry slump. The only way out of this no-win situation is to shift the Western economies more toward exporting. An increased savings rate could be used to create a liquid core to provide continuing finance for exports. Such savings should go into the capital markets and not be tied up uselessly in mortgages.

In the United States the problem of relatively low savings rates ties in with the larger problem of restructuring and modernizing the economy to bring it in line with current reality. It will be impossible to regain the initiative lost to the Japanese unless government, business, and labor can form a troika instead of pulling in opposite directions. To do this, a national consensus must emerge in the form of an industrial policy. Unfortunately, the concept of such a policy has been turned into a political football. This is too vital an issue to allow it to become attached to one party's ideological ragbag, as just one more weapon in the electioneering arsenal. The Democrats are offering various versions of the idea as a panacea for all economic ills. There is a gleeful undertone to much of their rhetoric, hinting that business has once again led the country astray, and that it is up to the descendants of the New Deal to put the economy back on course. Many businessmen and conservatives view these proposals with alarm, and reflexively spurn industrial policy as a new form of government interference. But it need not be so. The issue of a national industrial policy becomes polarized when one assumes that government and business are natural enemies, that all cooperation is collusion, that government has a holy mandate to keep an eternal vigilance over the supposed rapacity of business, or that business has a sacred duty to fight for the rights of free enterprise against the incursions of a bloated bureaucracy. All such rhetoric has become archaic, indeed dangerous. If government and business, and business and labor, continue fighting the old battles when the real issues have moved on to a different plane, the outlook for America is truly bleak.

Industrial policy as it has been practiced in Japan is neither an unholy alliance of big business and big government, nor a curtailment of business's legitimate freedom. Business and government leaders in Japan do not have an adversary relationship. Rather, the government is continually researching and investigating economic, technological, and business trends to get as accurate a picture as possible of current trends, so that the country will be prepared to meet problems before they become crippling. Some observers have counted it a demerit of the system that the predictions and recommendations have not always been correct. (For example, Sony was at one point advised to get out of electronics.) But a strength of the system is that business not only has access to government advice but also has the freedom to reject it if a company feels strongly that the proposed action is not in its best interests.

Japanese industrial policy has shaped the general direction of the nation's economy, but obviously no democratic government could hope to bring every single special-interest group in line with its policies. No government anywhere can hope to be always right in all details. The successful general direction of Japanese policy is proof of its effectiveness. The task of the fifties was rebuilding and modernization, that of the sixties to achieve international dominance in steel and shipbuilding (and, by extension, in other heavy industries as well), and that of the seventies to begin a shift toward high technology while maintaining their world-market leadership in various categories of consumer goods. The eighties have so far seen a continuing emphasis on high tech, and a constant commitment to shifting workers out of—and getting rid of excess capacity in—industries that are becoming obsolescent. None of this has been easy and painless. Some doomsayers have predicted that Japan will begin finding it more and more difficult to achieve its objectives, and point with an unbecoming satisfaction to its poor record of technical innovation, its budget-deficit problems, the rising incidence of juvenile delinquency (from a practically nonexistent to an infinitesimal occurrence), and other disturbing trends. But the fact is that the Japanese are already concerned about these present and potential problems. They are not standing still, and are constantly evolving new solutions to problems as they are anticipated.

Thus Japanese industrial policy is not a series of mandates handed down from an ivory tower but a continuing process that comes together every five years in order to allocate research and development and other resources to the most strategic industries. If an industrial policy is ever adopted in the United States, it must be done the Japanese way, not used as an excuse for government interference. Government sponsorship of industry is what is required, *not* government control. At the other extreme, laissez-faire is not the answer either. Considering that Japanese industry can draw on research and long-range economic forecasting backed by the vast resources of the government, industries that compete with Japan will find it difficult to do so if they cannot draw on a similar array of resources.

One example of the radical difference in attitude between the Japanese and the American governments is the functioning of their respective export-import banks. The Japanese Ex-Im Bank is aggressive, and has a plentiful and ready supply of yen to distribute to customers. The bank helps the medium-sized exporter, but its major objective is to finance megaprojects competitively. This has greatly aided Japanese companies, which have managed to begin displacing many of the Western companies that have traditionally undertaken such huge projects. In contrast, the U.S. Ex-Im Bank is something of a stepchild, whose primary function up to now has been financing the sale of airplanes to developing countries. It is not an aggressive lender, it doesn't always get enough money, and it can never be sure of getting the necessary funds on time. It has not been able to finance American projects at competitive rates. Heretofore, the Ex-Im Bank has had to assign priority to the goal of remaining self-sustaining, to the detriment of its ability to finance projects competitively. Competitive financing must become the bank's main priority. In addition, it should be able to employ mixed financing in conjunction with the Agency for International Development (AID). Such financing would allow it to offer better credit terms and would further the twin objectives of giving development assistance and according U.S. exporters the same level of government support as that received by Japanese and other foreign exporters.

Beefing up and restructuring the Ex-Im Bank is just one of the actions that should be taken in order to actively promote trade, rather than the benign neglect that has prevailed until recently. The United States needs a counterpart to Japan's Ministry of International Trade and Industry (MITI). The Reagan administration has lent its support to a proposal to reorganize the Office of the Trade Negotiator and the Department of Commerce. Senator William Roth of Delaware is backing legislation that would make it a reality, and the American Chamber of Commerce has gone on record in favor of the new department, known as DITI, or the Department of International Trade and Industry. This new department could, if given a proper mandate, provide the climate for export orientation in the United States and be a force linking government and industry, thus breaking down traditional barriers of mistrust. DITI should be a department whose responsibility is to fight *for* industry and trade, rather than *against* them. Currently three senior committees oversee trade, and this state of affairs leads to confusion and duplication of effort. The United States needs to present a united front in matters of trade policy, planning, and implementation. If DITI is to rival MITI, it must be powerful and prestigious, and its secretary an important figure whose opinion counts in policy making, with ready access to the President. If DITI can draw on high-caliber people to serve as long-term staff, professionals with language skills who become area specialists, American trade negotiations and export promotion efforts would become far more effective.

The essential difference between the United States' and Japan's foreign policies is that Japan always considers trade first, whereas we have often ignored the impact of our actions on trade. Not that we should become as single-mindedly export-oriented as Japan has been; that would be to adopt the same policies we have been so vigorously condemning. While Japan is working on moving away from its over-emphasis on exports, the United States and Europe should be going in the other direction, attempting to increase exports and public awareness of their importance. One would hope that we could meet somewhere in the middle and end up with a more healthy world economy.

Japan has repeatedly tried to divert U.S. and European attention from the bilateral-trade situation during trade negotiations, insisting that the bilateral picture is misleading, and that only the multilateral figures—which would include oil—are significant. The multilateral situation *is* important, but it, too, misleads. When comparing two similar economies, such as the American and Japanese, it is valid to take note of dramatic imbalances in trade. The trade deficit with Japan is a symptom of a system that is off balance. These imbalances spell unemployment, which leads to calls for protectionism—and that is in the long-term interest of nobody. Refusing to talk about bilateral trade will not make the problem go away. It is one more symptom of the widening gap between Japan and the United States, which has been caused by these same festering trade disputes.

One of the factors that continue to create obfuscation and obstruction in U.S.-Japan negotiations, and relations in general, is the extent to which the Japanese have succeeded in lobbying for support among influential people in Washington. This is not necessarily wrong or immoral, but it remains a fact that there is a Japanophile group of U.S. journalists, government officials, and various other influential professionals who always emphasize the positive side of Japan publicly and privately. Such people are supporters of Japanese interests in the American legislative process; again, this is not in itself evil, but when a lobbyist is not perceived as a lobbyist his views will not be seen in the proper light or taken with the requisite grain of salt. There is a gray area between personal convictions sincerely expressed and paid lobbying. Many of these Japan-lovers fall in between the two extremes, and this ought to be more widely known. The situation is unbalanced, in the sense that there are no U.S. lobbyists in Tokyo except those maintained by a few private companies to look after their interests. Japan sends many people to Washington to keep tabs on legislation affecting it, and we ought to be making similar efforts in Tokyo.

This lack of attention to furthering American interests in Tokyo is just one symptom of the disorganization of American trade policy, which demonstrates the need for a reorganized Department of Trade as a spearhead for a new trade policy. As mentioned previously, American trade negotiators tend to descend on Japan with a Calvinistic fervor of self-righteousness, but are met with endless caution and politely superficial *tatemae* statements. Negotiations between two sovereign nations with extensive economic and other interests in common ought to be conducted in an atmosphere of sober, workmanlike commitment to steady progress in achieving mutually beneficial results. At present, the Japanese stall and the Americans cry wolf.

One of the major reasons for the inefficiency of the current system is that not enough time is spent on negotiating. The U.S. trade representative flies in and out of Tokyo with the aim of extracting the maximum amount of concessions in the minimum amount of time. This method does achieve some progress, but it would be far better if negotiations were conducted in a more pedestrian manner in the interest of steady progress, achieved with a minimum of international rancor. One way to do this would be to set up individual industry task forces, composed of industry and government experts, which would meet as often as once or twice a week to identify problems and work out solutions. There could be an annual or semiannual review of each task force's progress. These committees would tackle problems on the basis of in-depth knowledge of their particular industry, which would allow an organized, clear-sighted approach to negotiating. In addition, negotiators meeting frequently with their counterparts would become more sensitive to the problems and concerns of the other side.

Yet another symptom of the chaos in U.S.-Japan trade policy is the unrealistic exchange rates. High U.S. interest rates have inflated the dollar, while the yen is kept artificially low by the Japanese reluctance to liberalize its regulations governing foreign participation in the yen market. The United States may have to continue to suffer the effects of high interest rates while the budget deficit remains enormous, but an organized commitment to consider the impact of fiscal and monetary policies on trade could ease the situation in the long run. Tokyo's policy, on the other hand, has no similar justification.

There is no reason for the yen to be kept at an unrealistically low rate of exchange. This gives an unfair advantage to Japan in promoting its exports; with the strong competitive advantage the Japanese enjoy in terms of product quality and service in the markets they dominate, this protectionist policy is clearly outmoded and unjustified.

Japan, the United States, and Europe have far to go in ironing out differences and learning to work in closer cooperation. Perhaps the Europeans have the furthest to go in adapting to the economic and political realities of today, but if the United States shows the way, the EEC may recognize the necessity of following. The free-market countries bear the responsibility of maintaining an open atmosphere in international trade. A return to the beggar-thy-neighbor policies of the thirties would be suicide. Instead, there must be a new partnership of cooperation between the West and Japan, a partnership in which there would be room for the newly industrialized countries as they advance to join the ranks of developed nations. The developed nations have a responsibility not only to support one another, but also to aid the lesser and underdeveloped countries, with the ultimate aim of eliminating such distinctions.

With their tremendous capabilities and unquestioned dominance in many industries, the Japanese are not worried about foreign competition. Whenever the Japanese have competed seriously, Western firms have simply crumpled. Indeed, Japanese firms should welcome a strengthening of Western competitiveness, since it would lessen the danger of protectionist backlash. Western managers pay too much attention to failure; it's time to look confidently at what works rather than to examine fearfully what has failed. Business people are beginning to realize this, especially in the United States. Our instinct has always been to respect and admire success, and this may prove our salvation in the long run. The new partnership of nations must begin at the business level; mutual respect and understanding cannot be achieved until the Japanese economic "miracle" is demystified— and imitated, where appropriate.

As many commentators have pointed out, the world economic center of gravity is shifting from the Atlantic to the Pacific. In recognition of this, a Pacific Economic Community (PEC) should be established. It would serve as an integrated economic union for the promotion of free trade in the Pacific area. The PEC would offer tariff incentives, and work out common trade policies for its member nations. The formulation of such policies would not be easy, but even if it took twenty years the advantages gained would be worth the effort.

The ultimate goal of a new partnership, including the Pacific Economic Community and the EEC, would be a coordinated industrial policy. Such a policy would determine where a particular technology or industry could most profitably and effectively be developed, and be an international force for maintaining long-term economic stability. The perfect partnership would produce a harmonization of industrial policies, Official Development Assistance, exchange rates, and all other factors affecting international economic development throughout the developed world. The alienation between the Third World and the developed nations is increasing. It can be alleviated only if developed countries commit themselves to working out their differences in the context of an effort to promote not only mutual economic advantage but also the long-term economic progress of the South.

A first step on the road to this admittedly somewhat utopian vision is that the United States cede leadership in Asia to Japan. We have already virtually given up economic leadership, and Japan has been undertaking ever-greater responsibility for development assistance in the region. Ultimately, Japan will inevitably begin taking on responsibility for the defense of the area as well, though this may take a long time because of the past atrocities that are still fresh in many living memories in Asia. But the shadow of the past will lift eventually; the Japanese have effectively gained by peaceful means what they had sought to win by going to war, so the old enmities will eventually become academic.

Throughout, this book has emphasized the need for Westerners to study Japan in order to work more effectively with its people and to learn from their successes. Such study not only will improve the Westerner's ability to do business with or compete against the Japanese, but will also yield rich dividends in the sphere of international relations, where the stakes are far higher than the concerns of individual businesses.

GLOSSARY

Because this glossary is included only as a convenience to the reader, the definitions given below are not intended to be either complete or definitive. Terms are defined briefly, and only as I have used them in the text. Many of them could have other meanings in other contexts.

aisatsu a formal visit—for example, a brief call on the chairman or president of a Japanese company before getting down to discussing business with his subordinates.

banzai literally, "Ten thousand years." Similar to "Hurrah."

batsu faction.

buchō department head.

daimyō feudal lords during the Tokugawa shogunate who had virtually complete control over their own domains.

dōkyūsei "Old Boys"—people who have graduated from the same school or college.

dōmei alliance.

FTC Fair Trade Commission. Administers antimonopoly laws, reviews international contracts for "fairness" to Japanese party.

fukushachō vice president.

futon   a sort of cotton quilted mattress-cum-sleeping bag that most Japanese use instead of a bed. It is spread out on *tatami* mats at night and stored during the day.

gaijin   foreigner, usually of European origin. Considered by some to be a derogatory term.

geisha   traditional female entertainer, skilled in traditional Japanese performing arts.

gimu   obligation.

giri   duty.

go   a Japanese board game played with dark and light stones—as subtle and difficult as chess.

gyōsei shidō   "administrative guidance." Advice or orders given by government ministries to private firms, usually in an informal manner.

hai   literally, yes, but actually, in certain contexts, it can mean only passive acknowledgement that the addressee is paying attention.

haragei   literally, "belly language." Nonverbal communication used to communicate true intentions. Often aggressive in business context.

hara kiri   literally, "belly slitting." Vulgar word for ritual disembowelment. Polite term is *seppuku.*

hiragana   phonetic alphabet used to write Japanese words not written in *kanji* (q.v.) or *katakana* (q.v.).

honne   truth, the reality that lies behind superficial utterances.

ichiryū-gaisha   number one company.

irasshaimase   the greeting "Welcome."

JETRO   Japan External Trade Organization. Provides support for Japanese business all over the world, and furnishes information on same to all inquirers.

jichō   deputy department head.

jōmu-kai   managing directors' meeting.

jōmutorishimari-yaku   managing director.

jōmu   managing director (shortened form of *jōmutorishimari-yaku*).

kabuki   a type of traditional Japanese drama.

kachō section chief.

kai group, club, meeting.

kaisha company.

kaichō chairman (of a company).

kaigi business meeting.

kana phonetic alphabet used in writing Japanese.

kanji Chinese characters, used along with *kana* to write Japanese.

kao face. Japanese sense of personal honor and respectability.

Kasumigaseki the financial center in Tokyo.

katakana one of two phonetic alphabets used in conjunction with *kanji* characters to write Japanese. Used for foreign words.

kimochi feelings. Important even in business in Japan.

kobun client, protégé, "godchild." Person who is attached to a leader *(oyabun)* of a faction. The *oyabun* looks after his *kobun* and receives loyalty in return.

kun term of address, suffixed to name, indicates the male person addressed is either an equal or a subordinate.

mado no hito "window people." These are Japanese who have lifetime employment but have failed, and are given a desk by the window and nothing to do.

meishi Japanese business calling card. Absolutely necessary for all business people, foreign and Japanese, in Japan.

MITI Ministry of International Trade and Industry. Japanese government ministry responsible for Japanese industrial policy and promotion of Japanese industry.

MOF Ministry of Finance.

nemawashi literally, preparing the ground. Process of consulting all concerned parties and garnering support for a course of action.

ningen kankei "human relationships." Very important to Japanese.

nintai patience, in almost mystical sense.

ofuro Japanese hot tub. Traditional Japanese bath.

on obligation.

oyabun   patron, "godfather," leader of a faction.

ringi seido   document announcing new course of action which must circulate and collect seals of approval from all involved. Formalizes a decision.

rōmaji   Roman script, Latin alphabet.

ryokan   traditional Japanese inn.

sama   term of address placed after surname. More respectful than *san.*

samurai   warrior-aristocrat in feudal Japan. A privileged class that was abolished after the Meiji Restoration.

san   most common respectful term placed after surname of man or woman. Similar to Mr. or Ms..

sarariman   salary man. White-collar worker.

semmonshōsha   specialized trading company, trader in limited number of commodities. Opposite of *sōgōshōsha.*

semmu   executive vice president.

seppuku   ritual disembowelment.

shachō   president.

shitenchō   manager of a branch office.

shinyō   trust.

shōgun   hereditary warlord. (The Tokugawa shogunate ruled Japan for three centuries.)

sōgōshōsha   general trading company. One of nine huge companies forming the nucleus of a linked network of companies (see *zaikai*). Up until recently these companies have handled most of the foreign dealings of Japanese industry.

tatemae   superficial appearance or utterance, opposed to *honne* (q.v.). Attitude adopted in order not to offend.

terebi   television.

torishimari-yaku   director.

wa   social harmony. An important concept.

zaibatsu   literally, "plutocrat." Pre–World War II industry in Japan was dominated by certain merchant families, called *zaibatsu,* that controlled industrial empires by means of holding companies that held all stock in trust for family members.

zaikai   literally, "financial circles." Modern descendant of *zaibatsu*. Zaibatsu families are now out of power, but the companies that were formerly linked maintain more or less close relationships, sometimes by such means as interlocking directorates, sometimes by more informal means.

BIBLIOGRAPHY

Recommended reading is indicated by an asterisk.

American Chamber of Commerce in Japan. *Living in Japan.* 9th ed. Tokyo, 1981.

*————. *Successful Entry into the Japanese Market.* Tokyo, 1981.

————. *U.S. Manufacturing Investment in Japan Executive Summary.* Tokyo, July 1979.

*————. *U.S. Manufacturing Investment in Japan: a Study.* Tokyo, July 1979.

————. *U.S. Manufacturing Investment in Japan White Paper.* Tokyo, February 1980.

Ballon, Robert J., and Eugene H. Lee, eds. *Foreign Investment and Japan.* Tokyo: Sophia University and Kodansha International, 1972.

*Benedict, Ruth. *The Chrysanthemum and the Sword.* Tokyo: Charles E. Tuttle, 1976.

Bush, Richard. *Exporting to Japan: A Practical Guide.* Tokyo: American Chamber of Commerce in Japan, 1981.

*Christopher, Robert C. *The Japanese Mind: The Goliath Explained.* New York: Simon & Schuster, 1983.

*Doi, Takeo. *The Anatomy of Dependence*. Tokyo: Kodansha International, 1977.

Downs, Ray F., ed. *Japan Yesterday and Today*. New York: Bantam 1969.

Drucker, Peter F. *Management: Tasks, Responsibilities, Practices.* New York: Harper & Row, 1974.

Forbis, William H. *Japan Today: People, Places, Power*. Tokyo: Charles E. Tuttle, 1976.

High Adventure in Joint Ventures Revisited. Tokyo: American Chamber of Commerce in Japan, 1972.

A Hundred Things Japanese. Tokyo: Japan Culture Institute, 1976.

*Japan Business: Obstacles and Opportunities. (Prepared by McKinsey & Co. for the United States–Japan Trade Study Group). Tokyo: President Inc., 1983.

Japan Echo, Vol. X, Special Issue on Technology, 1983.

Japan 1982, an International Comparison. 1st ed. Tokyo: Keizai Koho Center (Japan Institute for Social and Economic Affairs), 1982. (Published yearly.)

Kahn, Herman, and Thomas Pepper. *The Japanese Challenge*. Tokyo: Charles E. Tuttle, 1976.

*Kamata, Satoshi (trans. Tatsuru Akimoto). *Japan in the Passing Lane*. New York: Pantheon, 1982.

Kawasaki, Ichiro. *Japan Unmasked*. Tokyo: Charles E. Tuttle, 1976.

*Nakane, Chie. *Japanese Society*. New York: Penguin, 1977.

Pascale, Richard Tanner, and Anthony G. Athos. *The Art of Japanese Management*. Harmondsworth, Middlesex: Penguin, 1982.

Program on U.S.-Japan Relations: Annual Report 1980–81. Center for International Affairs, Harvard University.

*Reischauer, Edwin O. *The Japanese*. Cambridge, Mass.: Belknap Press, 1977.

*Richardson, Bradley M., and Taizo Ueda, eds. *Business and Society in Japan*. New York: Praeger, 1981.

Roberts, John G. *Mitsui: Three Centuries of Japanese Business*. New York: Weatherhill, 1974.

Singer, Kurt. *Mirror, Sword, and Jewel.* Tokyo: Kodansha International, 1982.

Vogel, Ezra F. *Japan as Number One.* Tokyo: Charles E. Tuttle, 1982.

Wilkinson, Endymion. *Misunderstanding: Europe versus Japan.* Tokyo: Chuokoronsha, 1982.

Woronoff, Jon. *Japan: The Coming Economic Crisis.* Tokyo: Lotus Press, 1982.

———. *Japan: The Coming Social Crisis.* Tokyo: Lotus Press, 1982.

Yoshino, M.Y. *Marketing in Japan: A Management Guide.* New York: Praeger, 1975.

Chapter 1 The Basics: Social and Cultural Motivations

1. Ray F. Downs, ed., *Japan, Yesterday and Today* (New York: Bantam, 1969), p. 79.
2. Taizo Ueda and Bradley M. Richardson, eds., *Business and Society in Japan*, pp. 70–71.
3. "Fujitsu; Bugged by Software," *Economist*, January 29, 1983.
4. Edwin Reischauer, quoted by Jon Woronoff in *Japan: The Coming Social Crisis* (Tokyo: Lotus Press, 1982), p. 289.
5. Woronoff, p. 162.
6. Edwin O. Reischauer, *The Japanese* (Cambridge, Mass.: Belknap Press, 1977), p. 224.
7. Ibid., p. 214.

Chapter 3 The Japanese Language: A Key to Understanding

1. Reischauer, *The Japanese*, p. 381.
2. Ibid, p. 387.
3. Norman H. Tolman, "Aisatsu," in *A Hundred Things Japanese* (Tokyo: Japan Culture Institute), p. 126.

4. Reischauer, p. 383.

5. Endymion Wilkinson, *Misunderstanding: Europe versus Japan* (Tokyo: Chuokoronsha, 1982), p. 293.

Chapter 5 Four Essential Concepts: *Nintai, Kao, Giri, On*

1. Ruth Benedict, *The Chrysanthemum and the Sword* (Tokyo: Charles E. Tuttle, 1976), pp. 98–99.

2. Ibid.

3. Ibid., p. 103.

4. Ibid., p. 134.

5. Reischauer, *The Japanese*, pp. 152–53.

6. John G. Roberts, *Mitsui: Three Centuries of Japanese Business* (New York: Weatherhill, 1974), p. 395.

7. Ibid., pp. 398–99.

Chapter 7 The Japanese and Contracts

1. Robert J. Ballon and Eugene H. Lee, eds., *Foreign Investment and Japan* (Tokyo: Sophia University and Kodansha International, 1972), p. 39.

2. Richardson and Ueda, eds., *Business and Society in Japan*, p. 152.

3. Ibid., p. 150.

4. Carl Green and Hisashi Owada, "The Legal Framework: An Agenda," in *Annual Report 1980–81* of the Program on U.S.-Japan Relations, p. 51.

5. Ballon and Lee, p. 204.

Chapter 8 *"Hai"* Means "I Hear You"

1. Jane A. Corddry, "Hara," in *A Hundred Things Japanese*, p. 102.

2. Reischauer, *The Japanese*, p. 136.

Chapter 9 The Decision-Making Process

1. Richardson and Ueda, eds., *Business and Society in Japan*, p. 3.

2. Peter F. Drucker, *Management: Tasks, Responsibilities Practices* (New York: Harper & Row, 1974), p. 469.

3. Ibid.

4. Richard Tanner Pascale and Anthony G. Athos, *The Art of Japanese Management* (Harmondsworth, Middlesex: Penguin, 1982), p. 111.

5. Richardson and Ueda, p. 9.

6. Ballon and Lee, eds., *Foreign Investment and Japan*, p. 55.

7. Reischauer, *The Japanese*, p. 135.

Chapter 10 Japanese Business Strategy in Japan

1. *Japan Business Obstacles and Opportunities* (Tokyo: President Inc., 1983), p. 30.

2. Chie Nakane, *Japanese Society* (New York: Penguin, 1977), p. 95.

3. "The Pheasant That Flies Gets Shot," *Stanford Magazine*, Winter 1982, p. 41.

4. Ibid.

5. *Japan Business*, p. 16.

6. Peter McGill, "Why Japan Sends Its Samurai Managers to a Training Hell," London *Observer*, June 19, 1983.

Chapter 11 Japanese Business Strategy in Foreign Markets

1. Quoted in Roberts, *Mitsui*, p. 265.

2. Quoted in ibid., pp. 487–88.

3. Delivered before a seminar on high-technology industries in Washington, D.C., February 1, 1983. Reprinted in *Speaking of Japan*, March 1983, p. 13.

Chapter 12 Japanese Trading Companies and Japanese Banks

1. In a speech delivered at the Foreign Correspondents Club of Japan, Tokyo, February 4, 1982. Reprinted in *Speaking of Japan,* August 1982, p. 28.

2. John Roberts, "Megaprojects in a Changing World," *Pacific Business,* Summer 1983, p. 9.

3. Ibid., p. 4.

4. Ueda and Richardson, eds., p. 80.

5. Quoted in Roberts, p. 16.

Chapter 13 How to Hold On to Your Market

1. Letter to the Editor, *Japan Times,* February 1, 1983.

2. *Newsweek,* June 27, 1983.

3. Richardson and Ueda, eds., *Business and Society in Japan,* p. 86.

4. Drucker, *Management: Tasks, Responsibilities, Practices,* p. 455.

5. James S. Balloun, "Real Lessons from Japan," *Speaking of Japan,* August 1981, p. 10.

6. Ibid., p. 15.

7. Drucker, pp. 45–46.

Chapter 14 Playing the Harp

1. Richardson and Ueda, eds., *Business and Society in Japan,* p. 8.

Chapter 17 Working in a Japanese Company

1. *Journal of the American Chamber of Commerce in Japan,* July–August 1979, pp. 51–55.

Chapter 18 We Need Each Other

1. Wilkinson, *Misunderstanding,* pp. 274–75.

2. *Newsweek,* October 3, 1983.

INDEX

Abbott, Trevor, 225
Abbott Laboratories, 165, 187
accountants, 222, 240
advertising, 145–46, 152–53, 159, 237–38
ageism, 99
Agency for International Development (AID), 288
agricultural quotas, 243–44
aircraft industry, 10, 62, 186, 197
aisatsu (formal visit), 101
Alpha Therapeutics, 165–66
alphabets, 48–49
ambiguity, 20
American Chamber of Commerce in Japan (ACCJ), 86, 98, 100, 220, 227–28
Anti-Monopoly Act, 143
apologies, 259
Art of Japanese Management, The (Pascale and Athos), 20, 122, 125, 133, 142, 194, 258
Ataka Trading Company, 169, 172, 180, 194
Athos, Anthony G., 20, 122, 125, 194, 258
attorneys, 94–95, 97, 158, 240
Australia, 181–82
automation, 190–91

automobile industry, 152–53, 187, 191, 192–93, 195, 281
   commodity tax on, 250
   quality standards for, 242–43
   working conditions in, 259, 260–62

Ballon, Robert J., 124
Balloun, Jim, 199, 200
Bank of Japan, 93–94, 183
Bank of Tokyo, 179
Banking Act, 143
banks, 147–48, 157, 177–83
   export-import, 180, 287–88
   as go-betweens in negotiation, 98, 178
   as information source, 127
baseball bats, 246–48
batsu (factions), 11, 13–14, 122–23
Bayha, Tom, 178–79
beef, 243–44
Benedict, Ruth, 67–69
blackmail, 10–11
blue-collar workers, 259–62
bowing, 26–27
branch office manager *(shitenchō)*, 177, 258–59
brand names, 137–38, 152–53
bribery, 10, 11, 62, 70–71

British Chamber of Commerce in Japan, 228
Brother Industries, 148
buchō (department chief), 12, 15–16, 44, 46, 51
Bucyrus-Erie/Komatsu joint venture, 62, 96, 228–29
Buddhism, 20, 21–22*n*
Bush, Richard, 245*n*
Business and Society in Japan (Richardson and Ueda, eds.), 6–7, 95, 194
Business Negotiations with the Japanese (Tung), 102–4
business trips, length of, 112
Business View, 266

calling cards *(meishi)*, 26–28, 38, 46
cartels, 140–41, 149, 151
Carter, Jimmy, 277–78
Celanese Corporation, 10
chairman *(kaichō)*, 46, 213, 215
chemical industry, 10, 197
China, 12, 17, 48–49, 96, 174, 229, 269, 274, 277
Christianity, 6
Christopher, Robert, 205, 254, 272, 277
Chrysanthemum and the Sword, The (Benedict), 67–69
clerical workers, 262–63
clothing, 37, 61–62
Coming Social Crisis (Woronoff), 19
commodity tax, 250
communication, 255–56
    apparent digressions in, 53, 56–57, 78–80
    in exporting to Japan, 240–41
    form versus substance in, 58–60
    haragai (stomach language) in, 107–8, 231
    role playing in, 60–61
    wa (harmony) in, 62
    see also language; speaking
company parties, 12–13
competition
    in educational system, 18–19
    in gift giving, 34–35
    government support of research and development and, 145
    market share in, 140–41

mention of, in meetings, 31
    ningen kankei (human relationships) and, 77
    strategy development and, 148–49
    in training of managers, 149–50
computer industry, 9, 192, 195–96
conference rooms, 28, 208, 209
Confucianism, 21–22
Connely, Robert F., 250
Conover, Donald ("Skip"), 252–53
consensus building *(nemawashi)*, 23, 124–25, 126
consultants, 98, 110–11, 212, 249–50
consumer appliances and electronics industry, 152, 158–59, 164, 223
contracts, 91–104
    Japanese government procurement, 249–50
    joint venture, 227, 228–29
    negotiation of, *see* negotiation
    nintai (patience) and, 64–65, 101
    review of, 93–96, 101, 227
conversation, 56–57
copper, 172
Corddry, Jane A., 107
corporate culture, 125, 206, 214–15, 221, 263–64
counter-purchase agreements, 175
courtesy calls, 215–17
credentials, 97–98
criticism, 65–66, 257–58
cross-licensing agreements, 114, 188
customs duties, 244–45

Daiei Supermarkets, 134–36
daimyō (feudal lord), 7
Datsun, 153
decision-making, 23–24, 109, 118–29
    corporate culture in, 125, 214–15
    courtesy calls and, 215–17
    maintaining contact and, 211–17
    management style and, 205–7, 209–10
    patience and, 65, 128–29
    techniques for smoothing Japanese, 210–15
    Western versus Japanese styles in, 120–22
defense, 106–7, 153–54, 272, 275–76, 292

Demming, W. Edwards, 141–42, 159
demotions, 259
department chief *(buchō)*, 12, 15–16, 44, 46, 51
Department of International Trade and Industry (DITI), proposed, 288
dependency, 64, 74
Dewey, Thomas E., 158
direct investment, 164–66, 172
    bank role in, 182
    through joint ventures, *see* joint ventures
    liberalization of, in Japan, 93–94
    trading company role in, 171–73
director *(torishimari-yaku)*, 46
distribution system, 134–39
    access to, through joint ventures, 220–21, 223–24
    as nontariff barrier, 282
    pricing in, 136–37, 146–47, 162, 192, 237
Dizer, Bill, 41–42, 49
Doi, Takeo, 64, 74
dōkyūsei (old boys), 76, 123
Domei (alliance), 106–7
Dow Chemical, 221–22, 230–31
Dress, Tom, 165–66
Drucker, Peter, 120, 198, 200, 206
dye-manufacturing industry, 162

Eastman Kodak, 252
Economic Planning Agency, 143
education, 18–19
    advertising and, 146
    of business managers, 149, 170, 200–1
    dōkyūsei (old boys) and, 76–77
    in language, *see* language
    role of, in Japanese meritocracy, 260
efficiency, Japanese view, 208–9
eigoyasan (English-speaking incompetents), 53
electronics industry, 152, 158–59, 164, 223
embassies, 210, 211, 239, 246
emotion, 22, 30–31, 57–58
employees (Japanese company), 254–68
    see also group orientation
England, 175, 199, 220, 239

equipment leasing, 183
ethics
    blackmail and, 10–11
    bribery and, 10, 11, 62, 70–71
    industrial espionage and, 9, 10
    see also group orientation
Ex-Im Bank of Japan, 180, 287
Ex-Im Bank of the United States, 287–88
exclusive distributors, 137–38
executive managing director, 213
executive vice president *(semmu)*, 46
Export Trading Company Act, 176, 240
exporting to Japan, 236–53
    contractual restrictions on, 96
    history of growth of, 153–55
    need for increased, 280
    nontariff barriers in, 245–51, 281–82, 290–91
    in strategy development, 190

face, *see* kao
factions, 11, 13–14, 122–23
Fair Trade Commission (FTC), 95–96, 227, 228–29
    see also Ministry of International Trade and Industry
fast-food franchises, 173, 224–25
feudalism, 6–7, 21
Fifth of the Month Clubs, 163
firing, employee, 258
first refusal rights, 114
foreign exchange rates, 250, 290–91
Foreign Investment Law (Foreign Capital Control Law), 93, 219
foreigners *(gaijin)*, 17–18, 47, 80
Fuji Bank, 178–79
Fujihara, Ginjiro, 154
Fujita, Den, 224–25
fukushachō (vice president), 46, 233
futon (cushioned sleeping bag), 37

gaijin (foreigner), 17–18, 47, 80
gairo (roaming employee of a foreign firm), 71
General Electric, 190, 240
General Motors, 192–93, 279
generalists, 170, 200
generation gap, 12, 44–45

gifts, 33–35, 36, 86
    concept of *giri* (duty) and, 69–71
    exchange rates and value of, 250–51
    record-keeping for, 35, 70
giri (duty), 64, 67, 68–73, 82–83
go-betweens, 98, 176–78, 210
go competitions, 36
golf, 33, 35–36, 83–85
government, Japanese, 142–45
    bank role in finances of, 179
    business information from, 110, 162
    Fair Trade Commission of, 95–96, 227, 228–29
    industrial policy and, 286–87
    involvement of, in foreign contracts, 93–94, 96
    Japan External Trade Organization (JETRO), 110–11, 157–58, 162, 210, 239
    Ministry of Agriculture, 243
    Ministry of Finance (MOF), 183
    Ministry of Health and Welfare, 249
    Ministry of Transportation (MOT), 242
    procurement contracts of, 249–50
Green Cross Corporation, 21–22, 24, 165–66, 215
gross national product (GNP), 169, 184, 276
group orientation, 5–14
    giri (duty) and, 64, 67, 68–73, 82–83
    homogeneity of people and, 16–17
    on (obligation) and, 64, 67–68
    self-confidence and, 22–23
    self-distrust and, 14–16
    special considerations and, 265–66
    work schedule and, 12, 259
    xenophobia and, 14, 17–18, 96, 281–83
Grove, Andrew S., 279
gyōsei shidō (administrative guidance), 96

hai (yes or I hear you), 106
handshaking, 27

haragei (stomach language), 107–8, 231
Hasegawa, Norishige, 45
High Adventure in Joint Ventures (ACCJ), 228
hiragana (phonetic alphabet), 49
Hollin, Ben, 266
home, entertaining at, 38–39
honne (truth), 58–60

IBM, 9, 195–96
ichi-ryū gaisha (number one company), 141, 152
India, 55–56, 159, 172–73
individualism, 13, 15–16, 31, 62, 118–19, 254, 261–62
Industrial Bank of Japan, 180, 182
industrial espionage, 9, 10
industrial policy, 285–87, 292
Industry Club of Japan, 142
information, 157, 160–61
    on corporate culture, 125
    from embassies, 210, 211
    on exporting to Japan, 245n
    from Japan External Trade Organization, 210
    from the Japanese government, 110, 162
    on joint ventures with Japan, 227–28
    sources of company, 127–28
    see also research
inns, Japanese, 36–37
Intel Corporation, 279
interpreters, 31–32, 49–54, 57–58, 107
interruptions, 56
investment, *see* direct investment
Irasshaimase (Welcome), 69–70
iron-ore, 172, 173, 182–83
isolationism, 274, 275, 281–84
Itoh Trading Company, 172, 180

Japan, Inc., 142–43, 163
Japan-America Society, 256–57
Japan as Number One (Vogel), 19, 23, 141, 184
Japan Business: Obstacles and Opportunities (McKinsey & Company), 228
Japan Echo, 257

Japan in the Passing Lane (Kamata), 260

Japanese, The (Reischauer), 261, 274, 284

Japanese Consumer Product Safety Law, 247

Japanese Mind, The (Christopher), 205, 254, 272

Japanese Society (Nakane), 26, 141, 256

Japanese Trade Crusade, 153–54

Japan's Choice: Conflict or Cooperation (Zimmerman), 164

JETRO (Japan External Trade Organization), 110–11, 157–58, 162, 210, 239

Johnson Company Ltd., 223

joint ventures, 218–35
    decision-making techniques in, 23–24, 128
    third country, 173, 181–83

jōmu (managing director), 16, 46, 61, 213

kachō (section chief), 12, 46

kai (group), 139

kaichō (chairman), 46, 213, 215

kaigi (discussion meeting), 29–30

Kamata, Satoshi, 259, 260, 261

kana (phonetic alphabet), 48–49

kanban system (inventory control), 193

kanji (Chinese characters), 12, 48–49

kao (face), 27, 64, 65–66, 69
    avoiding insults to, 73
    company size and, 147
    form and substance in, 58–60

Kao Soap Company, 66, 139, 230

katakana (phonetic alphabet for foreign words), 49

Kawashima, Katsuji, 148

Keidel, Albert, 6–7, 182

Keidanren (Federation of Economic Organizations), 13, 45

Keizai Koho Centre (Japan Institute for Social and Economic Affairs), 173

kimochi (feelings), 62

kimono, 37

Kissinger, Henry, 277

kobun (faction protégé), 13–14, 122–23

kokujin (black people), 17

Korea, 18, 175, 272

Koyama, Hachiro, 223

labor costs, 193

language
    English
        Japanese knowledge and use of, 42, 44–45, 49, 52–53, 283–84
        pace of speech in, 32, 52
        use of interpreters and, 31–32, 52–54
    Japanese, 41–54
        age and style of, 44–45, 51
        competence of foreigners with, 47–48, 49, 53–54
        difficulty of learning, 45, 48–49
        importance of learning, 41–42, 52–54, 255
        names in, 27, 45–46
        origins of, 42–43
        rank in, 43–44
        as screen around culture, 47–48
        titles in, *see* titles
        use of interpreters and, 31–32, 49–52
        written form of, 48–49
    see also communication; speaking

laser-beam effect (marketing), 160–61

leadership, 15, 21–22

lecturing, 30–31, 113, 284

lesser developed countries (LDCs), 157, 175, 182, 278, 292

letters, 210–11, 240–41

lettuce, 243

Liberal Democratic Party (LDP), 6, 14, 236, 243–44, 272

licensing, 224
    cross-licensing agreements, 114, 188
    Japanese preference for, 218
    of Japanese products, 159
    negotiation process for, 110
    relative profitability of, 218–19

lobbying, 158, 289–90

Lockheed, 10, 62

loyalty, 24

mado no hito (window people), 113n
management style, 198–99
    attitude toward foreign employees and, 254–55, 257–59, 262, 265
    joint ventures and, 221
    Theory J, 206–7, 208–10
    Theory X, 206, 207
    Theory Y, 205–6, 207–8, 209
management techniques, 197–201
    archaic forms of, 278–81
    long-range strategy in, 199, 279–80
    management style in, *see* management style
    removing labor-management barriers, 198–99, 278–79
    welfare of employees and retirees, 199–200, 207
    for Western managers in Japanese companies, 257–58
    see also employees (Japanese company)
managing director (*jōmu*), 16, 46, 61, 213
Mansfield, Mike, 273, 277
manufacturers
    bank equity in, 147
    innovation by, 190–91
    plants of, in client countries, 164–66, 172, 187, 260–62, 280
    trading companies and, *see* trading companies
    see also direct investment
manufacturing rights, 114–15
market research, 189–90
market share, 140–41, 152
    see also strategy
market testing, 238
marketing, 145–47
    advertising in, 145–46, 152–53, 159, 237–38
    of exports to Japan, 237–40
    laser-beam effect in, 160–61
    trading companies in, 169–70, 171, 176–77
    using foreign techniques for, 224–25
Masuda, K., 222
Matsushita, Konosuke, 125
Matsushita Electric, 125, 151, 158–59
McGregor, Douglas, 205–6

McKinsey & Company, 139, 228, 244
meetings, 25–32, 38
    contacts prior to initial, 210–11
    dress for, 61–62
    exchanging calling cards before, 26–28, 38
    follow-up arrangements for, 211–12
    greetings at beginning of, 29, 38
    Japanese management style and arrangement of, 206–7, 208–10
    maintaining contact between, 211–17
    negotiation, *see* negotiation
    ningen kankei (human relationships) and, 76, 77–81
    socializing after, *see* socializing
Meiji Restoration, 6, 7, 44, 169
meishi (calling cards), 26–28, 38, 46
meritocracy, 260
Mexico, 173
mikan (tangerines). 243
military, *see* defense
Mimura, Yojei, 173
minimum annual purchase clauses, 114–15
Ministry of International Trade and Industry (MITI), 94, 95, 144–45, 163, 288
    see also Fair Trade Commission (FTC)
MIPRO (Manufacturers Import Promotion Council), 239
Mishima, Yukio, 23
Misunderstanding (Wilkinson), 4, 63, 275
Mitsubishi Electric, 9, 172
Mitsubishi Trading, 153, 173
Mitsui, 157, 158, 172
Mitsui Bussan (Mitsui Trading), 72, 153, 171
Monday Clubs, 163, 174
Morita, Akio, 45, 152, 158, 164, 215, 252
motorcycle industry, 188–89
Myers, Steven D., 264

Nagase Trading, 252
Naito, Ryoichi, 21–22, 24, 165, 215
Nakane, Chie, 26, 141, 147, 256, 267
Nakasone, Yasuhiro, 107, 179, 276
names, 27, 45–46

natural resources, 171–73
negotiation, 97–117, 103
    composition of teams for, 99,
        104, 105, 116, 284–85
    corporate culture and, 125
    decision-making process in, *see*
        decision-making
    of joint ventures, 231
    problems in process of, 284–85,
        290
nemawashi (consensus building), 23,
    124–25, 126
newly industrialized countries
    (NICs), 183, 271, 272
nightclubs, 17, 40, 86
NIH (Not Invented Here) syndrome,
    111
Niizeki, Yasutaro, 72–73
ningen kankei (human relation-
    ships), 75–87, 216
    see also socializing
nintae (patience), 30–31, 56, 64–65,
    74, 101, 128–29
Nippon Airlines, 62
Nippon Miniature Bearing Com-
    pany (NMB), 165
nisei, 16
Nissan, 152–53, 190, 193
Nixon, Richard, 158, 277
Nomura Research, 110
nontariff barriers (NTBs), 245–51,
    245–48, 281–82, 290–91

Occupation authorities (SCAP), 181
Oda, Hideo, 144–45
Official Development Assistance
    (ODA), 157, 175, 278
ofuro (hot baths), 36–37
Ohira, Masayoshi, 106, 179
Ohmae, Kenichi, 149–50
oil, 45, 174–75, 289
Olmer, Lionel, 163
on (obligation), 64, 67–68
oranges, 243
Ouchi, William, 194
oyabun (faction leader), 13–14, 71,
    122–23

P notes (promissory notes), 72–73,
    138
Pacific Economic Community (PEC),
    291–92

packaging, 147, 237–38
parties, company, 12–13
Pascale, Richard Tanner, 20, 122, 125,
    194, 258
patience *(nintae)*, 30–31, 56, 64, 74,
    101, 128–29
Pearl Harbor, 20
Perry, Admiral Matthew, 7, 269
personality, 128–29
personnel, information on, 127–28
pharmaceuticals industry, 165–66,
    187, 191, 214–15, 219–20, 222–23,
    225–26, 230–31, 248–49
praise, 29
president *(shachō)*, 46, 59–60, 123,
    124, 214, 215
pricing, 136–37, 146–47, 162, 192, 237
*Procedure Manual for Tenders to the
    Government of Japan* (Connely),
    250
Procter & Gamble, 138, 220
product testing, 242
profitability, 218–22, 230
promotions, 265–66
protectionism, 164, 166, 245–51, 275,
    281–82
punctuality, 31, 35–36

quality circles, 260, 281
quality control, 141–42, 154, 158–59,
    194–95, 242–43, 260, 281
quotas, 236, 243–44, 243

racism, 17–18, 264
rank
    attendance at meetings and,
        28–29
    as barrier to communication,
        198–99
    contracts and, 98–99
    conversational style and, 57
    decision-making process and,
        212–14
    in exchange of calling cards
        (meishi), 27–28
    face and use of, 59–60
    in gift giving, 34
    Japanese management style
        and, 208, 209–10, 263
    labor-management relations
        and, 259–62, 278–79
    in language, 43–44

ningen kankei (human relationships) and, 77
role playing and, 61
Western attitudes to, 278–79
see also titles
Rankin, Bruce, 166
raw materials, 155–56, 171–73
Reagan, Ronald, 278, 288
refrigerators, 236–37
Reischauer, Edwin O., 9, 19, 21, 42, 49–50, 61, 69, 117, 129, 261, 274, 284
religion, 19–22
research
    consumer, 145–46
    on corporate culture, 125
    importance of, 65
    before initial meetings with Japanese, 210–11
    intelligence networks for, 156–57, 160–61
    on Japanese companies, 38
    for negotiation process, 110–11
    ningen kankei (human relationships) and, 80–81
    see also information
restaurants, 32–33, 39, 69–70
retailers, 136
retirees, 200, 221, 233–34
return on investment (ROI), 220, 221
Richardson, Bradley M., 92, 95
ringi seido (document for making decisions), 123–25, 126, 210
risk, 120–21, 171–72
Roberts, John, 72–73, 181–82
role playing, 60–61
rōmaji (Latin alphabet), 49
Roth, William, 288
royalty payments, 114–15
ryokan (Japanese inn), 36–37

sales company, 134
sama (term of address), 45–46
samurai (warrior), 6, 21
san (term of address), 27, 45–46
sansei (third generation born abroad), 16
sarariman (salary man), 43
Saudi Arabia, 174–75
savings, personal, 144, 182, 285–86
Schering-Plough, 121
Schlegel Engineering, 252–53
scientific management, 206, 207

Scotch whisky, 34, 250–51
Searle, G. D. 121
Sears, Roebuck, 236–37
section chief *(kachō),* 12, 46
Seiko, 160
semiconductor industry, 194, 195–96, 266
semmonshōsha (specialized trading companies), *see* trading companies
semmu (executive vice president), 46
seppuku (ritual disembowelment), 8, 23, 119
sexism, *see* women
shachō (president), 46, 59–60, 123, 124, 214, 215
Shepherd, Mark, 50
Shimizu, Norihiku, 143–144
Shintoism, 19, 20–22
shinyō (trust), 91–92, 95, 97, 115, 182
shipping industry, 156
shitenchō (branch office manager), 177, 258–59
Showa era, 44–45
shuntō (Spring Struggle), 241
Seiyu Supermarkets, 134–36
Simul International, 50
sincerity, 74, 265–66
site selection, 225
Snowden, Larry, 41
socializing
    dining out as part of, 32–33, 39
    entertaining Japanese guests, 37–40, 71, 85
    gift giving in, 34–35, 36
    golf and, 33, 35–36, 83–85
    importance of, in establishing *ningen kankei* (human relationships), 81–83
    trips to *ryokan* (Japanese inns), 36–37
sōgōshōsha (general trading companies), *see* trading companies
Sony, 151, 152, 158–59, 164, 215, 260–61
Spain, 192–93
speaking
    impatience and, 30–31, 56–57
    interruptions in, 56
    "lecturing" style of, 30–31, 113, 284
    pace of, 31–32, 52

see also communication; language

Spirit of Japanese Industry, The (Fujihara), 154

Spring Struggle (shuntō), 241

Stanford Research Institute (SRI), 110, 121

statistics, quality control, 141–42

status, *see* rank

strategy, 199, 279–80

    Japanese, 133–67

        in foreign markets, 152–67

        in Japan, 133–50

    Western, 184–201

Successful Entry into the Japanese Market (ACCJ), 228

Sumitomo Bank, 178, 180

Suntory, 251

superiority complex, Western, 264

Suzuki, Zenko, 179

Taisho era, 44, 50

"Tale of the Forty-seven *Ronin*," 7–9

Tanaka, Kakuei, 10

tatamae (superficial appearance), 21, 58–60, 105–6, 117

tatami (straw mat), 37

taxes, 143–44

    commodity, 250

tea, 37, 38

technology

    industrial espionage and, 9, 10

    information available on, 110–11

    transfer of, 186–88

telephones, 241

television, 100, 146, 158–59

Texas Instruments, 192

textile industry, 164, 171

Theory J, 206–7, 208–10

Theory X, 206, 207

Theory Y, 205–6, 207–8, 209

Theory Z (Ouchi), 133, 142, 194

third country ventures, 173, 181–83

Third World, *see* lesser developed countries

titles, 46

    buchō (department chief), 12, 15–16, 44, 46, 51

    fukushachō (vice president), 46, 233

jōmu (managing director), 16, 46, 61, 213

kachō (section chief), 12, 46

kaichō (chairman), 46, 213, 215

semmu (executive vice president), 46

shachō (president), 46, 59–60, 123, 124, 214, 215

torishimari-yaku (director), 46

toiletry industry, 237, 238, 241

Tokugawa Ieyasu, 6

Tokugawa shogunate, 6–9, 21

Torii Yakunin, 223

torishimari-yaku (director), 46

Toyo Menka, 171

Toyota, 134, 158, 193, 194, 259, 260, 261

trade shows, 238–39

trading companies, 168–77

    bank relationships with, 180–81

    equipment leasing and, 183

    as go-betweens in negotiation, 98, 176–77

    information networks of, 156–57, 160–61

    promotion of foreign products by, 239–40

    role of, in international growth, 153

trust *(shinyō)*, 91–92, 95, 97, 115, 182

Tsurumi, Yoshi, 119, 123–24

Tung, Rosalie L., 102–4

Ueda, Taizo, 92, 95

unions, 261–62

United States

    attitude of, to Japan, 269–70, 273–74, 276–79

    banks of, 177–78

    defense spending by, 275, 276

    discriminatory certification of exports to, 246–48

    education of Japanese in, 170

    growth of Japan compared with, 184–85

    interdependency of, with Japan, 270–73

    Japanese banks in, 179

    lack of trading companies in, 175, 176, 240

    management style in, 198–99

need for industrial policy in, 285–86

profitability of Japanese joint ventures with, 220

proposed Department of International Trade and Industry of, 288

trade policy promotion by, 288–90

venture capital, taxes and, 143–44

vice president *(fukushachō)*, 46, 233

Vogel, Ezra, 19, 23, 141, 184

vulnerability, 120–22, 145, 148, 283–84

wa (social harmony), 21, 62, 151

watch industry, 160

wholesalers, 134–39

Wilkinson, Endymion, 4, 52, 63, 275

women

as clerical workers, 263

as contract negotiators, 99, 285

employment of, in Japanese companies, 262–63, 266

as executives, 40, 86–87, 266

language used by Japanese, 43

socializing with, 17, 36–37, 39–40, 83, 86–87

work permits, 266–67

World War II, 17–18, 20, 44–45, 85, 153–55, 269, 273–76

Woronoff, Jon, 11, 12, 19

xenophobia, 14, 17–18, 96, 281–83

Yamanouchi Pharmaceutical, 191

Yoshino, M. Y., 181

yukata (Japanese garment), 37

zaibatsu (industrial groups), 168, 181
see also zaikai

zaikai (financial circles), 10, 72–73, 100–1, 100n, 163

banks in, 177, 179–82

information networks of, 157, 160–61

role of, in Japanese foreign expansion, 163–64

shipping line control by, 156

trading companies and, 168–69, 171, 174–75, 176–77, 180–81